Green Peony and the Rise of the Chinese Martial Arts Novel

SUNY series in Chinese Philosophy and Cultures

Roger T. Ames, editor

Green Peony and the Rise of the Chinese Martial Arts Novel

Margaret B. Wan

STATE UNIVERSITY OF NEW YORK PRESS

Published by
STATE UNIVERSITY OF NEW YORK PRESS
ALBANY

Printed in the United States of America

For information, contact
State University of New York Press, Albany, NY
www.sunypress.edu

Production by Ryan Morris
Marketing by Michael Campochiaro

Library of Congress Cataloging-in-Publication Data

Wan, Margaret B.
Green peony and the rise of the Chinese martial arts novel / Margaret B. Wan.
p. cm. — (Suny series in chinese philosophy and culture)
Includes bibliographical references and index.
ISBN 978-0-7914-7701-4 (hardcover : alk. paper)
ISBN 978-0-7914-7702-1 (pbk. : alk. paper)
1. Martial arts fiction, Chinese—History and criticism. 2. Chinese fiction—Qing dynasty, 1644–1912—History and criticism I. Title.
PL2419.M37W34 2009
895.1'3087—dc22 2008021309

10 9 8 7 6 5 4 3 2 1

To my family

Contents

Illustrations

Tables

Figures

Acknowledgments

THIS BOOK WAS INSPIRED BY an interest in popular literature and oral performance, which I pursued in my Ph. D. dissertation at Harvard University.

I am indebted to Patrick Hanan for being the best advisor and mentor one could ask for. He encouraged me to follow my research interests off the beaten path, and his high standards and unfailing support have been an inspiration to me throughout my scholarly career. He is an impeccable scholar, a great teacher, and a true gentleman.

Numerous scholars refined my ideas by reading various stages of the manuscript: Sarah M. Allen, Roland Altenburger, Cynthia Brokaw, Chen Jianhua, Liangyan Ge, Rania Huntington, Keith McMahon, Stephen Owen, Emmanuel Pastreich, Meir Shahar, Joanna Handlin Smith, Shang Wei, and Ellen Widmer. They gave generously of their time and expertise, and their critiques have been invaluable as this project developed. My thanks also go to Chen Pingyuan of Beijing University for his helpful advice. My colleagues at CHINOPERL, including Lindy Li Mark and Fan Pen Chen, have heard many presentations on this material; I am grateful for their insights. While working on this book, I have enjoyed the friendship and support of my colleagues at the University of Utah, especially Fusheng Wu, Richard Chi, and Janet Theiss.

The research for this book depended on materials in many libraries. My thanks to the staff at University of Utah Marriott Library (especially the interlibrary loan staff), the Harvard-Yenching Library, Dartmouth College Library, University of California at Berkeley's libraries, University of Chicago's Regenstein Library, Beijing Normal University Library, Beijing Library, Beijing University Library, Chinese Academy of Social Sciences Library, the Drama Research Institute of the Chinese Academy of Arts, Fudan University Humanities Library, and Shanghai Municipal Library. The staff at Capital Library (Beijing) deserve special mention for accommodating my frequent requests; without the unique materials discovered there this would be a very different book. Shum Chun at the Harvard-Yenching Library and Wu Ge at Fudan University Humanities Library were especially helpful in locating obscure materials and sorting out difficult dating issues.

This project received financial support from the Andrew Mellon Foundation, as well as a semester of research leave from the University of Utah. For these I am grateful.

Portions of chapters 2 and 5 previously appeared in "The *Chantefable* and the Novel: The Cases of *Lü mudan* and *Tianbao tu*," *Harvard Journal of Asiatic Studies* 64.2 (December 2004), 367–97. I thank the editors for permission to reprint these here.

Nancy Ellegate and Ryan Morris, editors at State University of New York Press, have been a pleasure to work with and have helped make this a better book. I would also like to thank the anonymous readers of the manuscript for their useful suggestions. Any errors remaining are mine alone.

Finally, I thank my family for everything, especially my parents for their encouragement of my far-flung love of Chinese culture, and my in-laws for their support. My husband Mike in many ways made this book possible. It is to them I dedicate this book.

Chapter 1

Introduction

Green Peony and the Martial Romance

THE MARTIAL ARTS NOVEL is the most widely read genre of Chinese fiction today, avidly consumed throughout the Chinese-speaking world and beyond. As essentially the only genre of traditional popular fiction to have survived beyond the imperial era in China, it is the oldest genre of Chinese popular fiction still being written.[1] Its origins remain obscure, however. While scholars recognize the martial arts novel as a major genre in the Qing, even specialized histories of the martial arts novel do not agree on when or how the genre began to take shape in the Qing.

Studies of the traditional Chinese novel tend to ignore popular genres like the martial arts novel, and instead focus primarily on the masterworks and lesser works that are still of high literary quality. For this reason, the martial arts novel has not received the kind of attention it needs to unravel it origins and intricacies. It is important because it was not only some of the most widely read fiction of its age, crossing boundaries of geography and social status; its prevalence in oral performance and easily understood performance texts also allowed it to reach people of almost every level of education. Its close relationship to both performance genres and the most elite literary fiction provides a unique opportunity to examine both common threads and significant differences between these milieus.

Let me begin by defining the martial arts novel. Modern critics vary widely in their use of the term "martial arts novel," the only common ground being fiction about martial heroes. The English translation does not do the

Chinese term justice; martial arts comprise only half of the term *wuxia*. The modern author Liang Yusheng explains martial arts (*wu*) are simply the means, while a kind of heroism akin to chivalry (*xia*) is the goal.[2] In fact, before the term *wuxia* appeared in the late Qing, the term used to discuss these novels was simply *xiayi*, "heroism and altruism." Martial arts fiction therefore has less to do with the description of fighting than with the ideal of martial heroes.

This ideal often forms the thread that binds together thematic studies of martial arts literature.[3] In a syncretic view derived from a range of genres spanning several centuries, James J. Y. Liu defines his "Chinese knight-errant" in terms of a set of values: altruism, justice, individual freedom, personal loyalty, courage, truthfulness and mutual faith, honor and fame, and generosity and contempt for wealth.[4] While he argues that the ideals of Western knights were similar in many respects, Liu also recognizes the differences between the two groups. In contrast to European knights, who were a distinct social class owing loyalty to the king, he argues that Chinese knights came from all walks of life, were often disruptive to society, and owed loyalty only to a *zhiji* ("one who appreciates you"). Anyone could be a knight in China; there was no particular organization and no religious affiliation. In contrast, European knights were tied to the Christian religion, which dictated many of the rules of their order. They were expected to be refined in their manners and were associated with courtly love. The Chinese knight, on the other hand, was often portrayed as crude and blunt, and would generally find women anathema.[5] Because of these differences I prefer the term "martial hero" to "knight."

From antiquity, the concept of the martial hero in China formed a counterpoint and potential challenge to Confucian relationships. The disregard of protocol and indifference to the hierarchy of relationships is obvious from the stories of martial heroes and assassins in the *Shi ji* (Records of the historian) and other early texts. On the other hand, martial heroes go to spectacular extremes to live out their own values, thinking nothing of dying for the cause. This ruffled Confucian feathers: If you will die for a complete stranger, what can you do for your parents? Still, even the martial hero's apparent freedom is circumscribed by a code of ethics centered on revenge, requiting favor, and righting injustice.[6]

While these thematic approaches address some of the concerns of martial arts literature, they provide little sense of the martial arts novel as a historical genre.[7] A satisfying literary history must go beyond the thematic to find a specific form for specific content.[8] How did the martial arts novel develop?

Before exploring that issue we must ask, What is a "novel" in China? Scholars conventionally use the Western term novel to refer to long prose narrative fiction in China. This use is supported by similarities in form and technique. In general, the narrative method employed by the Chinese novel bears comparison to realism in the West. Andrew Plaks notes its "exhaustive attention to fine details, maintenance of an orderly scheme of temporal movement, articulation of a consistent narrative perspective—i.e. point of view, and emphasis on credibility in motivation and personality."[9] However, there is no one Chinese term that precisely matches the word "novel." A variety of terms refer to the works of long prose fiction that are the subject of this study, each carrying its own connotations. The term commonly translated as novel, *xiaoshuo*, originated over a thousand years before the first long prose fiction in China and traditionally encompassed a wide range of materials. Ban Gu (32—92), compiler of the bibliography in the earliest dynastic history, explained the term *xiaoshuo* as follows:

> The *xiaoshuo* school probably evolved from the office of petty officials. The works were street talk and alley gossip, made up by those who engaged in conversations along the roads and walkways. Confucius once said, "Although a petty path, there is surely something to be seen in it. But if pursued too far, one could get bogged down; hence the gentleman does not do so." Still, he did not discard them. Being something upon which those of lesser knowledge touched, they were collected and not forgotten, on the chance they might contain a useful phrase or two. They are really the discourses of rustics and eccentrics.[10]

From the beginning the term *xiaoshuo* carried connotations of marginality or even frivolity, something which "the gentleman does not do." Up until the sixteenth century it was "an all-embracing category into which those texts deemed unfitting for other clearly defined categories were conveniently dumped."[11] As the novel took shape in sixteenth-century China as long vernacular fiction, the term *xiaoshuo* was applied to it. Thus not only was the novel in China traditionally placed outside the canon of serious literature, but also by implication of the term *xiaoshuo* it was something on which one should not waste time. This passage also spawned the term "petty officials" (*baiguan*) for these narratives, which carries similar connotations.

The Chinese novel grew out of historical narrative. This early kinship is reflected in terms like "unofficial history" (*yeshi*) and "popular elaboration" (*yanyi*). History in China served as a repertoire of moral models, positive and negative. As such it held a central position in Chinese culture, so association with history could elevate or justify other narratives. "Unofficial history" conceives of the novel as "leftover" history, justifying these narratives on the grounds that they provided information the official histories left out. The term "popular elaboration," which appears in the titles of many narratives, claims to retell history in a more accessible form. Some of the *yanyi* narratives are indeed popularized history, but even those that are fiction "justified their writings by emphasizing their effectiveness in terms of popular historical education (claiming that formal historiography was too difficult for and inaccessible to the common reader)."[12] The novel's supplementary relationship to history meant that it could serve the same moral purpose, but it also implied a subservient position for the novel.

Many of the earliest Chinese novels, including *Sanguo yanyi* (Three Kingdoms), strive to faithfully present historical facts while incorporating legend and lore.[13] Some, like *Shuihu zhuan* (The water margin), claim a historical framework but "make no pretensions to be serious history," focusing instead on the exploits of a hero or brotherhood.[14] Martin Huang argues that one way to look at the development of the novel in China is to see it as a process of "dehistoricization," in which each of the great novels critiqued its predecessors by dealing with a less historical and more intimate subject. Whereas the scope of *Three Kingdoms* is the fate of a dynasty, that of *The Water Margin* is the rise and fall of a band of outlaws, while *Jin Ping Mei* focuses on the fortunes and domestic squabbles of one family. As the focus narrows to the individual, the settings and concerns also shift to the private.[15]

A similar pattern appears in the development of the Chinese novel beyond these masterworks, although the chronology is not as neat. Among the earliest novels, more "responsible" historical novels coexisted from the very beginning with a looser branch, known as the military romance (*yingxiong chuangqi*).[16] As the novel freed itself from history, other favorite themes grew into genres, including scholar-beauty romances (*caizi jiaren*) and novels on the supernatural. Over the next two hundred years each of these thematic genres would spawn scores of novels. Scholar-beauty romances became the most popular theme in novels of the seventeenth and eighteenth century, while military romances burgeoned through the nineteenth century.

The mid-seventeenth century was a defining moment for the novel in China. *The Water Margin* and *Three Kingdoms* attracted the interest of iconoclastic intellectuals who argued for the legitimacy of the novel as literature. They edited and published new editions of these novels replete with literary criticism and detailed commentary that demonstrated the artistry of each novel. Such criticism shaped the aesthetic of the traditional novel in China, an issue to which I will return in chapter 4. These critics struggled to raise the status of their chosen novels by calling them "books of genius" (*caizi shu*) and ranking them on a par with the greatest literary works China had produced. Still, these advocates of the novel tend to elevate a particular work at the expense of the genre, arguing that *this* work shows excellence and cannot be compared with ordinary novels.[17]

Most novels never received the kind of serious attention lavished on *Three Kingdoms* and *The Water Margin*. As a consequence, the definitions of thematic genres, which encompassed the vast majority of novels, remained largely implicit. Since in late imperial China the novel fell outside the canon and, therefore, beyond the scope of most bibliographers,[18] there was traditionally no need to define the novel as a form, much less divide it into constituent thematic genres. Genres can still be discerned in the conventions of titles and the grouping implied by the works mentioned in a particular preface, but this does not constitute explicit genre criticism. Modern genre criticism in China began only in the late Qing. Thus it is not surprising that the term for the martial arts theme, *wuxia*, also appeared during this period.[19]

The serious study of martial arts fiction in China began with Lu Xun.[20] In *Zhongguo xiaoshuo shilüe* (A brief history of Chinese fiction, 1924), Lu Xun devotes a chapter to martial arts and court-case fiction, and although he never offers a formal definition for the genre, his discussion set the corpus of works and the general approach for future research.

Lu Xun's extensive discussion of *Sanxia wuyi* (The three heroes and five sworn brothers, 1879) and *Ernü yingxiong zhuan* (Moral heroes and heroines, 1878) explains why those two works appear consistently in later scholarship as representatives of the genre and are often portrayed as the earliest martial arts fiction. He presents them as exemplifying two different varieties of the martial arts novel intended for different audiences. He posits the novel's audience bifurcated in the Qianlong reign period (1736–1795); up to that time, everyone read the four classic novels, but when *Honglou meng* (Story of the Stone) became popular it replaced *Three Kingdoms* in the eyes of the literati, while the common people still preferred *Three Kingdoms* and *The Water Margin*. With changing tastes the genre of martial arts fiction evolved, producing two streams, *Moral Heroes and Heroines* for the literati and *The Three Heroes and Five Sworn Brothers* for the folk. I will return in chapter 5 to the question Lu Xun's model raises about the relationship between "popular" and "literati" literature in the mid-Qing.[21]

Lu Xun's most influential observation about martial arts fiction concerns the judge as a central figure (fig. 1.1). He observes that *The Three Heroes and Five Sworn Brothers* seems to retain the flavor of *The Water Margin*, but goes on to say this is only superficially true; in spirit the two works are quite different. Even though their intention is to relate tales of brave martial heroes helping people and saving their country, the later works differ in that there is always a famous official who directs all the heroes, in this case Judge Bao.[22] The judge serves as the structural framework around which the novel is built. Because they are the judge's helpers, the heroes work inside the system instead of being outside society and opposed to the government. This is a far cry from the famous heroes in *The Water Margin* who were "forced to climb Mount Liang."

Nearly all studies of the martial arts novel give a nod to *The Water Margin* as a precursor or early example of the genre and then start in the Qing with different works. For example, among recent histories of martial arts fiction,

Figure 1.1 Judge Di Renjie, from the 1800 editon of *Green Peony*

Liu Yinbo starts with *Shi Gong an* (Cases of Judge Shi), while Wang Hailin suggests the martial arts theme was revived in the novel at the end of the Jiaqing or the beginning of the Daoguang reign period (around the 1820s).[23] However, he does not discuss these novels, beginning his analysis instead with *Moral Heroes and Heroines*. This gap is due to the influence of Lu Xun's pioneering study.

Even more than Lu Xun's chronology, however, later work on martial arts fiction has been dominated by the political implications of his analysis. If the rebels in *The Water Margin* are praiseworthy for rebelling against feudal society, then the heroes of martial arts fiction are reprehensible for capitulating to it. This stance also explains why the genre was not given much scholarly attention in China from the 1950s to the 1970s. Although newspaper and journal articles continued to appear, most of them dismissed the novels as politically incorrect or "feudal." Much of the criticism of martial arts fiction in China has revolved around the question of values, from a Marxist point of view.[24]

As a major genre in the Qing, the martial arts novel deserves attention in its own right. Previous studies ignore the early development of the martial arts novel and, thereby, fail to acknowledge the complexity of the genre and its rich relationship to other genres of fiction. I will show that the early martial arts novel sheds light on the relationship between the popular novel, literary fiction, and other popular narratives such as *chantefables* in the nineteenth century. It demonstrates the enormous mutual influence of genres that are usually treated separately. This has implications for our understanding of "genre" in both senses of the word: as the formal and aesthetic conventions of the novel and as an entity defined thematically by shared content—what could be called a "subgenre" of the novel.

This study traces the origins of the martial arts novel to the late Qianlong period. To chart its development, I examine ten essentially unstudied novels published between the late eighteenth century and 1850, placing them in the context of the literary and performance-related genres out of which they grew. Because they prominently feature love stories, I call this corpus the "martial romance." I focus on *Lü mudan* (Green peony, 1800), one of the earliest examples, as representative of the genre.[25]

Green Peony opens with Empress Wu Zetian on the throne. She exiles the young crown prince, despite protests from loyal generals. The novel then turns to its protagonist, Luo Hongxun, the scholarly son of a martial official. Hua Bilian, the martial daughter of a notorious bandit, falls desperately in love with him at first sight. Luo refuses to marry her, ostensibly because he is already betrothed. Three proposals of marriage and three refusals provide the structure for the plot. Every time Luo refuses a proposal he runs off to play the hero—with disastrous results. Whether he tries to save Hua Bilian's family from a local despot, rescue a widow from a rapist, or avenge his ser-

Figure 1.2 Collective portrait, from *Green Peony Drum Ballad* (Jinzhang shuju edition)

綠牡丹鼓詞
像一
花碧蓮
駱弘勳
花正芳
余謙
一七

vant in a martial tournament, his attempts at heroism always end in disaster. Twice he is brought to court on false charges springing from these attempts. Each time he is saved by bandits or pirates, but his association with them simply incurs the wrath of powerful scoundrels and gets Luo into more trouble. After he refuses the third proposal of marriage, the bandits set up a funeral ruse; leading Luo to believe his mother and fiancée have died, they trick him into coming to their stronghold. Captured and framed as a bandit, he is then escorted toward the capital. Along the way, martial artists seeking revenge ambush him. At the last minute he is saved by pirates and travels with them to find his mother. He marries Hua Bilian and his original fiancée, and all the heroes go to the capital. Their pretext for entering the capital is a special women's examination that Empress Wu is inspired to hold after a green peony blooms in her garden, whence the title of the novel. With the aid of Judge Di they defeat the wicked officials in league with Empress Wu and restore the rightful emperor to power. All of the villains having been brought to justice, the emperor enfeoffs the heroes and everyone lives happily ever after (fig. 1.2).

Even this brief synopsis suggests that *Green Peony* incorporates elements from previous popular fiction: the scholar-beauty romance, the historical novel, and court-case fiction. How does it relate to these genres?

Relationship to Court-case Fiction

The relationship between court-case novels and martial arts novels has been a vexed question ever since Lu Xun discussed them in a single chapter. What are the differences between them? Are the terms synonymous, or is there a basis on which to distinguish them? Following Lu Xun's lead, most histories of the martial arts novel claim that the two strains came together in the Qing to form the "court-case adventure" novel (*gongan xiayi*).[26] However, the many important exceptions make it unreasonable to lump all Qing martial arts novels together as court-case adventures.[27]

Let me quickly outline the development of court-case fiction. Patrick Hanan defines it as "works in which the judicial solution (of some crime or other social disorder) is of central importance."[28] Its history is too long to go into here. While the court-case theme was popular from at least the Song dynasty on, it attained spectacular popularity in the Ming in the form of collections of short tales, the most durable collection being *Longtu gongan* (Longtu's court cases).[29] Thereafter, no major new works of court-case fiction appeared for over a century, until the theme reappeared, much changed in both form and content, around the turn of the nineteenth century as a genre of the novel.[30]

A comparison of *Green Peony* to *Cases of Judge Shi*, an early court-case adventure novel,[31] suggests a close connection between the two works. Besides typical features of the court-case adventure novel, such as the judge figure, *Green Peony* and *Cases of Judge Shi* share several subplots and one character, Pu Tiandiao.[32]

Despite these similarities, *Green Peony* does not fit the category of court-case adventure novel. *Green Peony* and *Cases of Judge Shi* treat similar situations from opposite perspectives. In *Cases of Judge Shi*, the courts dispense justice; heroes are admired, but they must strictly uphold the law. In contrast, in *Green Peony* the courts suffer from corruption, so the bandit heroes must step in to right injustices. Thus while in *Cases of Judge Shi* the hero Shi Zhong (Huang Tianba) acts in his official capacity to stop his bandit friends' attempt at a jailbreak, the bandit heroes in *Green Peony* successfully break their friends out of jail. Furthermore, in *Green Peony* the judge plays a fairly minor role. Judge Di Renjie appears only in the last twenty chapters of *Green Peony* and, rather than solving everything neatly, he simply lets the protagonist Luo Hongxun out of prison. He does not even try the case; in fact, one interesting feature in *Green Peony* is that the bandits hold their own court.[33] Far from directing the heroes, Judge Di is hardly involved in the final raid on the capital that restores the throne to Emperor Zhongzong.[34] Whereas in *Green Peony* the reader sympathizes with the outsiders, in court-case novels he sympathizes with the government. Official justice works better in the court-case novels than in the martial romance.

Should the court-case novel and the martial romance be considered different genres? To what extent are differences in values significant to generic distinctions? Lu Xun does not categorize genres based on values; consequently he recognizes significant relationships between works with conflicting ideologies, such as identifying *Dangkou zhi* (Quell the bandits) as a reaction to *The Water Margin*.[35] In contrast, Bakhtin's theory of genre in Western literature posits that each genre uses language to imply a certain set of values.[36] I will demonstrate below that particular values lie at the core of genres of Ming-Qing fiction like the scholar-beauty romance and the historical novel. Moreover, the martial romance and the court-case novel differ in structure as well as values. While the better-known court-case adventure novels are long, episodic, and generate endless sequels, the martial romance novels are generally relatively short and self-contained.[37]

If we consider the martial romance and the court-case novel separate genres, how do we account for their similarities? The simplest way would be direct borrowing. However, in the case of *Green Peony* and *Cases of Judge Shi*, there is not enough textual evidence to support such a claim. Rather, we must look to their common roots.

Signs of the influence of Ming and Qing court-case story collections appear in the plot and structure of both the martial romance and the court-case adventure novel. Many subplots in *Green Peony* and *Cases of Judge Shi* recall stories in *Longtu's Court Cases*.[38] The idea of structuring long court-case adventure novels around a single judge may also stem from Ming court-case story collections, as Chen Pingyuan suggests.[39] However, without evidence of textual borrowing such similarities cannot prove that either the martial romance or the court-case novel derived directly from court-case stories. They are thematically but not textually related.

A further tantalizing connection between *Green Peony* and *Cases of Judge Shi* is in their relationship to *chantefables*, ballads which alternate between prose and verse. *Chantefable* versions of both exist,[40] and the same merchant, Baiben Zhang, sold *chantefable* versions of both *Cases of Judge Shi* and *Green Peony*, suggesting that by the Daoguang or Xianfeng period (1821–1862) they participated in the same milieu.[41] These *chantefables* underscore the close relationship performance genres bore to both the martial romance and the court-case novel. Two of the earliest martial romance novels, including *Green Peony*, are clearly adapted from *chantefables*, as I will demonstrate in chapter 2.[42]

Thus both the martial romance and the court-case adventure novel derive thematically from earlier court-case story collections, while historically they developed in close relationship with performance genres. They simply developed in different directions, a point I will take up in chapter 2.

Similar questions are raised by the relationship between *Green Peony* and other thematic genres. While much effort has been expended on the relationship between martial and court-case fiction, its relationship to two other genres of popular fiction current at the time, the scholar-beauty romance and the historical novel, is hardly ever mentioned.

The Element of Romance

Green Peony is structured around a romance of sorts. The predominant model for romance in fiction and drama of the seventeenth and eighteenth centuries was the scholar-beauty romance, which typically centers on the courtship of a couple who are both brilliant and attractive. The Ming play *Lü mudan* (Green peony) by Wu Bing (1595–1648) is a typical example of the scholar-beauty romance theme, although the play bears no relationship to the Qing novel that is our focus here. In the play heroes and villains are distinguished primarily by talent; while the heroes write impressive poetry, the villains not only cannot write well, they can barely read.[43] Poetry plays a central role in the development of the romance plot; upon reading each other's poetry, the protagonists recognize talent and pursue the match.

In contrast, the Qing novel *Green Peony* contains few if any meetings of the lovers, exchanges of poetry, or the like. In the martial romance merely the idea of the betrothed sends the parties off on journeys that lead to various adventures, whether the man travels to marry his fiancée in her hometown or the woman narrowly escapes abduction or marriage to another man.[44] It is almost as if the earlier romance is emptied of its usual content, and all that remains is a framework.[45]

Lin Chen outlines the conventional tripartite structure of the scholar-beauty romance as: love at first sight, separation of the lovers by external forces, and a final reunion. These correspond to the three underlying values of the genre: free choice in marriage; loyalty and chastity in love; and a happy marriage for the lovers. There are also three scenarios for how the boy and girl meet. In the first scenario, the boy and girl both see each other, or the man admires the woman's poetic talent, or the man is looking for an outstanding woman. In any of the above cases they will get engaged secretly. In the second scenario, if the girl is choosing the man, her father or uncle must look for a suitable talented young man, and she must approve. In the third scenario, the man saves the woman, and they end up marrying through others' efforts.[46]

How does *Green Peony* utilize these scenarios? The nature of the debt *Green Peony* owes to the scholar-beauty romance will be examined in more detail in chapter 3, but for now let us look at the ways the boy and girl meet. In *Green Peony* the romance motif recurs three times; the boy and girl meet twice, and marriage is proposed three times. The repetition serves to incorporate all three of the methods of meeting. The first time she is looking for a husband (#2), and they see each other and are each impressed (#1). The second time they meet he saves her life (#3). The proposals also combine the various possibilities, since she chooses him herself but has her father propose rather than secretly arranging the match herself. The recurrence of these motifs allows *Green Peony* to incorporate most of the typical scenarios of the scholar-beauty romance.

The romance plot provides the backbone for the structure of *Green Peony.* For all the emphasis the structure puts on romance, however, there is very little romantic content. First of all, the boy consistently refuses the match. Secondly, although they meet twice, both meetings are in public, leaving little opportunity for direct interaction between the boy and girl. While poetry was so crucial to the scholar-beauty romance that they were satirized as being written simply as frameworks in which to show off the author's poetry,[47] in *Green Peony* no poetry is exchanged at all. *Green Peony* is exceptional among the martial romances in giving a psychological description of Hua Bilian's feelings for Luo Hongxun, from initial infatuation to secret bliss when he catches her in his arms after she falls off a roof.[48] However, Luo's feelings are rarely described. Instead the reader must infer his thoughts from his initial praise of her skill and his unfailing propriety. Except for two tantalizing scenes, the romance remains merely a framework. Even in these scenes, it is hardly made explicit in the same ways it was in the scholar-beauty romance.

For this reason *Green Peony* is unsatisfying to read as a romance, a fact that critics have noted.

Historical Fiction and the Military Romance

This odd reluctance shown by the boy reveals the influence of another genre on *Green Peony*. The work makes more sense if read in light of the lore of the woman warrior. The woman warrior is by no means new. As a romantic lead she appears in the late Ming, in chapters added to the Yuan Wuya edition of *The Water Margin*, as well as in accounts of the Yang Family Generals.[49] She develops in the military romance until her pursuit of a handsome general becomes a requisite element, while the object of her affections rarely requites them. As C. T. Hsia puts it, "While impressed by her beauty and power, the object of her love is usually too shocked . . . to acknowledge his interest."[50]

A preface which says *Green Peony* "imitated the unofficial histories (*yeshi*)" confirms its close relationship with the historical novel or military romance.[51] Critics have noted its typological similarity to a series of novels on the Tang Dynasty, including *Shuo Tang yanyi* (The tale of the Tang, 1736) and *Yishuo Fan Tang quan zhuan* (Another tale of rebellion against the Tang, 1753).[52] The rise and fall of Wu Zetian which begins and ends *Green Peony* also resembles a typical motif of the historical novel, the restoration of the dynasty after disturbances.[53] Moreover, in many editions *Green Peony* claims to be a sequel to the military romances on the Tang dynasty; it appears under the title *Fan Tang hou zhuan* (Later tale of rebellion against the Tang) and ends by referring to itself by that title within the text. How does *Green Peony* relate to these novels and genres?

The term "historical novel" refers to a heterogeneous group of narratives. All seem to share a general respect for historical fact, but the relationship between fact and invention differs from novel to novel and period to period. The difference between the definitions of the historical novel posited by Y. W. Ma and C. T. Hsia is instructive. C. T. Hsia says the historical novels "approximate the spirit and form of a popular chronicle," emphasizing their relationship with "serious" history.[54] Y. W. Ma, on the other hand, emphasizes the fictional aspect of these works, defining the historical novel as "a fictional work which embodies, in an artistic blending of actuality and imagination, a core of historically factual material, with allowance for inventiveness in both figures and events combined with respect for established facts."[55] The structure of the historical novel is based on a dynasty or a significant period within a dynasty, such as repelling invaders or restoring the dynasty after disturbances. It is generally characterized by moral seriousness and concern with instruction, either of historical events or, more often, of moral exempla.[56] Some of the earliest ones flaunt their relationship to serious history, especially

Zizhi tongjian (Comprehensive mirror for aid in government).[57] Indeed, some are essentially popularized history, and many of the narratives published in the Ming share little of the usual form of the novel; the storyteller's manner, for example, may be minimal or absent.[58]

C. T. Hsia identifies another related genre he labels the "military romance," which "make no pretensions to be serious history."[59] In general, the structure of the military romance centers on a hero or group of heroes and devotes much space to military campaigns and battles. Like the historical novel, the military romance relates grand events like the restoration of a dynasty or defense against invasion. Both genres draw on existing legends of heroes. I would suggest that both also center around the values of loyalty, brotherhood, and filial piety, even if military romances start to parody those values by the eighteenth century.[60] Thus the military romance and the historical novel both revolve around similar character types, such as the loyal general, although the military romance often exaggerates these character types.[61] In addition, the military romance makes much play of characters who do not appear in the historical record, such as women warriors and the scions of historic generals.[62]

A series of military romances appearing in the Qianlong period demonstrates the popularity of this genre. Four novels on the Tang dynasty, each a sequel to the last, generated fifteen editions in the Qianlong period alone and remained in print throughout the nineteenth century.[63] The last of the series, *Another Tale of Rebellion against the Tang*, relates the adventures of the general's scion Xue Gang (fig. 1.3). Labeling *Green Peony* as its sequel suggests that publishers were trying to capitalize on the popularity of this series. Despite appearing under the alternate title *Later Tale of Rebellion against the Tang, Green Peony* is not, strictly speaking, a sequel to *Another Tale of Rebellion against the Tang*.[64] The sequel title was only attached to *Green Peony* more than thirty years after its first appearance. Moreover, *Green Peony* does not act as a sequel. It shifts focus to new characters who do not appear in the previous narratives and shows what else was happening while Xue Gang was having his adventures during Empress Wu's reign. *Green Peony* thus could be considered at most a paraleptic continuation.[65] Yet that might be overstating the relationship, since only a paragraph at the beginning and the last four chapters of *Green Peony* are specifically indebted to *Another Tale of Rebellion against the Tang*. Even within the "shared" sections, the narrative shows more differences than similarities.

One of the most obvious differences between *Green Peony* and the military romance (*yingxiong chuanqi*) is the mode of fighting. James J. Y. Liu argues that a different degree of emphasis on the individual separates the martial arts novel and historical fiction. Whereas the heroes of historical fiction are generals conducting strategy on horseback, the heroes of the martial

Figure 1.3 Xue Gang, from the 1800 editon of *Green Peony*

arts novel tend toward fighting in one-on-one encounters.[66] The acid test of such a distinction is *The Water Margin*. Should *The Water Margin* be considered martial arts fiction? Many studies of martial arts fiction do include it and, undeniably, it has exerted a major influence. Chen Pingyuan notes that *The Water Margin* shaped the genre's description of fighting and its expressions of chivalry, but he also argues convincingly that at most only half of *The Water Margin* is a martial arts novel. Echoing James J. Y. Liu's argument, Chen observes that the heroes of *The Water Margin* may start as martial heroes, but in the course of the book become generals rather than avengers.[67]

The military romance (*yingxiong chuanqi*) also focuses on the battlefield as an arena in which generals display their strategy, martial prowess, and magic arts as they lead armies to victory. In contrast, *Green Peony* completely eliminates the hallmark of the military romance, magic battle; it eschews the supernatural and keeps everything on a mortal plane. Fights rarely occur on the battlefield. Instead, *Green Peony* primarily pits man against man (or woman) as a display of skill before crowds of appreciative onlookers in a tournament or similar setting. Even the battles and sieges to restore the dynasty focus on single-handed efforts rather than pitched battle. Thus, at a critical moment in the restoration effort, one man's heroic stand against hundreds captures the crucial pass:

> One of the [enemy] assistant brigade commanders yelled, "The bandit is about to open the gate, fire your arrows, what are you waiting for?" Before he had finished, arrows flew toward Hu Li thick as locusts. Hu Li had his back to the pass gate; facing the crowd, he used his two broadswords—up, down, left, right—to shield himself. To either side of him arrows piled up one or two feet high, and not a single arrow was able to strike him. After they had shot at him for the time it takes to eat a meal, all the arrows the soldiers had brought had been shot. They heard the officer order, quick, open the storehouse and bring arrows for them to use. Hu Li thought to himself, "I'd better take advantage of their being out of arrows to break the gate, what am I waiting for?" He turned around and broke the lock on the gate, but his left shoulder had already been struck by an arrow. The pain was hard for Hu Li to bear, so he couldn't open the gate wide, he just barely opened it a crack and yelled, "The gate is open, come in quickly, what are you waiting for?"[68]

Even this short passage prefigures the spectacle typical of later martial arts novels and films. Little wonder that such scenes of martial display were a mainstay of drama and performance texts on *Green Peony*.[69]

Once again, *Green Peony* resembles the genres it draws upon while carefully maintaining its own difference from them. Chapters 2 and 3 will explore more fully the relationship of the martial romance to the historical novel and military romance.

Implications

The above overview demonstrates that *Green Peony* draws on at least three genres of fiction without being subsumed by any of them. In this *Green Peony* characterizes a larger trend. The eminent bibliographer Sun Kaidi notes that at a certain point toward the end of each tradition, the scholar-beauty romance, the "loyal and righteous" subcategory of court-case fiction, and the historical novel all become concerned with "martial bravery" (*wuyong*) and the distinctions between them became correspondingly slight. Despite this observation, he refuses to establish a heading for "martial bravery"; since it is common to the last stage of all three traditions, he does not believe it has any characteristics by which it could be distinguished as an independent category.[70] I will argue for a different interpretation of this phenomenon.

Ferdinand Brunetière asserts that new genres always appear as a "dismemberment" and "extension" of previous ones.[71] Thus the extensive cross-fertilization among genres of popular fiction in eighteenth- and nineteenth-century China provided ideal conditions for the formation of a new genre. The question is how a genre can create something new out of older material.

One theory holds that genres tend to form systems. Their characteristics are often defined in opposition to one another, as genre and countergenre. Sometimes this is mutually beneficial, as genres energize each other by counterbalancing each other's values. Sometimes the opposed genres threaten each other by mutual criticism.[72] Either way, the genres form a dialogue over values, language, and technique. I will show the martial romance distinguishes itself from the genres it draws on by foregrounding this dialogue as it combines earlier motifs. *Green Peony* not only refuses classification as court-case fiction, military romance (*yingxiong chuanqi*), or scholar-beauty romance, but also plays the genre conventions off on one another.

By tracing the early development of the martial arts novel in the mid-Qing, we will see that while genre in the thematic sense is indeed useful to the understanding of popular fiction, these genres were never airtight boxes; there was frequent cross-fertilization between them. Still, their juxtaposition in *Green Peony* goes beyond this to reflect on the conventions of these genres. While *Green Peony* is first and foremost entertainment fiction, it is also the site of artistic play. This leads to questions about genre in its other sense. What defines the form and aesthetics of the novel in the nineteenth century? To what extent is that definition shared across the range of fictional practice?

Chapter 2 traces the development of the martial arts novel, focusing on the relationship between content and form. It examines a group of ten novels from the late Qianlong (1736–1795) to the Daoguang reign period (1821–1850), showing how previous genres of fiction interacted with performance genres in the formation of a new genre of popular fiction.

Parody of the genre conventions *Green Peony* draws upon is the subject of chapter 3. This chapter turns on the question of values. The major genres of popular fiction at the time, the scholar-beauty romance and the military romance (*yingxiong chuanqi*), are both predicated on adherence to certain codes of behavior. *Green Peony* self-consciously foregrounds the characters' attempts (and failures) to live by those codes, exposing the conflict between the conventions. It also explores the tensions between the values of court-case fiction and the military romance. On another level, *Green Peony* plays out the hidden potential in classic scenes in the Ming masterworks *The Water Margin* and *Three Kingdoms.* Thus it effectively functions as metafiction, highlighting the correspondence between the codes of behavior within the novel and the conventions of the genres themselves.

Chapter 4 argues that, while most of the popular fiction *Green Peony* draws upon presents itself as a model for life, *Green Peony* functions as a self-conscious novel. It shows that such literary reflexiveness is not merely the domain of the experimental novel; metafictional sophistication appears in popular fiction as well. *Green Peony* draws on an aesthetic informed by the masterworks of the Ming novel and the literary criticism that grew up around them, while critiquing the conventions and values of the thematic genres it builds on.

Chapter 5 returns to the question, How can we place the popular novel in nineteenth-century China? It discusses the relationship between the great novels of the Ming and Qing, popular fiction, and performance genres through an examination of their audiences, aesthetics, and cultural contexts.

Chapter 2

Formation of a Formula

> Every literary text is a product of a preexisting set of possibilities, and it is also a transformation of those possibilities. Therefore, literary study must operate by proceeding from the set of possibilities toward the individual work, or from the work toward the set of possibilities—which is, in fact, a generic concept.
>
> —Robert Scholes, *Structuralism in Literature*

By the time the martial romance began to develop in the late Qianlong period, the traditional Chinese novel was already mature. The "masterworks" of the Ming novel were readily available in print, and several of the great Qing novels were circulating in manuscript. The scholar-beauty romance had peaked, and the military romance (*yingxiong chuanqi*) was beginning to parody its own conventions. In other words, a great deal of fictional material was available, along with the accompanying conventions and forms. Because the martial romance comprises one of the last genres of traditional Chinese fiction to take shape, its formation also allows us to trace its relationships with the existing genres upon which it draws.

Where did the martial romance come from? This chapter will show that the martial romance brings together elements from diverse genres to form a new whole. Its challenge was to create a space for itself in the existing system of fictional genres, a challenge made greater by its reliance on the conventions, motifs, and character types established by other genres. Its formula develops through its search for a workable structure. For the purposes of this chapter, I will divide this formation into three phases of a roughly chronological progression: beginnings (ca. 1776–1814); formation of a formula (ca. 1808–1819); and formula and variations (1848–1851).[1] I will briefly outline these stages here before examining each in detail.

The earliest martial romance novels are adapted from *chantefable* texts or storytelling, drawing heavily on court-case fiction for both motifs and a general framework. But the addition of martial motifs changes the structure. The emphasis on righting wrongs taken from court-case fiction develops in the martial romance into personal feuds against corrupt officials. Unlike court-case fiction, the judge is not a central character or linking thread. In fact, his assistant's exploits are far more interesting than his own. While court-case fiction provides the early martial romance with a way to begin and end, the bulk of the plot lacks a clear structure.

The second group of novels creates the formula for the martial romance, incorporating a wider range of motifs while placing a new emphasis on structure. Some of the distinctive court-case motifs disappear, while a number of motifs from the military romance (*yingxiong chuanqi*) and the scholar-beauty romance are introduced. Such content brings with it competing structural devices, such as the romance plot and sworn brotherhood, which the martial romance tries to reconcile.

By the third stage, awareness of the formula drives the novels to find new "twists." Few new motifs are introduced. In fact, a number of motifs even fall into disuse. Those that remain are subject to variation, either in the form of a limited creativity that sees how far it can twist a motif, or by compressing a number of motifs into a single episode. Even the structure of these novels shows awareness of the genre conventions. Those that are not explicitly sequels still begin at the point where most previous martial romance novels end, with a national crisis, rather than building up from a personal feud.

All categories are somewhat arbitrary, but dividing the works historically this way reveals a progression leading to self-conscious play on the newly formed conventions of the martial romance. While much of this chapter will focus on "borrowing" or sharing of motifs between novels, it is not intended to be a source study. Rather I am interested in how these motifs are used or changed in these novels. What happens when the motifs from these three genres are combined? Do differences between the genres create tensions? Throughout this chapter, I intentionally use this body of texts to raise questions I examine in more detail in the following chapters on *Green Peony*. I shall give plot summaries as necessary, since these novels are essentially unstudied and plot is central to the issues under discussion.

Beginnings

Around the Qianlong period, the stories of the earliest martial arts novels appeared in *chantefable* texts and storytelling in different regions. *Zhenben*

Tianbao tu quan zhuan (The authentic picture of Tianbao lute ballad; hereafter *Tianbao Lute Ballad*) was printed in 1776, in Suzhou dialect, and apparently circulated before that (fig. 2.1).[2] The performance of *Shan e tu* (The chart of good and evil) by the Yangzhou storyteller Cao Tianheng is noted in the city memoir *Yangzhou huafang lu* (Reminiscences from the pleasure boats of Yangzhou, 1795).[3] A drum ballad version of *Green Peony* survives in the Palace Museum in Beijing, in the collection of the office responsible for dramatic entertainment for the Qing palace from the Kangxi period on.[4]

Before examining the relationship between the martial romances and these *chantefables*, a word of clarification is in order. Most *chantefables* carry labels that also denote oral performance traditions. Thus, for example, the term "lute ballad" (*tanci*) refers to a prosimetric genre performed in Jiangnan. In addition, it also is applied to texts. In the case of the lute ballad, scholars generally divide these texts into two forms: "performance-related" lute ballads, and "literary lute ballads" or women's lute ballads.[5] "Literary lute ballads" were written and copied primarily for reading rather than for performance. However, even performance-related lute ballad texts are "fakes," written to be read, and cannot be proven to be either scripts or transcriptions of performance; nonetheless, they bear a closer relationship to performance than do the "literary" lute ballads.[6]

By the Qianlong period *chantefables* were widely printed or copied for reading,[7] and it is as texts for reading that I shall analyze them below. However, the format of most *chantefables* would lend itself to a different reading experience than a novel. In the 1930s, Zheng Zhenduo noted that new drum ballads (or reprints of old ones) were appearing in waves; there was a drum ballad for nearly every well-known story. As Zheng stated, "From this you can see how much the Northern people love to read this kind of thing. They would not necessarily hear it performed; they could just hold it up and read it aloud to themselves to satisfy their craving."[8] This observation suggests that in Zheng's time reading printed *chantefables* could serve as a substitute for performance for those familiar with the tradition. When I use the term "performance texts" or "performance genres" below, performance refers only to the implied reading context evoked by many of the *chantefables*.[9]

Returning to the martial romance, are the *chantefables* on *Green Peony* and *The Picture of Tianbao* independent renditions of those stories, or are they textually related to the novels? If so, which is prior?

The Picture of Tianbao

Both the *Tianbao Lute Ballad* and the novel *Tianbao tu* (The picture of Tianbao, 1814)[10] share the same plot. The title derives from a portrait a damsel paints of the hero Tao Tianbao after he saves her; they marry in the end. The title character and the villain form the links in the episodic

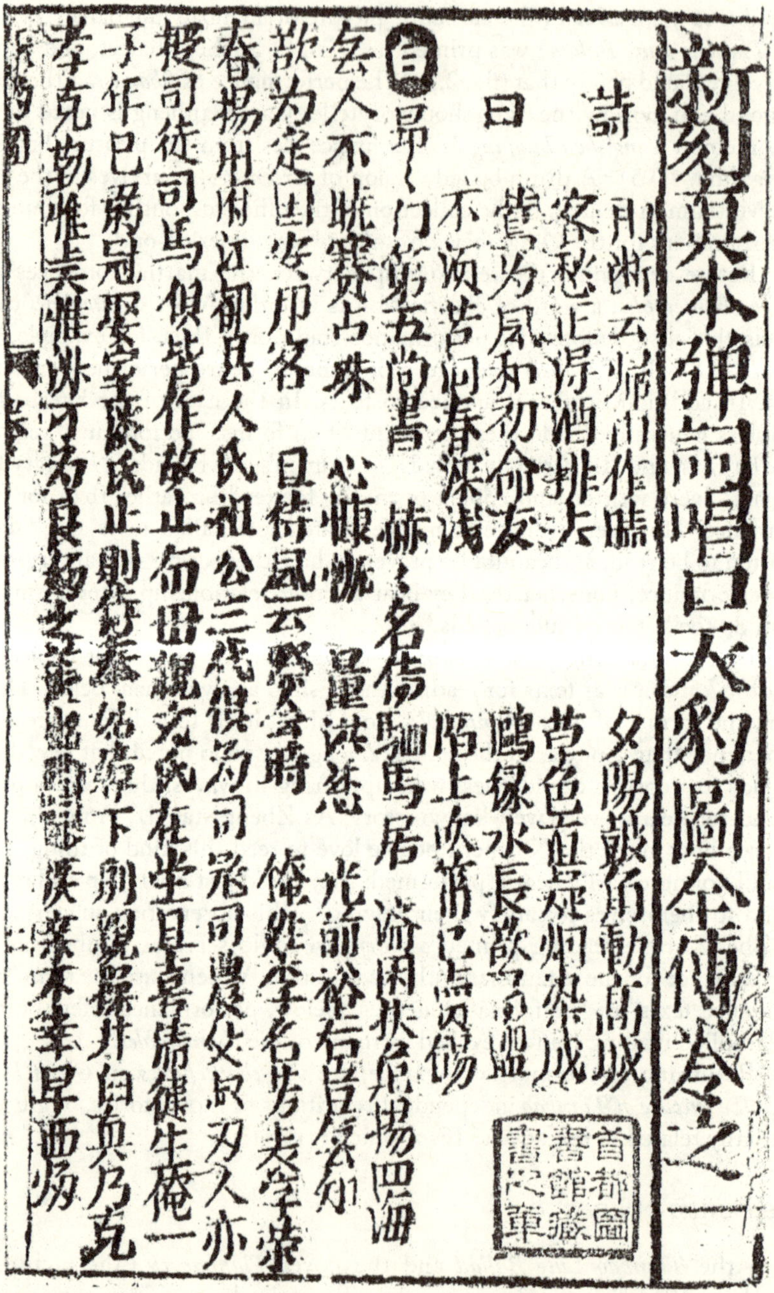

Figure 2.1 Title page and first page of the *Tianbao Lute Ballad*

乾隆四十一年新鐫

真本天豹圖

全傳

此書向無刻本外間所傳
俱係偽書今本坊購得
真本請名手重加潤色
關目句讀不同俗本
看辨之　飛春閣識

structure. A military official is executed for challenging the prime minister, and the official's wife and two children leave to live with relatives. On the way the official's wife dies; her son, Shi Bixian, becomes gravely ill; and the daughter, Shi Bixia, decides to sell herself into servitude to provide for her mother's funeral. She is seen by the prime minister's son Hua Zineng. He tricks her into coming to his manor, where he tries, unsuccessfully, to take her as his concubine. Li Rongchun, an official's son, goes to save her, but he is beaten and tied up by Hua Zineng's martial expert. Li is rescued by the maid Hong Hua. When Shi Bixian recovers, he goes to the Hua manor to find his sister; he ends up killing the martial expert. Li arranges a military post for Shi Bixian, and Shi Bixia is adopted into the Li family. On the way to his post, Shi Bixian meets some bandits; he becomes one of their leaders. When the martial expert's brother comes to avenge his death, he commits adultery with Hua Zineng's wife, née Qin. They are discovered by Hua's sister Hua Saijin, so Qin kills her. Judge Tian arrives, and Hong Hua presents Hua Saijin's murder case to him. He sends his protégé Tao Tianbao, the title character, to investigate and publicly punishes the adulterers.

Humiliated, Hua Zineng goes to the capital looking for revenge. He and his father forge a letter implicating Judge Tian and Li Rongchun as plotting a coup with Shi Bixian. Tian and Li are thrown in jail but broken out by Tao Tianbao, Shi Bixian, and his bandit gang. Imperial troops three times battle them at their mountain lair but are defeated. When they discover the prime minister is plotting to usurp the throne, Tao Tianbao and all the heroes go to the capital to rescue the emperor. The villains are executed. Li Rongchun clears his name. All the heroes are enfeoffed and married off.

In addition to sharing the plot, *Tianbao Lute Ballad* and the novel *The Picture of Tianbao* are textually related. That the lute ballad has the earlier date suggests that the novel adapted the lute ballad, a hypothesis supported by a close comparison of the two texts. Language characteristic of the lute ballad is present in the novel. One example concerns word order. For the sake of meter or rhyme the lute ballad frequently places the object in front of the verb using the particle *jiang* or *ba*. In this pattern *mai shen* (sell herself) becomes *jiang shen mai*. Standard grammar requires the verb be followed by something, but the ballad verse leaves the verb bare. Generally the novel respects the rules of grammar. In one instance, where the lute ballad has *ba Lu Jia guai*, the novel substitutes the more grammatical *jiang Lu Jia guai le*.[11] However, in several instances the novel copies the ballad's poetic license. Although such a construction is less common in prose, we find *jiang shen mai* and similar patterns in the novel *The Picture of Tianbao*.[12] Such patterns in the novel are vestiges of its *chantefable* origins.

Another tell-tale sign that the novel *The Picture of Tianbao* was derived from the *chantefable* is its frequent use of strings of elaborate similes and idioms. The action comes to a halt as the character delivers a monologue figuratively describing the situation. These are typical of the lute ballad. For example, one speech in the lute ballad is composed entirely of similies with similar meaning:

> Young Master [Hua Zineng] said, "Mrs. Hua [Miss Shi], I'm not afraid you won't submit.
>
> (Sings)
> You're *just like a fly in the spider's web*; how can you get out?
> *A fresh fish in water who's taken the hook and rod.*
> *A bird that's entered the cage* can't fly anywhere.
> *A lamb that's entered the pen* has no way to escape."[13]

Two of these similes appear in dialogue in the corresponding scene in the novel.[14] Thus *The Picture of Tianbao*'s lively dialogue, which has been praised by scholars of the novel,[15] derives directly from the lute ballad.[16]

Although the novel *The Picture of Tianbao* makes minimal use of verse, it borrows bits of verse from the lute ballad. At times the borrowings give the novel's prose a parallel rhythm.[17] The parallelism persists even when the wording echoes the lute ballad only faintly. In a passage where a maid fetches things, the lute ballad verse runs, "Hot water—in no time at all she had prepared a jug, while for a towel she chose patterned cloth" (*reshui dengshi bei yihu/ shoujin yikuai tiao huabu*).[18] The novel renders these two lines, "She poured a basin of hot water and got a towel" (*daole yipen reshui/ qule yitiao shoujin*).[19] The wording has significantly changed, but the parallel structure remains.

Besides the elimination of the verse, the most significant change from the *Tianbao Lute Ballad* to the novel is in the narrator's role. In both the lute ballad and the novel the narrator controls the narrative through "storyteller phrases" that shift the focus from one storyline to another or mark transitions between modes of presentation.[20] However, the narrator is more pervasive in the novel version than in the lute ballad. *Tianbao Lute Ballad* reads more like the script of a play than a traditional Chinese novel. Often it presents the dialogue without even indicating which character is speaking; speech markers like "he said" or "she thought" are not often used. The reader deduces from context which lines are whose. The narrator seems much less intrusive, partly because much of the action unfolds before the reader's eyes bit by bit rather than being summarized by the narrator in general terms. In *Tianbao Lute Ballad* action is directly shown; the narrator rarely intrudes to explain, comment, or pose questions to the audience. In the novel, action is primarily *told* by the narrator.[21] The novel also expands the narrator's role by adding explanations, or appropriating those presented by the characters in the lute ballad.[22]

The process of adaptation from the lute ballad to the novel *The Picture of Tianbao* is fairly straightforward. Little is omitted, and the rewriting rarely changes the meaning significantly. The novel primarily cuts out or paraphrases the verse and fills in the narrator's role. Is this the basic process of genre translation between the *chantefable* and the novel? To test the idea, the following section will examine a second pair of texts, in which the novel refashions the *chantefable* material more extensively than did *The Picture of Tianbao.*

Green Peony Drum Ballad

Sun Kaidi suggests that the novel *Green Peony* seems to have been adapted from a drum ballad.[23] Beyond close similarity of plot, *Green Peony Drum Ballad* and the novel are textually related. Slightly less than half the prose is the same in both works. The rest has been either partially or totally rewritten, but preserving the same order and details of plot and wording. Which was written first, the novel or the drum ballad? Since the drum ballad is undated, one cannot simply rely on the dates of the respective editions to settle this question.[24] A comparison of the verse sections of the drum ballad with the corresponding sections of the novel demonstrates the drum ballad is prior.

About one-third of the verse in *Green Peony Drum Ballad* is absent in the novel. In at least one case the omission of verse creates an anomaly in the novel. In a verse section in the first chapter of the drum ballad, the audience learns that Luo Binwang became a monk to protest Empress Wu's behavior, thus preparing the reader for the role he plays toward the end of the story in saving the hero, Luo Hongxun, and restoring the rightful emperor.[25] Since this verse was omitted in the novel, the novel does not mention Luo Binwang until chapter 44, when he suddenly appears identified only as a monk; only later in chapter 45 is his name revealed.[26] Likewise omitted from the novel is a verse that offers a clue to why Luo Hongxun finally agrees to marry the heroine, Hua Bilian. Although neither the novel nor the drum ballad explains this satisfactorily, the drum ballad comes closer to it in a decasyllabic verse in which Luo Hongxun is upset that the people at Hua's inn call him "son-in-law" (*guye*) but concludes that his mother may have agreed to the match.[27]

Further suggesting that *Green Peony Drum Ballad* came first is that the novel includes a pattern characteristic of the drum ballad. In order to stretch a line out to the necessary number of syllables, the drum ballad, like the lute ballad, often employs the pattern *ba* (or *jiang*) plus object plus verb; as in *ba jia huan* (return home), or *ba luo da* (hit the gong).[28] In one line of verse, the novel uses the pattern *jiang tai shang* for "mounted the stage" instead of *shang tai.*[29] Since this diction is unusual in conventional poetry, it is most likely that the drum ballad was the source.

The novel preserves bits of verse in ways that indicate the influence of the drum ballad. It often incorporates into its prose a line or two that clearly came out of a longer passage of verse in the drum ballad. While many of the snippets of verse that are preserved as prose can be discounted as set phrases, weightier evidence for the priority of the drum ballad is provided by the passages of verse preserved in dialogue in the novel. The novel again appears to draw material from the drum ballad in its use of a speech that has twenty-two lines in the drum ballad. Of these the novel keeps eight whole five-syllable lines as well as incorporating bits of several other lines into longer lines that preserve the rhyme.[30] Similarly, couplets in the novel often correspond to lines from longer passages of verse in the drum ballad. This duplication compellingly argues for the priority of the drum ballad. It is much less likely that the drum ballad borrowed one or two lines from the novel and composed eight or more lines to match than that the novelist chose one or two lines to preserve.

The verse from *Green Peony Drum Ballad* inspired unusual uses of verse in the novel. In the drum ballad, verse often describes emotion, a usage the novel adopts.[31] In fact, one critic praises the novel *Green Peony* for its detailed, realistic description of emotion.[32] Under the influence of the drum ballad, the novel *Green Peony* also uses verse to forward the action. This usage is quite rare but not entirely absent in novels; *Xiyou ji* (Journey to the West), for example, uses verse to describe action.[33]

The drum ballad verse further influenced the novel *Green Peony* by contributing some of its most vivid scenes, even when there is no discernible verbal influence. Perhaps because the drum ballad verse tends to focus on the characters' thoughts and feelings, it has provided the inspiration for many of the best episodes in the novel. An example is the scene in which Yu Qian tells Luo Hongxun that the villain Wang Lun has committed adultery with Ren Zhengqian's wife. The scene owes little verbally to the drum ballad, but it does develop an idea suggested by the verse in the drum ballad. The relevant scene in the drum ballad is as follows:

> Now Yu Qian, a lantern in his hand, entered their room angry. He threw the lantern down on the table—clunk!—and ducked to one side. Luo Hongxun stared at him and saw that Yu Qian looked angry, but he said nothing. Luo said, "Is there any tea?" Yu Qian brought over a cup of tea and plunked it down on the table, saying, "Master, have some tea." He almost broke the teacup. Luo Hongxun again stared at him and saw that Yu Qian was raging mad. Yu Qian said, "Master, in the future you shouldn't drink so much," in a tone of voice like an uncle chastening his nephew. Luo Hongxun couldn't help but get angry and yell, "You dog! Look at how drunk you are, and yet you are lecturing me!" Yu Qian said, "My drinking did no

harm. Your drinking did a lot of harm." The official's son said, "What harm have I done?" Yu Qian said, "If you hadn't asked, that would be that; since you have asked if I didn't tell you I would be cheating my master."

Before Yu Qian opened his mouth
His anger came to the surface.
Respectfully he said, "My master
This is no small matter.
It would be better if you hadn't mentioned it,
Bringing it up makes me bust a gut.
Wang Lun is the most depraved;
Everyone in the neighborhood says so.
He Shilai, the scoundrel,
Unscrupulously schemes for profit.
Both are no good
They do things without principles.
Knowing the two of them
How could you swear brotherhood?
You fell into his trap.
They used a plan to trick you.
You would never have seen through it;
You still thought they were your good friends."

Luo said, "How did he trick me?" Yu Qian said, "Master,

If I didn't tell you about this I would be angry,
But bringing it up makes me bust a gut.
How could you drink with him in the front room?
When you drink, you never get drunk.
Today of all days why did you crave liquor?
The two of you passed out at the table, dead to the world,
And because of this you fell into their clever trap.
The scoundrel Wang Lun is a lecher; he loves beautiful women.
He Shilai is avaricious, so he acted as a go-between.
Seduced, Wang Lun entered the back chambers;
He and that strumpet Madam He committed adultery.
I walked past their door after I went drinking.
I heard them making love, it's hard for me to speak of it."
Little Yu Qian had not finished telling everything
But when Luo Hongxun heard this much he blew his top.
He couldn't help but point and curse.
"Slave! There's no reason to what you say!
With this kind of thing it's hard to tell true from false.
If this got out, the consequences would be as weighty as a mountain.

First, slandering a good person as an adulterer is no trifle,
Second, a servant tricking his master is a crime hard to bear."
What a hot-headed official's son Luo is!
As he spoke he wanted to hit the loyal little Yu Qian.
In the back study, master and servant turn hostile.
In the next chapter the official's son swallows his anger and is bound.[34]

The novel follows the same plot down to the details. However, in a relatively concise passage it intensifies the drama of the confrontation. The italics in the following passage indicate language the novel shares with the drum ballad:

> *Now Yu Qian, a lantern in his hand, entered the* bed*room.* He put it on the table making a piercing sound; he was angry, so he couldn't help putting it down a little too hard. *Luo Hongxun* looked at Yu Qian and let it pass. Yu Qian then poured a cup of tea, came over in front of Luo Hongxun and *plunked it down on the table*, saying, "*Master, have some tea.*" *He almost broke the teacup.* Luo again glanced at him and let it pass. *Raging mad*, Yu Qian said, "*Master, in* the *future* you should drink less." When Luo heard these words, since Yu Qian's tone of voice was just *like an uncle* teaching *his nephew* a lesson, Luo unwittingly *got angry and yelled*, "*You dog!* Just *look* at how *drunk* you are, and yet you are exhorting *me!*" Yu Qian said, "Your *drinking did harm.* My drinking *did no harm.*" Luo Hongxun said angrily, "Tell me, what *harm have I done?*" Yu Qian said, "Since Master *asked me,* I'll tell it straight. Just now when you and Master Ren got drunk and fell asleep, *He Shilai*—that son of a bitch—*acted as a go-between* for his sister. *Wang Lun and Madam He* had a great time together." When Luo Hongxun heard these words, he yelled, "You beast! Where did you go to drink your rotten wine that you're lying to my face? Why don't you go to sleep!" After *Yu Qian* had been *cursed* out by Luo Hongxun, all he could do was *swallow his anger* and keep quiet, *muttering* to himself, "So I'm lying. In the future even if it turns into a matter that *roils rivers* and turns *seas* over, it's none of *my* business. Since he's close to Master, I could not but report it. I don't care anymore; I'm just going to mind my own business and go to sleep." Truly: "Each person sweeps the snow before their door / Never mind the frost on other people's roofs." So he *went to sleep* on the bed.[35]

The novel deftly heightens the confrontation by omitting Luo Hongxun's request for tea, thereby making Yu Qian's suggestion carry the force of an order. Repetition of words builds tension—Luo chooses to "let it pass" twice before becoming angry. The novel additionally expands the section toward the end where Yu Qian mutters to himself, and adds the summarizing couplet. Such selective rewriting and amplification pervades the novel. The differences in how the novel and the drum ballad treat a particular scene may be slight, but they are enough to affect the reader's impression of the scene and characterization.

Comparing these two passages raises the issue of the aesthetics of the *chantefable* versus the novel. Apart from the relative proportion of verse to prose in the two works, there are few fundamental differences between the drum ballad and the novel *Green Peony*. However, as the passage analyzed above suggests, innumerable minor changes accumulate to affect the reader's impression of the two texts. The novel *Green Peony* is more textually oriented than the drum ballad. I shall explore this distinction and its implications in more detail in chapter 5, but for now let me mention some of the distinctive features of the novel. The novel prizes conciseness; it uses repetition effectively to tie constituent elements together; and it creates a tighter overall structure by slight changes to the drum ballad. For example, the drum ballad emphasizes prolepsis of the ultimate outcome of the story over prolepsis from one episode to the next. When it does include the second kind of prolepsis, it tends to limit information to what will literally be seen in the next moment in the next scene. While the novel omits some of the prolepses pointing to the final outcome, it inserts prolepses into many episodes to prepare the reader for the following episode. These prolepses are usually quite subtle, consisting of an occasional line of dialogue instead of a highly noticeable comment or poem by the narrator. Even so, these medium-range prolepses tighten the structure of the novel compared with the short- and long-range prolepses of the drum ballad. One example is Pu Tianpeng's invitation, inspired by his gratitude, to Luo Hongxun to visit his home.[36] Even though the invitation is refused, it prepares the reader of the novel for the next episode, in which Pu Tianpeng has his band of pirates kidnap Luo Hongxun and bring him home so he might thank him. The drum ballad provides no such hint, so the kidnapping episode comes completely without warning.

The textual orientation of the novel *Green Peony* also shows in the passages it adds, which are often ironic reworkings of scenes from well-known texts such as *The Water Margin*. Even more striking is the novel's addition of self-referential and metafictional comments by the author, narrator, and characters, to which we shall return in chapter 4.

In summary, while both *The Picture of Tianbao* and *Green Peony* adapt *chantefable* texts, *The Picture of Tianbao* simply tailors its material to the novel's formal requirements, reshaping the verse to prose and modifying the role of the narrator, without significantly changing the meaning. *Green Peony* complicates the process of adaptation by adding irony and tightening the structure of the novel; it thereby alters the reader's understanding of the characters and meaning. While the two cases suggest a range of acceptable aesthetics for the novel as a genre, *Green Peony*'s success in reaching a wide readership implies that it was the more successful adaptation.

In addition, these two cases of adaptation suggest that, in the earliest stage, martial arts fiction may have formed and spread in *chantefable* texts before the novels existed. This raises the question: Are many of the martial romances derived from written *chantefables*? Certainly the relationship between these novels and *chantefable* traditions remains close throughout the Qing. As we shall see below, however, adaptation from *chantefables* was an important first step in the development of the genre, but once it established its own conventions, the martial romance generally developed independently from the *chantefable*.[37]

Martial Motifs

What characterizes the early martial arts novels as a group? The resemblances between the novels in this first stage of the martial romance mark them as products of a similar performance-related milieu, although each is related to a different local performance genre.[38] A comparison of *The Chart of Good and Evil*[39] and *The Picture of Tianbao* shows that motifs shared between the two novels make up at least 15 to 20 percent of the material in each novel. While the novels in this first stage share many motifs, there is no single overall structure that they all follow. Indeed, with the exception of *Green Peony*, the structure of these novels may strike the reader as weak.

These three novels draw on a similar stock of formulae, ranging from conventional descriptions, nicknames, and poems to plot motifs. For example, the villains in both *The Chart of Good and Evil* and *The Picture of Tianbao* are so notorious for kidnapping any woman they see that all the women hide whenever they go out. In *The Picture of Tianbao* the narrator explains,

> So when any woman saw he arrived she would scuttle like a mouse seeing a cat and disappear without a trace. A woman with nowhere to go would close her gate and shut her door. They gave him a nickname; everyone called him "Clear-Out-the-Streets King," because as soon as he came out, whole streets and lanes would fall silent, and not a soul would dare to oppose him. That's why everyone called him "Clear-Out-the-Streets King."[40]

This resembles the explanation in *The Chart of Good and Evil*, "There was not a single woman on the streets. Why was that? As soon as someone saw Pock-faced Li, every home would shut its doors, every place would close its gates, who would still dare to come out? So they didn't see a single woman."[41] Variations in these shared materials argue against textual transmission, since the same sound will be written with different characters in each novel. For example, in a verse appearing in both *Green Peony* and *The Chart of Good and Evil*, eight of fifty characters differ; most are phonetic substitutions, such as *shou* (head) for *shou* (hand).[42]

I am not suggesting that any of these novels borrowed directly, textually or otherwise, from any other. The three novels each adapted a different local performance genre, which would largely preclude direct influence among the novels. The shared motifs are established patterns that get repeated again and again, substituting new characters but changing very little overall. A comparison of an episode that the three novels *The Chart of Good and Evil*, *The Picture of Tianbao*, and *Green Peony* have in common demonstrates their similarities. The chart below outlines the major motifs constituting one episode shared by the three novels, the abduction and attempted rape of a martial woman (table 2.1). Note that the same motifs are employed in largely the same order in each novel, though other episodes may interrupt the sequence.

Table 2.1 The abduction motif in three early martial romances

	NOVEL AND CHAPTER		
INCIDENT	*Good and Evil*	*Picture of Tianbao*	*Green Peony*
woman's martial performance	4		2
villain's lust is aroused	4	1	2
she is invited in "to meet wife"	4		5
villain flirts with woman	4	1–2	5
she fights him		1–2	5
hero comes to save her	+	3	6
villain escapes	+	3	5
villain calls guard	+	3	
hero/heroine smashes up place		3	5

+This incident appears in conjunction with another attempted rape in chapter 9.

What makes the proposition of a shared milieu for these novels all the more convincing is that these motifs carry with them a startling amount of detail. For example, the abduction of a martial woman begins in both *The Chart of Good and Evil* and *Green Peony* with a martial performance by the heroine. Even the dialogue introducing the performance and the description of the heroine's clothes are very similar. The passage in *The Chart of Good and Evil* goes:

> Suddenly they heard the sound of gongs thundering in their ears, and asked what was happening to make all that ruckus. A servant came forward and bowed, saying, "Master, there's someone performing gymnastics at Guandi Temple."
>
> Li Lei said, "Old Shao, what's this thing called gymnastics?"

Shao said, "Master has never seen it?"

Li Lei said, "I have never seen it."

Shao Qing asked if they were men or women, and the answer was there were men, with one woman and one girl. Are they sexy? He said I just saw them, and she's fairly pretty and a Northerner, it's just that her skin is a bit dark.

Li Lei said, "Old Shao, I'd like to send someone to invite them home to perform."[43]

In *Green Peony* it is the two heroes, rather than the villain or his men, who see the performers first.

Suddenly they heard a clanging of gongs on the main road. Master Ren and Luo stood up and looked toward the road. They saw a throng of people surrounding a dozen or so men, all of them dressed in Shandong garb. Among them, there were also two women, one old and one young; the old one was around sixty, the young one only sixteen or seventeen. All of them were wearing old blue cotton jackets, except the young woman, who was dressed in thin green silk pants, bluish-white damask socks, and bright red silk shoes, but did not wear a skirt. In the middle was an old man, in his hand a big gong, which he clanged several times. Luo had watched for a while and had no idea what kind of people these were, so he asked,

"Elder brother, what does this band do?"

Master Ren said, "Little brother, this is something they do in Shandong, it's called acrobatics. In the south have you ever seen it?"

Luo answered, "Actually I never have."

Master Ren ordered Yu Qian, "Call that band over and ask them what they can do."[44]

The difference between the two passages is essentially that the passage in *Green Peony* gives a first-hand view of the troupe rather than a reported account. Indeed, when a full description of the girl is given in *The Chart of Good and Evil*, many of the details match another description in *Green Peony*: In both novels, the girl takes off an outer jacket to reveal inside an apricot colored top, a bright sash, green pants, and small feet.[45] In *Green Peony*, the villain also invites the troupe home to perform, but only after they have already begun performing in public.

Wang Lun watched with admiration as that girl rode the galloping horse and walked the tightrope. He turned to He Shilai and said,

"This girl's only fifteen or sixteen and her face and figure are well-proportioned, but I wonder if she's that sort?"

He Shilai smiled and said, "Master, you really are a noble scion; you don't even know the status of people like them. Anyone who gallops on a horse or walks the tightrope, or sells flowers, traveling to every province and county, does that just as a cover. All of them make their money doing

> *that* at night; which of them isn't 'that sort'? . . . If you're pleased with them today, tomorrow I'll go to their inn and invite them over. It'll be like a falcon eating a sparrow, no trouble at all."[46]

Although the actual program performed is different in each case, both women ride on horseback. Moreover, both performances are called off before they are finished, and both lead to the same result: The villain wants to sleep with the performer. The corresponding dialogue in *The Chart of Good and Evil* is much simpler than the passage given above from *Green Peony*. After watching, dazzled, as the women perform, the villain Li Lei asks, "'Old Shao, I want these two women. Do you think it can be done?' Shao Qing said, 'If Master wants it, there's no harm in trying.' When Li Lei heard that, he went with Beastface into the study to discuss matters."[47]

In order to get the women alone, in each case the villain says that his wife invites the women in. Thereafter the two stories diverge. In *The Chart of Good and Evil* the villain has his way; the women are brought to the "Western suite," stripped, and raped. A lawsuit follows; the women's relatives bring the villain to court, but the judge decides in the villain's favor.[48] Usually, however, the women are saved at the last minute, or save themselves. When a similar motif occurs in chapter 32 of *The Chart of Good and Evil*, the woman is saved. An underling informs the villain (here a bandit) about the girl, and he orders her captured. After his men capture her sedan, the bandit orders the bridal chamber prepared. However, this woman has more courage; she curses him and refuses to submit. Thereupon the bandit leader orders her stripped and beheaded, but one of his band members asks for another three days to talk her around. In that time she swears sisterhood with the bandit chief's daughter, who protects her until the heroes capture the villain's stronghold and all the stolen concubines are returned to their kin.[49]

In both *The Picture of Tianbao* and *Green Peony* the villain never succeeds. The woman herself fights back. One scene in *The Picture of Tianbao* shares elements with both the motifs from *The Chart of Good and Evil* just described. In *The Picture of Tianbao*, the martial woman Shi Bixia first arrives at the villain's home after having sold herself into servitude to pay for her mother's funeral. Despite her clear statement that she will be a maid but not a concubine, the villain has other ideas. He makes advances, clasping her waist; she then knocks him to the floor and curses him. He orders his maids to strip her and hold her down, but his other concubines intercede on her behalf. This is repeated three times, with the villain's advances and the heroine's blows becoming stronger each time. Finally one of the villain's concubines asks for three days to talk Shi Bixia around.[50] Thereafter he tries twice more to have his way with her, but always to no avail, and in the end she gains protection by swearing sisterhood with his sister.

Although the villain's advances in a similar scene in *Green Peony* are slightly less graphic, they still form recognizably the same motif. The martial woman, Hua Bilian, and her mother are invited into the back of the house, ostensibly by the villain's wife. When they get to the room that they are led to and see two men, they assume they are mistaken and ask their way. They are told that his wife's invitation was just a ruse, because the villain himself, Wang Lun, wants to meet her.

> Wang Lun saw Hua Bilian's face was flushed and looked even more beautiful than before, and he thought she was playing bashful.
>
> He said, "If you won't reject me, there's a banquet already laid, so please sit and drink with me."
>
> With that he tried to take Hua Bilian's hand in his.
>
> Hua Bilian cursed him out, "You bastard, you dare flirt with me!"
>
> Then she made a fist and was about to capture Wang Lun, and Mrs. Hua was about to grab He Shilai, when several servants happened to run in from outside the gate and block them. Wang Lun and He Shilai, seeing that their plans were ruined, went behind the screen and locked the door behind them. Then they escaped into the study.
>
> When Mrs. Hua and Hua Bilian saw the servants blocking them, allowing Wang Lun and He Shilai to escape, they got very angry and beat up the servants. Indeed:
>
> Those who met their feet dropped to the ground,
> Those who felt their fists fell facing the heavens.
>
> How could any of them be a match for this mother and daughter? With three blows and two kicks, they all were beaten and went scurrying in all directions. The two of them, mother and daughter, went into the hall searching for Wang Lun and He Shilai, but they saw the screen was shut tight and knew the men had hidden. So with one kick they tipped over the feast that laid at the eastern side of the hall and broke off the four legs of the table. They completely demolished all the antique objets d'art, as well as the tables, chairs, and other furniture in the parlor.[51]

The martial women prove more than a match for the villain and his men.

The above account lays out how one motif, the attempted rape of a kidnapped woman, is handled in three novels derived from different performance genres. At the level of structure, motifs are often closely associated with other motifs. In both *Green Peony* and *The Picture of Tianbao,* the attempted rape of a martial woman evokes the motif of a hero coming to save her. In each case, upon learning the woman's plight, the hero goes to the villain's house to rescue her. Once there, the villain suggests that he and the hero swear brotherhood. The two novels diverge with the hero's response.[52]

In *The Picture of Tianbao*, when Li Rongchun, the hero, arrives at the villain Hua Zineng's manor, they have a polite chat in which the villain suggests they swear an oath of brotherhood. The conversation soon breaks down, however, when the hero suggests that the villain release Miss Shi. The villain angrily orders a wedding banquet laid out, then strikes at the hero, who hits him and pins him down under his foot. The hero then "makes a fist and beats the servants so that they scamper in all directions, vanishing without a trace."[53] The hero releases the villain on the promise that he will release Miss Shi. Instead, the villain runs in, locks the door behind him, and calls out his resident martial artist, who comes out to find the hero smashing up the place.

> Li Rongchun waited a long time, but saw no one come out; he called a few times, but no one answered; so at that moment a fire flared up in his heart. He yelled,
>
> "Hua Zineng, you son of a bitch, since you won't release Miss Shi, I'm going to come in after you!"
>
> Still yelling, he picked up a rosewood eight-immortals table, and with a shake of his two hands broke off two legs. He wielded them in his hands and smashed to pieces the tables, chairs, and all the objets d'art arranged on the table. He even tore down and shredded the landscape paintings and calligraphy by famous artists hanging on the walls.[54]

The hero's rescue attempt in *Green Peony* resembles that in *The Picture of Tianbao*, but its constituent motifs are split among actors. The hero in *Green Peony* agrees to swear brotherhood with the villain. Thus, as seen above, the motif of smashing up the hall when the villain escapes is carried out in *Green Peony* not by the hero, but by the martial woman herself. Despite this, the motif is very similar in the two novels, right down to some of the wording.

The above discussion demonstrates that even in the earliest martial romances, the martial motifs are already well formed. The striking similarities between these motifs suggest that the texts are products of a similar milieu. A comparison of the structure of the three martial romance novels shows that there was considerable flexibility in their composition. In shared motifs, certain incidents may be added, left out, or acted by different characters in different novels.[55] Moreover, each motif carries a great deal with it, down to details of language and description. Still, the very different ways these materials are combined in the early novel shows a certain lack of consensus in the formative period of the martial romance.

From Punishment to Prevention

What influence does court-case fiction have on the martial romance, and what does the martial romance change?

The typical structure of court-case fiction consists of some or all of the following: "the background of the crime, the crime itself, its discovery, the identification of the criminal, his capture and confession, his sentencing and punishment."[56] Most of the time the crime is discovered after it has been committed, though the supernatural does facilitate rescue in a few cases in *Longtu's Court Cases*.[57] More often, the supernatural functions as evidence. Clues often come in dreams or by means of strange winds leading the judge to the scene of the crime. Such clues provide the information the judge needs to resolve impossible cases.[58] Otherwise, the plaintiff and defendant provide the evidence through their statements and written suits and countersuits. In the end the judge holds a trial and punishes the culprit. The judge is the one indispensable character in court-case fiction. Only he merits full characterization, while all other characters remain bare stereotypes.[59] Y. W. Ma recognizes the central role of the judge as "one of the most predominant features of *kung-an* fiction," evident from the earliest stories in the Yuan.[60]

While court-case fiction influenced the structure of *The Chart of Good and Evil*, the content is primarily martial.[61] *The Chart of Good and Evil* sandwiches martial adventures between an initial crime and the final punishment[62] and switches between a focus on the villain for the perpetration of the deed and a focus on the judge for its discovery and punishment. At the end, the novel returns to the court-case framework; the grievances that are perpetrated in the course of the novel are finally avenged by a judge aided by a group of martial heroes. However, much of the novel is simply theme and variation on the same local despot's attempts to rape women.

The martial romances expend great ingenuity on getting the heroes and heroines into dangerous situations and then rescuing them at the last minute. For example, the rape motif, in which a girl is abducted and forced to marry against her will, recurs six times in *The Chart of Good and Evil*, accounting for almost half the novel. However, martial heroes and supernatural elements constantly intervene, so each successive incident goes further than the last in disrupting the pattern. Thus while the first rape is successful, the second only appears to be successful. The third attempted rape is disrupted on the wedding night. The fourth victim attempts suicide when she learns of the engagement, thus preventing the wedding. In the fifth case the abduction itself is disrupted. By the sixth case the villain never abducts the girl he wants, but is given a substitute instead. Each repetition both repeats and varies the preceding pattern. This repetition with a difference illustrates the ascendancy of the martial motifs over the court-case crime motifs. In the martial romance, the crime usually remains an evil intent, rather than becoming a completed action.[63] Although one cannot posit a strictly chronological progression from *The Chart of Good and Evil* to *Green Peony* and *The Picture of Tianbao*, we have seen above that the martial motifs are more dominant in the latter two novels, so the villain never succeeds in violating the woman.

Since the hero and villain in the martial romance are not killed off in each episode, they can continue to appear throughout the novel. This contrasts sharply with earlier collections of court-case stories, in which the judge is the only main character to remain constant from episode to episode. As a consequence, the judge is no longer as central to the structure of the martial romance. For example, in *The Chart of Good and Evil* the judge appears very late in the novel and figures only in the last six chapters. However, in this novel the judge is still a central character once he appears. One sign of this is a switch in narrative style when the judge enters the action. Like a Western mystery, the reader learns only as much as the judge does. Whereas up to this point *The Chart of Good and Evil* had employed an omniscient narrator and multiple points of view, after introducing Judge Tang, the action follows him and is given exclusively from his point of view.[64]

In the martial romance, the hero gradually displaces the judge as the focus of the novel. In *The Picture of Tianbao* the judge appears about halfway through,[65] but after deciding one case, he becomes just another character and equally subject to the machinations of the villain. The good judge becomes little more than an excuse for the appearance of his protegé, the title character Tao Tianbao. He is a martial type, with Daoist training, who was dismissed by his teacher and sent to assist the judge. His adventures largely consist of saving people from villains' evil schemes. As the emphasis in the martial romance moves away from the intricacies of solving a case and focuses instead on standing up against corruption, it becomes an open question who can play the role of judge. Interest shifts from how the case is solved to how corruption will be overcome and justice served. The symbol of the judge's power in these novels is often a sword given by the emperor, which confers on him the power to execute first and report later.[66] Thus the "judge" can be a civil or military official, a bandit, or even an immortal.[67] This becomes increasingly apparent in the second stage of the martial romance, as shall be seen below.

Even motifs that once centered on the judge take other characters in the early martial romance. In the court-case stories, the supernatural often provides the judge with crucial information about injustice that leads to the solution of a case. In the martial romance, it continues to serve the same function but informs the victim's relatives instead of the judge. In *The Chart of Good and Evil*, dreams also serve to inform people of injustices, and strange winds take them where they ought to go. While Judge Tang's dream of all those wronged by the villain is typical of the court-case tale, he is not the only one to have such dreams. The ghost of one victim tells his mother what happened in *The Chart of Good and Evil*, and in *The Picture of Tianbao* another ghost appears in a dream to ask his brother for vengeance.[68]

In both *Green Peony* and *The Picture of Tianbao,* the judge does not even decide a case. The judge in *Green Peony* first appears about two-thirds of the way through the novel and turns the court case the outlaws bring to him back to the outlaws for judgment. Similarly, the judge in *The Picture of Tianbao* is so displaced that he does not even preside over the final trial of the villain, even though he is present; instead the mother of one of the heroes holds trial in the righteous bandits' stronghold. Chen Pingyuan comments on this phenomenon, suggesting one of the main functions of the judge in the martial arts novel is to provide official justification for the heroes' previous actions.[69] In other words, even in these early martial romance novels, the judge primarily plays a structural role.

The martial romance draws many of its themes and a general structure from court-case fiction. However, the increasing importance of the martial motifs shifts the emphasis away from discovery of a crime by the judge toward prevention of such crimes by the martial hero. Particularly for the first two stages of the development of the martial romance, changes in the role of the judge mark major changes in structure. In this first stage, the martial motifs change the structure of the plot. While the traditional court-case plot progresses from the commission of a crime to its discovery and punishment, in the martial romance the heroes prevent the crime from ever happening. This seemingly minor change has implications for both structure and characterization, since it places less emphasis on the judge than did court-case fiction.

The Formation of a Formula

The second group of martial romances consists of three novels: *Qun Ying Jie* (The Gathering of Heroes, no date), *Wanhua Lou* (The Pavilion of Myriad Flowers, 1808), and *Zheng Chun Yuan* (The Garden of Competing Beauties, 1819).[70] While introducing a wide variety of motifs from the military romance (*yingxiong chuanqi*) and the scholar-beauty romance, they also superimpose three different frameworks: the ongoing adventures of a judge and his assistant from court-case fiction; the romance plot; and sworn brotherhood as a structural device from *Three Kingdoms.* How do these competing structures come together to create the particular form of the martial romance?

A Clash of Genres

In *The Gathering of Heroes,* the clash of genres determines the structure.[71] The plot shifts abruptly between the scholar-beauty romance, court-case fiction, and historical fiction. The best way to demonstrate this is with a synopsis. *The Gathering of Heroes* begins like a scholar-beauty romance. A scholar sets off to marry his fiancée. However, when he befriends a martial type (Fan Zhongyan, on his way to the capital for the examinations) on the road, and swears brotherhood with him over his servant's objections,[72] he alienates his servant.

This departure from the norms of the scholar-beauty romance unleashes the lawless world of court-case fiction. Disgruntled, the servant decides to kill his master, take his engagement token, and marry his master's fiancée.[73] The murder is thwarted by supernatural intervention from a helpful local deity. By the time the scholar arrives at his father-in-law's, the servant has already married his fiancée—or actually a maid who substitutes for her. The true fiancée, warned by a dream, had opposed the match even though her father approved it. In accordance with her role in the scholar-beauty romance, she has escaped dressed as a man to look for her true match.[74]

The arrival of the real scholar threatens to expose the ruse and ruin the family's reputation.[75] So, in another motif from court-case fiction, they decide to frame the scholar for the accidental death of a maid they themselves killed.[76] The villain uses his influence to give the judge only three days to solve the case on pain of death. While the jailer frees the scholar and runs away with him, the judge brings the case before Judge Bao and the empress, listing the villain's misdeeds. The martial hero, who has just passed the imperial examination, is appointed to investigate the case. The villain is warned, however, and uses every means available to him to try to impede the investigation, including colluding with bandits.

Thus begins a series of close escapes and hide-and-seek adventures that are brought to a close halfway through the novel. In a nod to the conventions of the scholar-beauty romance, the servant, the fiancée, and the scholar all pass the imperial examinations under the same name, prompting the emperor to uncover their true identities.[77] Justice is then served; in punishment for their crimes the servant is executed and the villain implicated, prompting the latter to join forces with the bandits in full-scale rebellion.

At this point the novel switches models from the scholar-beauty romance to the military romance (*yingxiong chuanqi*). The second half of the book relates how the scholar and the martial heroes he has met during his adventures campaign against the rebels and eventually win. The hero must switch roles from the victimized scholar to the strategist and avenging general.

How are all these genres connected? Judge Bao appears a number of times at crucial moments in *The Gathering of Heroes*, connecting the various episodes and keeping the action going. On his first appearance in chapter 8, Judge Bao becomes our hero's advocate at the imperial court.[78] He convinces the emperor to send Fan Zhongyan to investigate the hero's case. In chapters 15 and 16 he intercedes on his behalf in the hearing presided over by the emperor that decides the hero's identity and fate. Then he suggests in chapter 18 that the scholar and all his martial friends be made generals. When they are nearly defeated in a battle of magic, Judge Bao arranges in chapters 26 and 27 for an imperial edict ordering the woman warrior Mu Guiying to come to the rescue. Judge Bao continually sets things in motion and then stands back. While the judge may seem to have a larger role in this second group of martial romances, he does not participate in the action so much as play a structural role in facilitating it.

Heroes and Brotherhood

In contrast to the episodic structure of *The Gathering of Heroes*, *The Pavilion of Myriad Flowers* achieves a tightly knit structure by centering on one character. C. T. Hsia notes that one reason for the success of *The Pavilion of Myriad Flowers* is that it can be read as the adventures of the general Di Qing. It was written after a number of other novels about him, so he had already attained the status of a legend.[79] The novel begins with intrigues at court before he was born, then relates his childhood, martial training, arrival at court, and the brash enthusiasm to fight corruption that gains him enemies.[80]

The bulk of the novel revolves around three court cases. The first is a suit against Di Qing for killing a high official's wastrel son.[81] When Di Qing is released, his enemy the high official tries to take revenge by sending him on a perilous mission to the front. Under a strict deadline, Di Qing is not only late arriving, he loses the supplies he was charged with delivering. He is tried a second time. He convinces the judge at the front to allow him to redeem himself in battle by leading a successful expedition against the enemy. As a result, the bad officials at the front are executed. Di Qing's motivation to enter the battlefield is not that of the typical military man, who is concerned with either winning glory or proving his loyalty to his country. Instead it is simply a way to prevail in court.

The third case arises when the widow of one of the men executed asks another corrupt official to get revenge against Di Qing. The injustice is revealed to Judge Bao by the ghost of the wife of the corrupt official, who is then revived to testify. Both of the corrupt officials are executed. Its classification as a military romance (*yingxiong chuanqi*) notwithstanding, the backbone of *The Pavilion of Myriad Flowers* is the court-case motif.[82]

The feud that runs throughout *The Pavilion of Myriad Flowers* stems from the episode in which Di Qing swears brotherhood with two heroes. The vows of brotherhood Di Qing and his friends swear are specified as "the vows of the Peach Garden."[83] The reference is reinforced when a tavernkeeper thinks they are the ghosts of the *Three Kingdoms* heroes, to whom they bear a striking physical resemblance.[84] As they are drinking in the tavern, in the gorgeously carved Pavilion of Myriad Flowers (whence the novel's name), they get in a fight with the wastrel son of a powerful official, and Di Qing accidentally throws him down to his death. All three heroes are arrested and brought to trial, but Di Qing's sworn brothers Li Yi and Zhang Zhong loyally take the blame, so he is released by a sympathetic Judge Bao. Although the brotherhood ceremony is clearly modeled on *Three Kingdoms*, it does not serve the same structural function in organizing the novel.[85] In *The Pavilion of Myriad Flowers* the ceremony seems almost a gratuitous reference to *Three Kingdoms*, and serves mainly to provoke the high official's wrath.

In contrast, the ceremony of brotherhood in *The Garden of Competing Beauties* structures the entire novel. The brotherhood ceremony occurs three times in *The Garden of Competing Beauties*, to form a brotherhood of nine.[86] Their vow, "We hope to live and die together" echoes the *Three Kingdoms* vows, "We don't ask to be born on the same day; our only hope is to die on the same day."[87] The brotherhood is even given supernatural justification. In the opening chapter of *The Garden of Competing Beauties*, a Daoist gives the martial hero Hao Luan three precious swords and sends him on a quest to find two other heroes upon whom to bestow the swords. While looking for heroes worthy of them, Hao Luan forms the brotherhood of nine. All of the stories related in *The Garden of Competing Beauties* are tied together by the fact that they implicate one of the nine sworn brothers. Once framed, the brother must be rescued through the other heroes' martial adventures.

In *The Garden of Competing Beauties*, the emphasis on heroism reduces the importance of court-case motifs. In fact, the court cases in the novel all result from the hero Ma Jun's love of justice. The first case occurs when he avenges the injustice that began the book by killing the villain and his henchman and presenting their heads at court along with the details of the case.[88] On two other occasions he serves the function that ghosts and dreams had served in the early martial romance, providing the judge with crucial information to solve difficult cases. When Ma Jun goes back to an inn to retrieve his sword, he finds it is being held as evidence in a murder trial. He approaches the judge in the middle of the night and informs him of the details, which he has learned from the perpetrator. The judge is then able to solve the case, and returns Ma Jun's sword. Later, Ma Jun returns to serving as the eyes and ears of the law and informs the emperor that his prospective son-in-law is an impostor. The emperor does not believe him immediately and jails both men, but Ma Jun redeems himself by saving the emperor from an assassination attempt.

Not only does the hero instigate the court cases, but a Daoist plays the structural role generally played by the judge, directing the heroes in their adventures. He ensures that the heroes are in the right place at the right time, for example, to save the emperor.[89] It is only in the penultimate chapter that he participates directly in the action, appearing in a battle of magical tactics.[90]

The second group of martial romances fulfills Chen Pingyuan's criteria for genre, that particular material match a particular form.[91] The way in which the martial romances combine these competing structures is still not completely fixed; each novel incorporates largely the same elements but places a different amount of emphasis on each. At this stage the oath of brotherhood comes to play an important role as impetus to the plot, provoking the feud with the villain that sets the hero's adventures in motion. Typically, the feud begins when the hero or his sworn brother prevents the villain from committing a crime.[92] In the end it is usually resolved in court, and the villains are punished. However, they are not punished for the incident that began the book. As the personal feuds that figured in the early novels escalate into national crises in this second group of novels, the villain is finally punished for crimes against the state (plotting rebellion, a coup, or an assassination).

How does this differ from the military romance (*yingxiong chuanqi*)? In other words, what did these competing structures change? In order to answer that, one must have a clear picture of the typical structure of the military romance, which Y. W. Ma characterizes as revolving around issues of "national security." These set "a brave and theatrical general who is highly romanticized or drawn on a scale larger than life, and his devoted subordinates as one group," in factional disputes against "a treacherous and towering minister, usually allied with influential eunuchs and other powerful court followers."[93] But such novels often end in tragedy, like the famous story of Yue Fei; "the hero, in his reluctance to negotiate, always fails to fulfill his heroic promise . . . The subsequent triumph of the malicious party, however temporary, completes the contrast of good and evil and confirms the ironic tragic quality."[94] Once again, just as in the first stage, the martial romance novels palliate the tragic aspects of the genres they draw upon and construct a new happy ending. In contrast to the novel of national security, the hero in the martial romance not only wins in the end but comes out ahead in each episode despite the villain's machinations.

Legends and Composition

The second group of martial romances were primarily composed as novels, rather than adapted from performance genres. Although *The Gathering of Heroes* and *The Pavilion of Myriad Flowers* have clear links to *nanyin* ballads, there is no evidence that the ballads preceded the novels.[95] Not only are the ballads themselves much later than the novels, but *nanyin* often adapted material from novels rather than vice versa.[96] The text of the *nanyin* on *The Pavilion of Myriad Flowers* states as much: "Now we'll tell of how Di Qing got his start/in the unofficial histories and novels it's already been written/there's no harm in adapting it to make a song-text."[97]

How does the method of composition affect these novels' relationship to each other and to other works? Although the novels of the second stage still share a significant number of motifs, they account for a much smaller proportion of each novel's plot than in the first stage. Moreover, a comparison of the same motif among second-stage martial romances shows very little shared language or description. These novels are no longer drawing on the same kind of pool of shared motifs as did the first stage. That is not to say that they are wholly original. Far from it.

Legend has always been one of the major sources of material for the military romance (*yingxiong chuanqi*), which "draw[s] to a significant extent upon a common heritage of hero-legends irrespective of whether these legends already existed in a written form or remained in a fluid state as oral tradition."[98] Even in the more "responsible" novel *Three Kingdoms,* the use of legendary material to supplement the historical facts is well established.[99] Of the novels we have discussed so far, *The Pavilion of Myriad Flowers* and *Green Peony* owe the greatest debt to the military romance. Their main characters derive directly or indirectly from legends, some of which had been elaborated in other novels before them; indeed, they were sometimes considered sequels or prequels to existing military romances.

The last few chapters of *The Gathering of Heroes* call up the legend of the Yang Family Generals. The heroes defeat the villains in magic warfare only with the assistance of General Yang's widow Mu Guiying. When Mu Guiying is requested to go to the battlefront, the Yang family matriarch refers to those in her family who have died for the country, and says Mu Guiying is too old to go.[100] In this way, despite the fact that Mu Guiying only puts in a cameo appearance in *The Gathering of Heroes,* the action in this novel is put in the context of the other legends of the Yang Family Generals. Indeed, one title for a *chantefable* version of *The Gathering of Heroes* declares its affiliation with the Yang Family Generals saga.[101] This legendary material may be attractively familiar to the reader, but it is simply grafted onto the novel.

The Pavilion of Myriad Flowers also draws on legend, but incorporates it as a frame for the whole novel. Drawing on the famous court-case story, Emperor Renzong claims his mother,[102] the beginning of the novel recounts the corruption that forced Emperor Renzong's mother to flee from the palace. It is connected to Di Qing through his aunt, who adopted the emperor as an infant after Empress Liu tried to kill him. At the end of the novel, the already famous scene in which the emperor's real mother is brought back to court is played out. Like the other martial arts novels in this second group, *The Pavilion of Myriad Flowers* uses a well-known story to place the new plot in a familiar framework.

The legendary material is increasingly well integrated within these novels. Except for *The Gathering of Heroes,* which still indulges in wholesale borrowing, they use the material from legend or other well-known novels as a familiar framework within which they can find a way to tell a new tale, or retell an old one from a different angle. *The Pavilion of Myriad Flowers* invents the story of its famous protagonist's youth,[103] while *The Gathering of Heroes* and *The Garden of Competing Beauties* create new main characters shaped to fit the needs of the emerging genre of the martial romance.

How does the structure of the second-stage martial romance novels reflect the change in method of composition? The discussion of structure above demonstrates an increased consciousness of the written construction of the novel. Skillful use of repetition augments the construction of the plot. When repetition occurs in the second stage of the martial romance, the repeated incidents are related. For example, in *The Pavilion of Myriad Flowers* there are three attempts in a row to kill corrupt officials, and three levels of generals defeated by the hero. Even trials come in twos and threes, with a corrupt trial followed by an upright trial of the same crime. All of the court cases in the novel are linked in both their cause and their results as well their placement in the novel. As soon as one case is decided, another arises out of it or is related to it. These escalating court cases form the framework of the novel's plot. The intricate pattern they construct, with each case growing out of and referring back to the previous one, would have been appreciated by the literary critics of the time as a way to add structure and meaning to the novel. In fact, *The Pavilion of Myriad Flowers* even includes chapter commentary that points out how it creates unity and resonance between episodes.[104] Thus a tighter structure in the second-stage martial romances reflects the change in method of composition.

As these novels integrate central roles and motifs into a common structure, they create the formula for the martial romance. This is borne out by C. T. Hsia's observation that *The Pavilion of Myriad Flowers* is the turning point in the creation of the martial arts novel.[105] It is no coincidence that the martial romance became a publishing staple after *The Garden of Competing Beauties.* The martial romance began to take off in the 1820s; from that point on such novels were published steadily each decade. The commercial success of *The Garden of Competing Beauties,* which spawned imitators, may have helped to establish the martial romance as a viable genre of popular fiction.

Formula and Variations

Such writing, perhaps all writing, eventually brings with it the drive for novelty. C. T. Hsia noted a similar tendency in his study of the military romance (*yingxiong chuanqi*). "[E]ach romancer, while inheriting the formulas from his predecessors, is also obliged to depart from the familiar and offer something new. . . . These innovations either refine, exaggerate, or render more comic a received plot situation."[106] As this tendency becomes apparent in the martial romance, it may truly be called a formula.

What evidence is there that the martial romance was already a formula at this point? The influence of the previous martial romances on this third group is unmistakable. The clearest example is *Da Han san he mingzhu baojian quan zhuan* (The complete tale of the pearly precious swords reunited three times in the Great Han Dynasty, 1848: hereafter *Three United Swords*), which is explicitly modeled on *The Garden of Competing Beauties.*[107] The last eight chapters of *The Garden of Competing Beauties,* about a search for the imperial son-in-law and the exposure of an impostor, form the framework of the first half of *Three United Swords.* The opening scene of *Three United Swords,* an episode on the lake, echoes chapter 10 of *The Garden of Competing Beauties.* The relationship is confirmed by several characters who appear in both.

In this third stage of the formation of the martial romance, the structure is fairly constant, and few new motifs are introduced. In fact, the number of motifs in use declines.[108] Except for *Three United Swords,* most of the novels in this third group present themselves as new by not invoking any specific stories. In contrast to the previous martial romances, they are self-contained works and avoid using characters from legend. As part of their self-containment, they insist on rendering a number of motifs that had previously simply been assumed to have happened before the novel began. For example, the enmity between the hero's father and the villain is always backstory in the early martial romance novels; often it is not clear how the enmity came about. In later novels, however, the enmity is acted out within the novel itself.[109] This tendency may be seen as early as *The Pavilion of Myriad Flowers*; it portrays how Di Qing's father died, a fire left him poor, and a flood separated him from his mother.[110] The third group of novels not only portray the catalytic incident but also make it increasingly solvable; rather than the hero's father being killed, he is exiled or sent on a border expedition while his children have their own adventures.[111] Indeed, the hero's search for his father becomes a new element in these novels. A perfect happy ending becomes possible. By incorporating and explaining its own assumptions, the martial romance succeeds in removing the remaining fangs from the traditions on which it draws.[112]

While most do not invoke specific previous stories, the novels in this third group do build on the developing conventions of the martial romance. Structurally, they begin when the others end. Rather than building up from a personal feud as did the previous martial romances, they start with a national crisis. Self-consciousness is evident in the novels' increasing attempts to avoid or vary previous motifs and incidents. The avoidance demonstrates an awareness that this type of incident has been used before in another work.

The search for novelty manifests itself in the variation of existing motifs, either in the form of a proscribed creativity that aims to take established motifs just one step beyond what has been done before, or by compressing a number of motifs into a single episode. *Three United Swords,* for example, shows a man kidnapped, dressed as a woman, and sold as a concubine, creating one more twist on *The Garden of Competing Beauties*.[113] In *The Garden of Competing Beauties* when the heroine is sold, the interest derives from whether her chastity will be preserved; she is saved by the buyer's wife. In *Three United Swords*, the interest lies in the novel's play on the reader's knowledge of such conventions. Since it is the hero who is sold as a concubine, however, the reader wonders not so much if his chastity will be preserved as when his identity will be discovered, although the two are linked: a threat to his "chastity" would expose his true identity. Dramatic irony drives the episode. As in *The Garden of Competing Beauties*, the buyer's wife prevents the buyer from taking him as a concubine and suggests he be given to their daughter as a maid instead. While the parents remain ignorant of the fact that he is a man, the daughter soon discovers his secret and they become lovers. Her lustful brother eventually uncovers the truth; when he attempts to rape his sister's "maid," he finds that "she" is a man. The chastity issue takes on a new relevance, applying now not to the attempted rape but to the affair itself. The man is sentenced to death (but rescued in the nick of time), and the girl dresses as a man to escape her father's suggestion that she commit suicide. The interest in this episode derives entirely from its play on the reader's expectations, which are conditioned by the formula of previous martial romance novels.

These novels also betray their awareness of the formula they work within by compressing several motifs into one in summary fashion, as if all the incidents are by this point so familiar to the reader that it is no longer necessary to develop each in its entirety. One short episode in *Yun Zhong Yan san nao Taiping Zhuang* (Yun, Zhong, and Yan stir up a ruckus three times in Taiping Zhuang, 1849),[114] for example, combines at least four motifs from previous novels. The villain's plan to kidnap the girl provides the impetus. The girl's cousin is actually working for the villain. Though he tries not to let on, the others know it and play different roles for his benefit: the maid plays the girl, the girl plays a man, and the mother goes along with the masquerade. When the villains seem to have kidnapped the girl, they have in fact kidnapped the maid. The maid is then saved, ostensibly by the bandits of Peach Blossom Mountain, who are led by none other than our hero dressed as a bandit. The whole episode takes only a few pages, with the novel alerting the reader that these roles and actions are "false."[115] Still these four conventional motifs (the maid being substituted for the girl of good family; the girl dressing as a man to escape; the villain dressing as a bandit to abduct her; and the hero preventing the abduction) change substantially by being combined. The girl dresses as a man not in order to leave home but to stay. The hero, not the villain, dresses as a bandit, and he does so not to abduct the girl but to rescue her. Moreover, the entire episode springs from the daughter's ploy to keep the villain at bay.

The novels of the third stage sometimes play on their reader's expectations by substituting roles within an established motif. *Yun Zhong Yan* characterizes one of the villains by casting him in the hero's role in the tavern fight motif. Yun Wen, the adopted son of an upright official, is drinking in a beautiful tavern when the waiter asks him to leave because the villain and his party are coming. He refuses, as a hero would, and the reader expects a fight. But instead, the villain's underling smoothes over the conflict and all of them become friends. The conflict never comes about. Because he reverses expectations and makes friends with the villains rather than fighting them, the reader realizes that he, too, is a villain. This realization depends on the reader's knowledge of genre conventions. As Heather Dubrow observed in *Genre,* "One of the most effective ways a writer can use genre is to evoke and intensify our generic expectations only to overturn them."[116] This is precisely what happens here. When a villain takes the hero's role, the motif no longer portrays the conflict of good and evil but throws into relief how the villain's actions differ from those of the hero.

The type of material the martial romance novels invoke changes at each stage, reflecting their method of composition and their context. In the first stage, the martial romances present the story being told as already familiar to the reader. This reflects their relationship with the performance genres. In the second stage, the author uses particular legends to frame his novel. This is a standard procedure in the Chinese novel, a way to present new material in a familiar manner. By the third stage no particular story or legend is invoked. Instead, the novels rely on the conventions of the martial romance. At this point it truly can be called a formula. The progression may also suggest a shifting audience for the genre, from those familiar with the first group of stories in other forms, to those more familiar with other forms of popular fiction, and finally to aficionados of the martial romance as a genre in its own right. Marketing and publication history supports this hypothesis to some extent. As we shall see in chapter 5, the most widely printed martial romances—*Green Peony, The Pavilion of Myriad Flowers,* and *The Garden of Competing Beauties*—all employ the rhetoric of fiction criticism to appeal to mainstream readers of the novel. In contrast, the third group does so only superficially and the other two novels of the first stage, not at all.

Genre Tensions

The question of roles addressed in the last section raises the issue of values. What happens when roles from the scholar-beauty romance, court-case fiction, and the military romance (*yingxiong chuanqi*) are placed side by side in the same novel?

The distinguishing characteristics of both scholar and martial hero are undermined. As early as *The Chart of Good and Evil,* a certain ambiguity appears concerning the definition of the martial hero, since sworn brothers fight on both sides and some martial types are loyal to an evil master. *The Chart of Good and Evil* amply shows that being martial or appreciating martial types is not necessarily the attribute of a hero. It presents a man who recognizes talent but puts it to bad use and who also uses unorthodox methods of recruiting. It thereby undercuts the ideal "mutual recognition" of heroes central to *The Water Margin*.

Our first exposure to a martial type in the novel evokes expectations of a righteous avenger, then inverts them as he is persuaded to work for the villain. When a group of merchants is discussing the villain Li Lei's misconduct in a tavern, Zhang Hai vows to make Li Lei leave.[117] Drunk, Zhang challenges and defeats Li Lei's martial artists. Li Lei's henchman Shao Qing suggests they kill Zhang Hai, but Li Lei shows his appreciation for martial types by insisting on Zhang Hai's surrender. Shao Qing has no choice but to go and hire new martial artists to fight him.

The men Shao Qing hires are a parody of the martial hero. They are starving and hardly have the strength to speak. At first they are reluctant to take the job since Zhang Hai has given them money in the past, but desperation wins out over principle. The new hires ambush Zhang Hai, beat him, and carry him to Li Lei's. Shao Qing then suggests they build a "fire jail" with which to subdue Zhang Hai. Threatened with certain incineration, Zhang Hai surrenders and goes to work for Li Lei. In a final twist, when he goes home to fetch his mother, far from reprimanding him for serving such a villain, she is happy.[118]

Of course, this could all be explained away by saying the villains' transgressions of conventions simply serve to reinforce those conventions. But even the heroes fail to uphold the ideal. While the villain's bodyguard at least honors brotherhood enough to spare a sworn brother in a fight, on two different occasions a hero and a judge falsely claim friendship or brotherhood to achieve their ends. Even more surprisingly, the other party believes them. These relationships, so crucial to the larger-than-life martial hero, are thereby devalued: "Over the years, [he] had sworn brotherhood with who knows how many friends. . . . How could he remember all of them?"[119]

If *The Chart of Good and Evil* effectively undermines the distinguishing characteristics of the martial hero, *The Gathering of Heroes* does the same for the brilliant scholar. An impostor, the brilliant scholar's own servant, proves as learned as the scholar; the only way to distinguish between them is by appearance. All the traditional proofs of identity are no longer valid—the engagement token is stolen, the servant can recite (and thereby appropriate) the scholar's genealogy, and for a while the examinations themselves actually further the impostor's claims rather than expose him.

Most of the novels maintain a clear separation between the roles of the martial hero and the scholar. However, simply by their juxtaposition, both roles are increasingly exposed as one-sided or even comic. The scholar's claims on skill and virtue are undermined by equally skilled villains, while the principle of love as the ultimate goal is reduced to marriage as a means to success. The fact that skill, be it literary or military, is not limited to good characters reduces their value as models. In earlier popular fiction, skill distinguishes the hero. The scholar could write circles around his rivals, and martial heroes recognized each other through the display of their abilities. In the martial romance, however, skill is no longer sufficient. The comic martial hero (*haohan*) may be skilled, but he is also nearly always foolhardy, hasty, or bumbling.[120] Conversely, the villains are often just as skilled as the heroes. Thus the increasing self-consciousness of the martial romance deflates characters from their previous status as the larger-than-life heroes of fairy tales to caricatures.[121] Some of the changes in characterization seem to arise from considerations of plot. But in looking for novelty, the novels pull at the seams of the conventions that had sustained previous genres for over a century.

The constant tension between the roles of scholar and martial hero also call attention to their conventions. *The Gathering of Heroes* draws a very clear line between the brilliant scholar (*caizi*) and the martial hero (*haohan*). The tension between them is verbalized by Wang's servant, who berates him for eating with a swordsman (*jianghu dao ke*): "Master, you've made no distinction between noble and base, good and bad! He's not your relative or old friend. Eating at the same table with this swordsman is a disgrace to your official family dignity!"[122] Even if the criticism is in the villain's mouth, it is still indicative of the assumptions being challenged. But again, the character types within the novel are not absolute; the swordsman the hero befriends is none other than the future prime minister, Fan Zhongyan!

Similarly, the scholar in *The Picture of Tianbao* views the martial hero Shi Bixian as a troublemaker. Though the scholar's wife is happy to adopt Shi Bixian's sister, she suggests they give Shi Bixian money and find him a job; otherwise he will implicate them. The martial hero, for his part, wants nothing to do with the official world. When the scholar Li Rongchun brings up the subject with Shi Bixian, he shows no desire to be an official. He says, "My dad was absolutely loyal in serving the country, but he was killed by that evil bastard Hua Jinzhang. Why would I want to be an official? I wish I could just bring him here and cut him into a thousand pieces! That's the one thing that would appease my wrath."[123] On the other side the officials and their relatives are openly concerned about the damage to their reputation that associating with bandits could cause.[124] This concern may be justified, since a letter from Shi Bixian at a bandit lair does get Li Rongchun arrested.

The tension between scholar and martial hero continues throughout the book. When the bandits are pursued to the river by imperial troops, the scholar Li Rongchun and the judge Tian Daxiu threaten to throw themselves into the river rather than fight the troops as the bandits are preparing to do. The situation is defused when a golden bridge appears from nowhere: Supernatural intervention mutes their objections to going with the bandits to their mountain lair.[125]

The Garden of Competing Beauties creates an open dialogue between the roles of scholar and martial hero. When Hao Luan meets the martial hero Ma Jun and learns he is a thief, he has misgivings: "I'm a dignified hero, how can I associate with a thief? Wouldn't that make all the heroes in the world laugh at me?"[126] But after Ma Jun relates his adventures, Hao Luan decides this is the man to rescue his sworn brother. The next day the same tension is exhibited when Hao Luan suggests to the others that they swear brotherhood with Ma Jun; they are reluctant, but go along. The scholars laugh at Ma Jun's appearance, but this laughter oddly validates Ma Jun as a martial hero.[127] Whereas previously anyone pretending to the role of scholar would be taken for a villain, Ma Jun's very inability to play the scholar now marks him as an authentic martial hero. The dialogue on roles goes both ways; the martial hero also talks back to the scholars. Arriving just in time to rescue a friend from execution, Zhou Shun thinks the martial hero Bao Gang is a fool to attempt a jailbreak in broad daylight and urges caution. Bao replies, "Most of what you say is a lot of cowardly bookworm talk!" and jumps into action.[128]

Finally, the awareness of these roles and conventions leads to their inversion. While in earlier novels characters may have been aware of other's roles, later novels allow the characters to be aware of their own roles. But at the same time the heart of these roles disappears; they are no longer grounded in stable values. The genre tensions in *Three United Swords* create a fictional world opposite to *The Picture of Tianbao.* When in *Three United Swords* Scholar Liu suggests that they swear brotherhood, the martial hero Bao Gang modestly demurs, saying Liu is an official's son, while he is just a crude martial type His self-effacing politeness runs counter to the tradition of brash, straight-talking martial heroes. Indeed, the martial heroes are not the men of the greenwood of earlier novels. When the martial hero Ma Jun meets up with robbers in a forest, he laughs at them and tells them they deserve worse than death for ignoring the laws of the land. However, the heroes' associations with the greenwood are not completely severed, either; despite his rhetoric Ma Jun temporarily joins them, although reluctantly. This betrays a dramatic change in the martial hero's attitude toward bandits. Banditry is no longer his first choice as a profession; it becomes a last resort.

The scholar's ambitions have changed as well. Whereas in the scholar-beauty romances the scholar regards true love as his highest ambition, in the third group of martial romance novels marriage is about power rather than love. Thus in *Three United Swords* when the princess is to throw an embroidered ball to find her husband, Scholar Liu decides to go because such a match would put him in a position to right the injustice against his father. To him it has nothing to do with love, though the princess does fall in love with him. This idea of working from inside the system is also reflected in the other two novels of this group, *Yun Zhong Yan* and *Da Ming quan zhuan Xiu qiu yuan* (*The complete tale of the destiny of the embroidered ball in the great Ming*, 1851: hereafter, *Embroidered Ball*). Although marriage to the princess plays an important role in the structure of both novels, it seems to be merely a means to air the hero's grievance, rather than a romance. In *Embroidered Ball*, revenge is even more important than romance to the structure of the novel.[129]

Only in this third group of martial romances does the question of power and ethics become a real concern. It will remain so throughout the Qing. Modern Chinese critics consistently fault martial arts novels for the martial hero's capitulation to the system. But in fact, this only became part of the formula relatively late. *The Picture of Tianbao* and *Li he jian lianzi ping* (Sword and vase)[130] concentrate on the extralegal exploits of the heroes, while *The Chart of Good and Evil* and *The Garden of Competing Beauties* run the gamut, legal to extralegal. The third group of martial romances goes nearly to the other extreme. Private revenge disappears, for the heroes are instruments of the system.

Since *The Garden of Competing Beauties* clearly provides the model for *Three United Swords*, the differences between the two works reflect the development of a genre. In *Three United Swords*, the hero seems caught in a power network, merely providing information to the emperor, who tests it. Essentially the novels have come full circle, returning to the early model of judge and assistant. In the first chapter of *Three United Swords*, Ma Jun seems to embody the ideal of the martial hero as the unselfish avenger of the people. He takes the law into his own hands to kill an official's son and save a kidnapped girl. Moreover, in *Three United Swords* the girl is a total stranger, in contrast with *The Garden of Competing Beauties*, in which the obligations of brotherhood prompt the hero to rescue her. This makes Ma Jun even more gallant than the previous heroes.[131] As a result of his daring, in chapter 2 Ma Jun is on the run from the law, reluctantly hiding on a bandit mountain. But by chapter 7, when he brings a case before the emperor, he becomes the agent of law. He saves Scholar Liu from the execution grounds in chapter 21 by using a letter from the emperor, and he nearly executes a local official for handling Liu's case badly.

The emphasis on working from within the system is nowhere clearer than when *Three United Swords* inverts *The Water Margin*. When Ma Jun's sister is first mentioned in chapter 20 of *Three United Swords*, she is the object of a bandit chief's lust. The episode is strongly reminiscent of the episode in

The Water Margin where Lu Zhishen saves a girl from a forced marriage to a bandit.[132] But here the hero saves her by writing a letter promising the bandit leader an official position if he gives up his attempts to marry her. It is presented as summary rather than scene, lacking the drama of Lu Zhishen disguised as a bride. Moreover, rather than appeal to him as a friend and fellow bandit, he appeals to him as a potential official colleague. The official world has taken over the greenwood.[133]

The martial romance novels play across genre boundaries. As I noted, Sun Kaidi refused to establish a heading for such hybrid martial novels in his bibliography, on the grounds that they lacked the characteristics of an independent category.[134] My analysis concurs that few of the motifs of the martial romance are original to the genre. Instead, the way in which these motifs are combined distinguishes the genre. The juxtaposition brought about by attempts to unify these disparate elements brings the differences between genres into sharp focus. The thorough hybridization of the martial romance novel makes it impossible for the novels to be read simply as scholar-beauty romance, as court-case tale, or as military romance (*yingxiong chuanqi*). By juxtaposing the motifs, roles, and values of these genres, their limitations become apparent.

Chapter 3

Parody and Roles in *Green Peony*

Green Peony was extremely popular from 1800 until the first decades of the twentieth century. Part of its appeal lies in its comic treatment of other genres. Like the other martial romances, *Green Peony* plays upon the conventions of the scholar-beauty romance (*caizi jiaren*), court-case fiction, and the historical novel. However, *Green Peony* goes beyond the simple juxtaposition of conventions and roles. In a series of "miscastings" that pervade *Green Peony*, a character who seems more appropriate to one genre chooses to involve himself or herself in a situation more appropriate to another genre. Although for nearly a century motifs from the historical novel had been incorporated into the scholar-beauty romance and vice versa, in these earlier novels the role and the character playing it were unified: A brilliant scholar was a brilliant scholar, a beauty was a beauty, and a hero (*haohan*) was a hero. Roles could be redefined as the traditions evolved, but the character was the role he played. In *Green Peony*, the disparity between the role and the character playing it serves to highlight the conventions being played upon, and effectively makes the characters "free agents" who can take up and discard roles as they see fit. They are not chameleons, however, so the discrepancy between their original characteristics and the role they are trying to play accounts for much of the comedy in the novel.

Let me give a quick illustration of the strategic use of a motif by a character: At one point in the novel a notorious pirate who has captured two adulterers announces that since he has nothing else to do that day, just for fun they should hold a trial. He then asks who would like to play the judge. Everyone defers to him, so he takes the role himself and plays it to the hilt. At first he calls attention to the difference between himself and the official judges by announcing, "Even though I'm not a court of law, I'm even stricter than the official law," and "I'm not an investigating official, so I have no power over you. I just want to understand this."[1] But his language mimics that of official judges elsewhere in the book,[2] the protocol is the same as in the official court scenes, and he even arranges for his men to simulate the tortures of the official court without the proper equipment.

The comedy of the scene derives from the contrast between the character of the pirate and the role he is playing as judge. This is an obvious example, since the pirate announces that he is going to play the judge, and by locking the suspects up and carefully storing the evidence, he shows that he has finished playing the role.[3] But a similar, though more subtle, "miscasting" underlies the romance plot that unifies the book. The awkwardness resulting from the conflation of genres is thematized in *Green Peony* by the woman warrior's pursuit of the unwilling official's son. The characters play with the conventions of previous novels by consciously playing roles, or setting up mock rituals.

Such conflation of genres throughout *Green Peony* acts as parody. Parody works by raising one set of expectations, then providing something else counter to those expectations. This contrast makes the parody comic, but more importantly it makes the reader aware of the expectations being evoked and thwarted. Moreover, in creating expectations for a particular text or genre, parody allows that prior text to speak for itself, while at the same time placing it in a new context that changes its significance. This creates a "double-coding," where the embedded, parodied text can be read both sympathetically, on its own terms, and also critically, in the terms proposed by the new work.[4] Thus, in M. M. Bakhtin's view, parody serves as a corrective double to more straightforward targets, "a critique on the one-sided seriousness of the lofty direct word."[5]

In exposing the conventions of these earlier novels, *Green Peony* plays a role similar to Bakhtin's Second Line novels. Bakhtin divides the history of the novel into two lines of development. The First Line novel organizes language and the human experience to present a one-sided view consistent with the values it upholds. It works by excluding or cleaning up lived experience and everyday language. In the Second Line novel, previous genres of the novel become "one language among other languages" and thereby take on "a parodic ring."[6] According to Bakhtin, the novels of the Second Stylistic Line test literary discourse either (1) through a hero who tries to live "according to literature"; (2) by a "laying bare of the device" through techniques like introducing the author inside the novel, or writing a "novel about a novel"; or (3) through parody.[7] This testing in the Second Line novel exposes the simple, "*exclusively* positive or *exclusively* negative" characters of the First Line novel by destroying "the rhetorical unity of personality, act, and event."[8]

The early scholar-beauty romance and the historical novel are similar to Bakhtin's First Line novels: they are highly stylized, use a somewhat elevated language, and present themselves as models for life. In contrast, *Green Peony* can be considered a Second Line novel in that it brings the previously transparent conventions of the scholar-beauty romance and the historical novel into focus through elaborate parodic play. Bakhtin's notion of the characters' ability to expose the one-sided "literariness" of previous role types undergirds much of my discussion of parody in this chapter. While the traditional scholar-beauty romance ennobles language and actions, taking propriety to extremes, and the historical novel imbues human action with a larger significance, *Green Peony* parodies the characters' standards of behavior.

Let me review the conventions of the scholar-beauty romance and the historical novel and consider, first, to what extent they present models for behavior; and second, to what extent these models are played upon as the genres converge. A wonderful, if contemptuous, account of these genres in the mid-eighteenth century is included in the frame story to *Story of the Stone*, as the Stone argues the merits of his book.

> Your so called "historical romances" [*yeshi*] consisting, as they do, of scandalous anecdotes about statesmen and emperors of bygone days and scabrous attacks on the reputations of long-dead gentlewomen, contain more wickedness and immorality than I care to mention. Still worse is the "erotic novel," by whose filthy obscenities our young folk are all too easily corrupted. And the "boudoir romances [*jiaren caizi*]," those dreary stereotypes with their volume after volume all pitched on the same note and their different characters undistinguishable except by name (all those ideally beautiful young ladies and ideally eligible young bachelors)—even they seem unable to avoid descending sooner or later into indecency.
>
> The trouble with this last kind of romance is that it only gets written in the first place because the author requires a frame-work in which to show off his love-poems. He goes about constructing this framework quite mechanically, beginning with the names of his pair of young lovers and invariably adding a third character, a servant or the like, to make mischief between them, like the *chou* in a comedy.
>
> What makes these romances even more detestable is the stilted, bombastic language—inanities dressed in pompous rhetoric, remote alike from nature and common sense and teeming with the grossest absurdities.[9]

Even if the Stone mentions the romance only to mock its stereotyped characters, action and language, the fact that he feels compelled to confront it at such length attests to the influence of this genre in the eighteenth century.

Indeed, the conventions of the scholar-beauty romance form part of the skeleton upon which the *Story of the Stone* is built. Moreover, the concern with the novel as moral exemplar shows that the standards for the characters in the novels were not radically divorced from those of society at large.

The prefaces to these kinds of fiction corroborate this sense of fiction as models for life. The standard justification for literature was that it served as a vehicle for moral instruction (*wen yi zai dao*). As Anne McLaren points out, this ideal is evident in the earliest (1494) preface to *Three Kingdoms*, which says:

> If you read about the ancients' loyalty, you will think about your own loyalty or disloyalty; when you read about their filiality, you will think about your own filiality or lack of it. Good and bad, permissible or not, all should be like this; only then will it be of benefit. If you only read and do not embody these in your own actions, that is not reading.[10]

Here the good reader emulates what he reads. In this way fiction could serve the same moral purpose as the official histories. The advantage fiction has, according to these prefaces, is its accessibility to ordinary people, not just scholars. The 1494 Yongyuzi preface to *Three Kingdoms* notes:

> In the composition of the histories, the principle is subtle and the significance profound. . . . [W]hen most people read (*guan*) them they often criticize them and put them aside and pay no further attention because they are not comprehensible to a broad readership (*butong hu zhongren*). Consequently with the passing of time the events of the ages become lost in transmission.[11]

The novel *Three Kingdoms* makes these lessons accessible; "the language is neither too profound nor too vulgar and it is almost equivalent to a history, so if you read and recite it anyone can learn a lesson from it."[12] This rhetoric became a standard apologia for fiction, with some commentators going so far as to compare fiction to the classics in its ability to impart moral wisdom.[13]

The preface to the military romance *Shuo Tang yanyi quan zhuan* (The tale of the Tang) echoes the standard apologia for fiction. It states that the classics and histories are too much work to understand, but this book can encourage good and warn against evil. In *The Tale of the Tang* "the words are straightforward and events and principles are separately laid out." Thus it constitutes "a good book that can benefit the world."[14]

The scholar-beauty romance *Haoqiu zhuan* (The fortunate union) takes this rhetoric one step further, suggesting that the novel presents moral models for propriety in love and marriage more clearly than the classic *Shi jing* (Book of songs). The phrase "fortunate union" in the title of the novel comes from the first poem in the *Book of Songs*, "Fishhawk," which the "Great Preface" holds up as the example of how literature shapes morality. According to the paradigmatic theory of the purpose of literature put forth in the "Great Preface," when people read "Fishhawk," they recognize the ideal marriage it depicts and their own responses conform to the values presented.[15] The preface to *The Fortunate Union*, however, daringly says that for a long time the principles of "fortunate union" have been unclear and there has been no way to revive them, until this novel came along. Much of the preface details how the novel illustrates that true love will not conflict with propriety (*li*) and virtue (*de*).

> It is not that he does not love, but the epitome of love creates respect; it is not that he is not intimate (*qin*), but extreme intimacy destroys the selfish (*si*). . . . In this case, how can it be that only the *Book of Songs* can sing of what makes a fortunate union? . . . Thus this compilation (*bian*) should be read together with "Fishhawk."[16]

No stronger statement could be made about the novel's function as a moral model for its readers.

The preface to an important collection of court-case fiction, *Longtu's Court Cases*, presents it as a slightly different kind of model. Rather than invoking the classics or the histories to assert its worth, it promotes Judge Bao as a moral example for present-day officials. After discoursing on Judge Bao's character, incorruptibility, and mercy toward ordinary people, it states, "I hope that those who act as 'father and mother to the people' will burn incense and read *Longtu's Court Cases*."[17] This use of fiction may not be so far-fetched. Ann Waltner's study of court-case fiction and court-case handbooks shows that the latter may well have been used as practical guides to "legal ethics;"[18] similarities between the genres suggest that these stories to a large extent shared that moral orientation. The preface to the early court-case novel *Cases of Judge Shi* borrows heavily from this preface to *Longtu's Court Cases*, often using the exact words and simply substituting Judge Shi's name for Judge Bao's. This suggests once again how strong a model the collection *Longtu's Court Cases* was for later works in the court-case genre. Beyond this, the preface to *Cases of Judge Shi* adds an additional purpose; it not only presents the novel as a model for contemporary officials but also opens its readership up to a more universal audience by aiming to let later "people of the world" know who Judge Shi was.[19]

Turning to the novels themselves, each thematic genre projects its own system of values. The conventions of the scholar-beauty romance highlight propriety (*li*), both in spectacular, extreme exhibitions of behavior and violations of conventional propriety. The heroine is a beauty who embodies talent and virtue. Often the only child of a gentry family, who educated her like a son, her primary concern is to marry someone worthy of her. The importance of propriety and chastity to the genre means the beauty often must go to great lengths to arrange an ideal match, for instance, by cross-dressing as a man, or communicating through intermediaries. Since a virtuous maiden should remain cloistered in the inner chambers, she must resort to these expedients to traverse that boundary. While she may have the opportunity to meet her love face to face, the genre rarely even allows the pair to hold hands.[20]

To take the famous scholar-beauty romance *Yu Jiao Li* as an example, a good marriage is the goal of all the characters, while everything else, including career, is secondary. The scholar spends most of his energy (and most of the book) finding a suitable wife. What distinguishes heroes from villains is the means by which the match is pursued. Heroes abide by the social conventions and impose even stricter restrictions on themselves; witness the young man who refuses to make any other match while he is waiting for a reply from the family of a girl to whom he has proposed. While *Yu Jiao Li* allows some bending of the rules, such as a heroine dressing as her "brother" to offer her own hand to a handsome scholar (fig. 3.1), the villains are those who violate social conventions by selfishly trying to persuade engaged persons to marry someone else. They relentlessly target the scholar and beauty, who do what they must to avoid these unwelcome matches. The standard of behavior for the characters corresponds with the ideal standard of behavior of its readers.

Another early scholar-beauty romance, *The Fortunate Union*, places righteousness in opposition to marriage by incorporating a martial hero and heroine. *The Fortunate Union* is almost the opposite of the novel of manners since the hero and heroine's virtue lies precisely in refusing to marry. The very fact that the hero and heroine have met (by chance) is in their minds an obstacle to their union. She says their noble deeds—each has saved the other's life—should not be sullied by self-interest; he declines even to discuss the matter and leaves town. As he explains, their relationship to that point was not that of a man and a woman, but of friends who truly understand one another (*zhiji*).[21] Later their parents approve the match, but even after the wedding the couple does not consummate the marriage until an imperial investigation has cleared their names of any suspicion of impropriety. By changing the protagonists from a couple with literary talent to a couple with martial skills,[22] *The Fortunate Union* emphasizes the conflict between the hero's selfless values, in which friendship is paramount, and his conception of marriage. In this way it anticipates *Green Peony* playing on the conflict of values that results from the juxtaposition of the martial with the romance,[23] but unlike *Green Peony* it preserves the unity between character and role.

Since the historical novel was considered a popular elaboration of the historical record, it laid claim to history's role as moral exemplar,[24] as we have seen in the prefaces. The Stone's criticism quoted above confirms this claim even as it focuses on the historical novel's failure in this regard. Significantly, the Stone's main objection seems to be to the interpolation of the element of romance. Just as the scholar-beauty romance incorporated martial episodes,

Figure 3.1 The beauty cross-dresses to meet the man she admires, from *Yu Jiao Li*

love stories also found their way into the historical novel. The shift in the historical novel from personal vendettas to "affairs of the heart" began with *Romance of the Sui and Tang* (*Sui Tang yanyi*, 1695).[25]

In the military romance this romantic element developed into a standard trope: the woman warrior as a foreign princess who falls in love on the battlefield and pursues a Chinese general.[26] The strongest model for the forward woman warrior in the military romance is Mu Guiying of the Yang Family Generals saga.[27] Does the incorporation of romance reveal tensions with the core values of the military romance? While Mu Guiying's prime concern is finding a worthy husband, the object of her affections thinks only of his duty to his country. After she captures the Song general Yang Zongbao on the battlefield (fig. 3.2), we see him through her eyes: she "saw that he had bright eyes

Figure 3.2 (a) Mu Guiying capturing Yang Zongbao, from *Yang Jia Fu yanyi* (top) and (b) *Nan Bei Song zhizhuan* (bottom)

孟良桂英

二人交戰

一根來與我作斧柄可伏其人則可成事不然去亦無益實
曰既師父務要此木用小可即前往求之五郎曰爾去索取
此物吾當准備俟候良即辭五郎徑望木閣寨來恰遇寨主
乃定天王沐羽之女小名木金花別名木桂英生有勇力前
嘗極精曾遇神授三口飛刀百發百中是日正與部下出獵
射中一鳥落於孟良面前良拾得而去行來數步忽有五六
嘍囉赶來叫聲好將其鳥還我饒你一死孟良听得停住脚
嘍囉近前一齊發作被良打得四分五落走去良又行一望
之地嘍囉報與木桂英部衆追至良聞後面人馬之聲知是
賊兵赶來取出利刃挺身待之一伏時桂英大罵誅不盡狂
夫敢來此處相鬥那孟良更不答話舞刀來戰桂英舞劍迎
之二人在山脚下連鬥十數合孟良刀怯退步便走桂英不
赶遂殺入把住路口孟良進退無計謂曰吾[illegible]時馬[illegible]

桂英捉獲

宗保而去

所閉路放我過去嘍囉[illegible]爾來鎖路頭誰不知要過木閣寨
者得下買路錢爾若無[illegible]一年也過不去孟良自思有緊急
事只得脫下金盔當買路錢嘍囉報與桂英桂英令放路與
過孟良離却此地徑回寨見六使道知至木[illegible]木閣
寨主難敵又將金盔買路[illegible]說了一遍六使曰似此如之奈
何宗保曰小兒與孟良同走一遭六使曰恐爾不是其敵宗
保曰自有方略即日引孟良率軍二千來到寨外索戰木桂
英聽得全身慣帶部衆鼓譟而出宗保曰聞爾山後有降龍
木二根乞一根借我破陣事定之日自當重謝桂英笑曰其
木的有[illegible]得中[illegible]刀二柄盡付爾宗保大怒曰捉此賊人自
往伐取乃挺鎗直奔桂英桂英舞刀來迎兩騎相交二人戰
上十餘合桂英賣個破綻拍馬便走宗保乘勢追之轉過山
坳一枝箭到宗保坐馬已倒桂英殺回將宗保捉之而去孟

and delicate eyebrows, white teeth and red lips, and his words were impassioned, so she secretly thought if I could get him for a spouse I wouldn't have lived in vain."[28] While this description shows her attraction to Yang Zongbao, the absence of any physical description of her underscores the different value systems in play. She is ruled by romantic sentiment (*qing*), while he agrees to the match in order to fulfill his duty. He had been sent to get some magic wood needed in battle, so when he hears the proposal of marriage he thinks it would be best to say yes to save the country. Still, when his father learns he accepted Mu Guiying's proposal, he is enraged by what he perceives as his son's "giving in to private lusts (*yu*) and forgetting his sovereign and relatives."[29] From this perspective, the threat of Yang Zongbao accepting a match with Mu Guiying is that he could be distracted from his duty by desire. In the end his father accepts the match, though the novel never spells out his reasons, and Mu Guiying agrees to surrender and fight for the Song.

This episode suggests the dangers of romantic love, and many of the issues implicit in it are played out in greater detail in later military romances. Indeed, romance (*qing*) is often conflated with sex (*se*) or desire (*yu*),[30] and romantic attraction is seen as a challenge to both loyalty (*zhong*) and filial piety (*xiao*), two of the central values espoused by the military romance.

The later military romance *Yishuo Hou Tang zhuan sanji: Xue Dingshan zheng Xi Fan Lihua quan zhuan* (Another tale of the later Tang, third collection: Xue Dingshan's western campaign and Fan Lihua; hereafter *Later Tang Third Collection*) explicitly dramatizes the implications of this motif. In one instance, the woman warrior Du Xiantong proposes to the general Xue Dingshan on the battlefield, but he refuses the match twice. His first concern, that it would be unseemly for him to marry a "bandit," invokes the issue of loyalty. After she captures him, she proposes and he refuses again. He refuses a third time on the grounds that it would be disloyal and unfilial to marry while his father and country are in danger. This seems to internalize the kind of criticism made by Yang Zongbao's father. Only when the matchmaker points out to Xue Dingshan that his mother agreed to the match does he consent.[31]

Still his father, Xue Rengui, is enraged when he finds out, saying that as a general his son should have died rather than submit to Du Xiantong. The father links the issues of filiality and loyalty, lamenting, with this kind of a disobedient son, how can I manage the country when I cannot manage my own family? What is implicit in earlier examples becomes explicit here. The father's tirade spells out the perceived dangers of romantic attraction in a general. The son's acceptance of the match is seen as unfilial, as having the wrong priorities (self over mission), and as evidence of a weakness for women that could affect his abilities as a general and thereby undermine his loyalty to the country.[32]

This episode also explains why the woman warrior is accepted despite the perceived dangers of romantic attraction. Although Xue Dingshan's father initially refuses to recognize their "wild union" as a legitimate marriage, he is eventually persuaded that Du Xiantong and her brother would be assets fighting on his side and a genuine threat if sent away. Her virtue is considered in passing, but trumped by her skill. In other words, their marriage is justified in terms of loyalty (*zhong*)—for the good of the country—rather than romantic love (*qing*).

Fan Lihua's pursuit of the Chinese general Xue Dingshan in *Later Tang Third Collection* epitomizes the challenge of romantic love (*qing*) to loyalty and filial piety.[33] C. T. Hsia comments that in this episode Xue and Fan take courtship to such extremes that Xue almost becomes the hero of a comedy of manners.[34] In fact, it becomes a parody. While Xue's punctilious refusal to marry would be appropriate in a scholar-beauty romance, the conventions of the military romance make it ridiculous, in contrast to Fan's disregard for propriety.

Unlike the martial heroes in *The Water Margin* and earlier military romances who see no moral obstacle to arranging their own marriages, Xue holds Fan up to Confucian conventions. Fan's actions originally seem as alien to Confucian values as could be. She violates the prescribed conduct toward parents, brother, and ruler. In order to pursue Xue, she goes beyond renouncing the match her parents have made; she even kills her own father and brothers, then defects to join the Tang army. Fan proposes to Xue three times; each time he refuses her and curses her for her forwardness in proposing her own match.[35]

Nevertheless, Xue is portrayed as in the wrong. Fate is on Fan's side; before they even meet, she has been told by her teacher, an immortal, that she is destined to marry Xue Dingshan. Moreover, in the name of propriety Xue violates some of the conventions himself. When Fan saves Xue's life, convention calls for Xue to befriend her as his benefactor. Rather than gratitude, however, he repays her with curses. Xue calls Fan disloyal and unfilial,[36] but ironically he can hardly be called filial either. Since his parents support the match, in refusing to marry Fan he repeatedly defies their wishes.[37] His father even throws him in jail to punish him for his stubbornness.

Fan's disregard for propriety is also vindicated by describing incidents from her point of view. The reader sees her "adopt" a young man whom she met on the road, and therefore knows their relationship is platonic. Xue, however, doubts her chastity and refuses to consummate the marriage when he learns of the young man after their wedding ceremony. His objections seem unreasonable, so his father throws him in jail again.

Even the Chinese emperor is on Fan's side. Ironically, it is the "loyalty" that Xue Dingshan constantly espouses that forces him into accepting a marriage to Fan Lihua. The emperor orders Xue to gain Fan's military assistance on pain of death; only then does Xue put aside his objections. As he approaches her home, Fan fakes her own death in order to win him over.[38] After three unsuccessful proposals, it takes a drastic ruse to make them man and wife. Only by tricking Xue does Fan finally win his trust.

In this instance, desire on the part of the hero becomes a more credible question. While in earlier iterations of this motif the attractiveness of the woman warrior registers either through narratorial description or through the eyes of foil characters known for their lust, in this case Xue Dingshan's own thoughts voice his attraction to Fan Lihua. When Xue Dingshan first sees Fan Lihua he thinks, "Even though my wife Du Xiantong is pretty, she doesn't compare. My sister Jinlian isn't even one in ten thousand times as pretty." Still, Xue reminds himself that he already has two wives.[39]

The episode inverts the counter forces, loyalty and filiality, since Xue's father agrees to the match with alacrity in hopes of gaining Fan Lihua's formidable skills for their side. When Xue Dingshan rejects her after the wedding, his father urges him to reconcile, saying none of the men are her equal. Xue Dingshan's duty would be to obey his father and marry her. Instead, Xue mouths pieties which attempt to hold *her* up to those standards. Once again, Xue Dingshan internalizes the criticism usually lobbed at the general, in this case by adamantly refusing the match. His refusal appropriates the discourse usually voiced by the father, applying it not to himself but to the woman warrior. This misappropriated discourse becomes comic, but it also seems hollow. Xue Dingshan is clearly not impervious to romantic attraction, but denies it by adamantly refusing to marry Fan Lihua and by invoking the discourse of loyalty, filiality, and chastity. If the refusals to marry in *The Fortunate Union* stem from high-mindedness, in *Later Tang Third Collection* they become plain stubbornness dressed up in Confucian rhetoric. His value-laden claims are no longer taken seriously. Not only does Fan Lihua fight back against Xue's accusations on their wedding night, but Xue's whole family also sides with her.

The courtship of Fan Lihua and Xue Dingshan parodies all five cardinal relationships. This supports C. T. Hsia's observation that the convention of the foreign woman warrior pursuing a Chinese general "consciously exploit[s] this love situation as a clash between two ways of life,"[40] barbarian versus Chinese. In so doing, this episode not only parodies the conventions of earlier military romances, but it also reverses the expectations of the scholar-beauty romance. The woman warrior serves as the mirror image of the proper beauty, opposite to her in most respects but still putting sentiment (*qing*) first.

The example of the woman warrior illustrates how genres of fiction function as complementary or even rival systems. Each thematic genre has its own focus, which emphasizes certain values over others. The value system of different genres may even contradict each other. For example, while the hero in a scholar-beauty romance would put love (*qing*) above all else but preserve propriety, the martial hero generally treats it with suspicion and contempt and usually does not concern himself with propriety. The military romance portrays desire as an exploitable weakness and an inherent challenge to the central values of loyalty to country and filiality. However, it gives the foreign woman warrior complete license to follow her heart; she not only violates propriety with impunity but can ignore Confucian duty, even to her parents, to do so. In contrast, the leading lady of the scholar-beauty romance manages to reconcile love with propriety and Confucian virtues. The genres frequently offer diametrically opposed perspectives.

Playing the Wrong Part

Green Peony uses the convention of the military romance to contrast two different ways of life, but instead of playing foreign customs against Chinese customs, it plays the military romance against the scholar-beauty romance. The protagonists originally live in separate worlds inspired by these two genres, but once they meet, those worlds collide and each tries to play a role from the other genre.

Luo Hongxun is initially characterized as a typical martial scholar, in a passage that invokes the conventions of the scholar-beauty romance.

> There was a man of Yangzhou named Luo Long, style name Tengyun, a peerless hero, whose martial skills were refined and strong. He had earned a military degree in the imperial examinations, and his first position was as the Brigade Commander of Dingxing County. So he brought his wife and son with him to Dingxing County to take up his post. The old man and his wife were around forty years old, and they only had one son. Their son was only thirteen, with a square face and big ears, and great stature. He was also naturally intelligent, and extraordinarily strong. The old man and his wife loved him like a treasure, and named him Binhou, style name Hongxun.[41]

Luo Hongxun is the cherished only son born to an upright official late in life. Status is a matter of being born to the right family, and of virtue and talent. The fact that Luo Hongxun soon loses his father also tallies with the standard portrayal of the romantic hero.[42]

When the plot proper starts a few years later, Luo remains true to this characterization insofar as he insists on being faithful to his original fiancée, but he wants to be a hero (*haohan*), and that is his problem (fig. 3.3). In the course of the novel he is often praised in terms of being a hero (*haohan* or *yingxiong*),[43] but when it really counts, he is considered a noble scion (*gongzi*) who should not be exposed to too much danger. In the outlaws' eyes, "He's still very young, and has the temperament of a noble scion; how can he compare with you and me who have experience with formidable enemies?"[44]

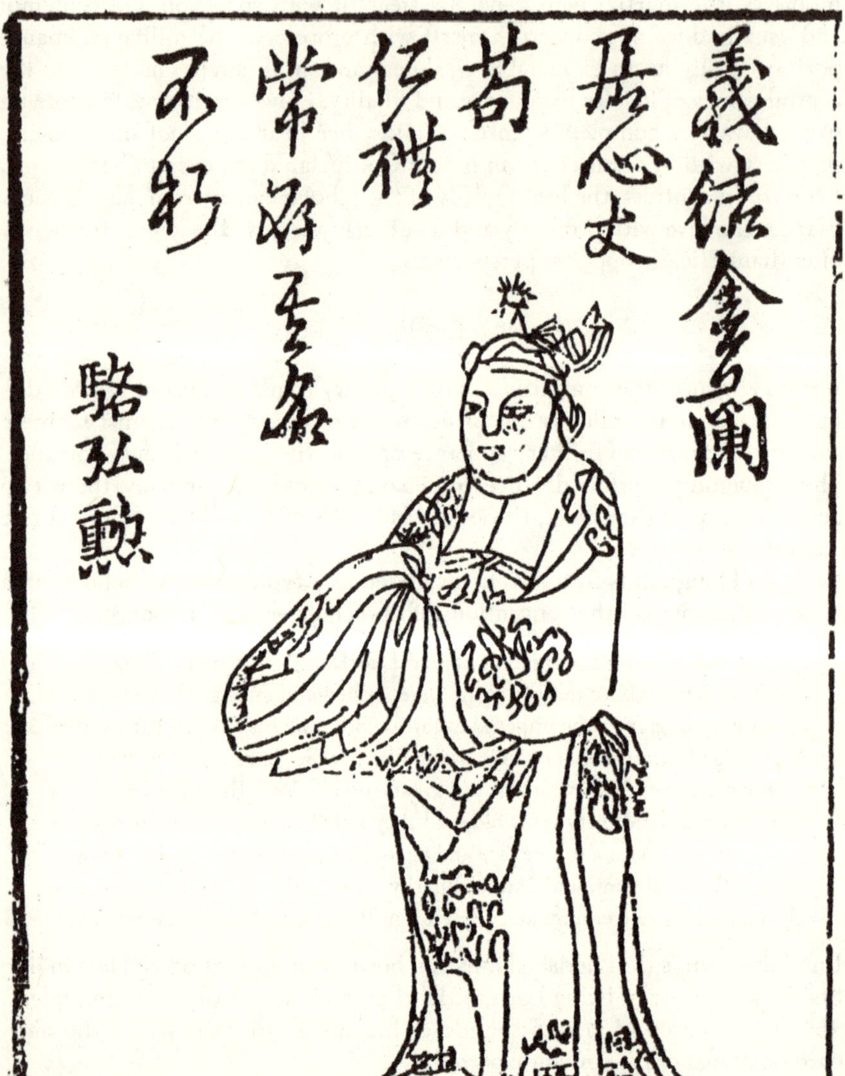

Figure 3.3 The protagonist of *Green Peony*, Luo Hongxun, portrayed as (a) a scholar in the 1847 edition (left) and (b) as a martial hero in the 1892 edition (right)

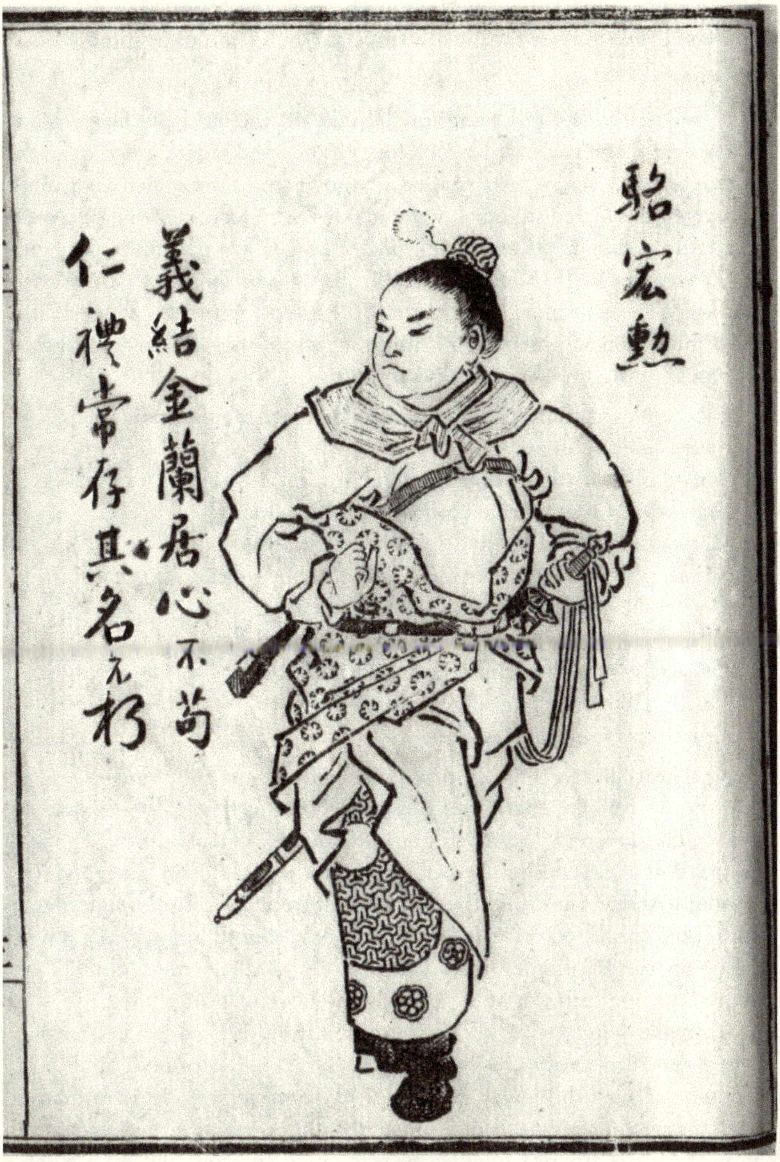
駱宏勳
義結金蘭居心不苟
仁禮常存其名不朽

His pursuer, Hua Bilian, is the daughter of a notorious bandit. She first appears when she and her family are traveling in search of a suitable husband for her.

> They saw that young girl stand up and take off the outer old blue cotton jacket. Inside she wore a short apricot silk robe and a dark green damask vest. A bright red crepe sash was tied around her waist over green silk pants. She wore jade colored silk stockings and flower-red shoes showing off a pair of golden lotuses just three inches long. Her hair was pulled up in a bun, but not ornamented with flowers, and from her ears dangled a pair of gold earrings. She was neither short nor tall, a little over five feet tall . . . With the combination of colors in her clothes, she was a multicolored butterfly no one could resist. There's a poem to prove it:
>
> Cicada-like hairbuns pile forming clouds above the mountains of
> her painted brows,
> A natural beauty in the mortal realm.
> Born with looks that could topple states and cities[45]
> Her lovely face makes fish dive and birds fall.[46]
> She seems a new lotus blossom reflected in the water,
> as graceful as lotus buds overlooking the spring.
> Elegant in simplicity when she eschews cosmetics,[47]
> Delicately, she sometimes dots on a beauty mark.
> Floating like three birds descending,[48]
> Graceful as five clouds swirling.
>
> The girl heard her father's command, and neither hurried nor rushed came over to the front of the horse. She put her hand firmly on the saddle, and neither grasping the mane nor climbing on a stool, she just tapped her hand and leaped into the saddle. As her left hand held the reins, she pressed with her knees and the horse began trotting; with her right hand she flicked the whip a few times, and the horse seemed to fly. While it was galloping, the girl jumped up and knelt on the saddle, doing a "child bowing to Guanyin" act; the whole audience broke into cheers.
>
> To make a long story short, she did this three times, one after the other, and also performed "hiding oneself in the stirrups,"[49] and "Tai Gong catching fish."[50] Her effort was extraordinary, each performance outstanding. When she had finished the three passes, she dismounted and sat on the troupe's bundles to rest. Soon someone put up a tightrope. After the girl had rested a little while, she stood up, tightened her sash, and mounted the tightrope. Walking forward and retreating backward, her tiny golden lotuses walked the tightrope as if she were on level ground. As Ren and Luo watched in admiration, Luo couldn't help yelling, "Just the tightrope act is worth eight taels of silver!" Ren echoed, "Not bad!"

> She was doing her routine on the tightrope when she suddenly heard someone cheering in a voice like thunder. She looked up—it was the two heroes in the pavilion who had asked her to perform: one with a swarthy face and a red beard, and one with a square face and big ears. The one with a square face and big ears was only about twenty, with a white face and broad forehead, a tiger-like back and ursine waist, a stately figure, dignified and awe-inspiring. To see him was to love him. The man praised the girl's extraordinary skill, while the girl loved the man's startling bearing and appearance.[51]

She falls for Luo as soon as she sees him and convinces her parents to propose. This sets up the tension between her original character as a woman warrior and her aspirations to the role of beauty (*jiaren*) (fig. 3.4).

The narrator then introduces the Hua family: The father is a notorious bandit chief and the mother a woman warrior with the nickname "tigress" (*mu dachong*).[52] They met on the road, fought each other and married. In contrast to these clearly martial roots, the narrator describes Hua Bilian as an only child who was schooled in literature from an early age and learned martial skills from her parents and uncles. They did not want to marry her off to just anyone, and for her part she made up her mind (*li zhi*) that she would only marry a hero (*yingxiong haojie*).[53] When she finally finds Luo, she does not pursue him or propose to him herself, as a woman warrior would, but combines two common formulas of the scholar-beauty romance by choosing him herself but having her parents propose.[54] Hua Bilian clearly knows how a proper beauty should act; she is not bound by the role before she finds a suitable match, but consciously tries to live up to it afterward.

The backbone of the novel is a pattern of three proposals by Hua Bilian's father and three refusals by Luo. The main obstacle to Hua Bilian's romance is not her parents, or even any meddling villains; it is her prospective fiancé's objections. This resembles the woman warrior trope in the military romances. But rather than take action like a woman warrior, Hua Bilian gets lovesick as befits a proper beauty, worrying her parents into acting on her behalf. Her very passivity signals her choice to play the demure beauty, a role she is not always able to maintain.[55]

Sometimes her failure is due to her parents' demands. When they arrive in Yangzhou intending to propose to Luo a second time, her father volunteers her to catch a monkey in return for a reward. Hua Bilian thinks,

> What did we come here for today, that you're forcing me to make a fool of myself? Since Mr. Luo lives in this city, if he sees me, do you think he is going to like me climbing around up there? This match is going to fall through again.[56]

She puts the successful conclusion of a match with Luo above all else—she is no longer the willing acrobat of chapter 3—but she cannot very well talk

Figure 3.4 Hua Bilian, portrayed (a) as a woman warrior in the 1800 edition of the *Green Peony* (left) and (b) as a beauty in the 1892 edition (right)

卷碧蓮
巾幗爲尊有賢有仁是英是傑
堪勝古人守閨守訓常秉大倫

back to her father.[57] Hua Bilian's thoughts show a shift in her viewpoint. Earlier she had no qualms about displaying herself and her skills, and indeed that is how she and Luo noticed each other. Her desire for Luo now makes her try to adopt the rules of propriety befitting the beauty. Her father, on the other hand, justifies his order using the discourse of the martial hero—he says he cannot go back on his word. By the standards of the beauty, however, it is outrageous to put his daughter on public display and knowingly subject her to the gaze of the villain who commissions this performance.

While she is chasing the monkey on top of a pavilion, the roof collapses and she falls down—perhaps playing the beauty has affected her skills as a woman warrior. But when Luo saves her, she reveals a woman warrior's forwardness by pressing herself against him, although she is quickly reminded of the impropriety of her actions by her mother. She returns to her role as proper beauty, swearing to marry only the man who has saved her life—another conventional trope.[58]

In some respects, this episode encapsulates the romance plot and the duality of the main characters' roles. If the monkey can be taken as a displaced object of desire,[59] Hua Bilian's trying to catch it is analogous to her trying to catch Luo. In each case when she actively tries to catch the object of her desire, she fails, and Luo ends up catching her. She literally falls out of her position as woman warrior into the role of the beauty in the scholar-beauty romance and finally gets Luo by accident. Thus, as long as she is trying to catch him, she is a woman warrior, despite any play-acting to the contrary; it is only when she fails to catch him that she becomes a demure beauty, resulting in marriage.

Ironically, Luo can accept the Hua family as friends under the code of the hero (*haohan*) and even praise Hua Bilian when she is exhibiting her martial skills. But when she tries to step into the role of the proper beauty to match him as brilliant scholar, he refuses her. It is significant that unlike the generals in the military romance, he never raises any specific objections regarding Hua Bilian; he is simply concerned about his good name. Perhaps Luo's attitude to the match is conditioned by some of the ideals of the scholar-beauty romance; overtly by his loyalty to his original fiancée, and implicitly by the expectation that the hero will marry his two wives at the same time, in effect making them co-wives of equal status. But it seems that he protests too much. He does not see himself as a "brilliant scholar," and he himself says that his ambitions do not lie in such things as a wife and concubines.[60]

As if to prove that his ambitions lie elsewhere, every time he refuses a proposal he runs off to play the hero—with disastrous results. Significantly, when Hua Bilian's father hears how Luo has handled his discovery that a friend's wife has committed adultery, he says, "hiding the bad and encouraging the good as you did, that's what a gentleman (*junzi*) would do."[61] It is obviously not what a hero (*haohan*) would do, however, and Hua goes on to chide Luo for leaving his friend in a dangerous situation. Luo's role as hero is further undermined the next time he sees the Hua gang coming into town and wants to hide from them rather than deal with another proposal. His cousin must convince him that he has an obligation as a friend at least to entertain them, berating him, "Are you ever rude! (*wu li*) . . . It's a good thing we're cousins, so I can't suspect you; if we were just friends, and I saw you being this callous, I wouldn't be your friend any longer!"[62] Luo's impulse to hide rather than deal with another proposal from the Huas would be understandable in his original characterization as a scholar. However, his pretensions to the role of hero, under which he befriended the Huas, require him to treat them hospitably. His cousin voices the expectations of righteousness (*yiqi*) so central to the martial hero's ethos. Luo steps back into role and plays the martial hero in saving Hua Bilian when she falls from a roof, as I have mentioned. The crowd greets his feat with cries of approval and calls him a hero (*yingxiong*), but his heroics also make him the target of a local bully's wrath.[63] After refusing the third proposal from the Huas in no uncertain terms, he goes off to capture the villain Wang Lun, but jeopardizes his mission by stopping to play the hero and save a widow from rape. He is later praised for having done what a hero (*haohan*) should do;[64] that may be true, but Luo makes the mistake of telling the woman his name rather than remaining anonymous as a hero should, a mistake that leads to his being framed by the culprit. He also shows the mindset of a noble scion by insisting on showing up when summoned to a court investigation, rather than following the heroic ideal of ignoring the law.

These examples illustrate that while Luo may see himself as a hero and get himself into situations appropriate to that role, he is rarely able to carry it off, leaving noticeable gaps between his role and his character. However, his playing the hero challenges his original identity. When an upright official is called in to save Luo from being framed by villains, he says "[Luo] is the descendant of an official. He should be studying his proper occupation in order to make a name for himself. How is it that he is consorting with these bandits and pirates?"[65] Consorting with the outlaws makes him less of a scholar in the eyes of the official. By trying to play the hero, he fails to live up to the scholar's role he was born to, and risks rejection by his own class.

What may have permitted this sort of miscasting in the first place is the pattern of three proposals and refusals found in both the scholar-beauty romance and the military romance. Its use in *Green Peony* recalls both antecedents. Thus each action can be read in terms of multiple expectations based on the interpretation of the pairing of the two parties: as martial beauty and martial scholar or as woman warrior and general. Each of these pairs is able to account for some aspects of the situation, but no single pairing can account for all aspects.

Hua Bilian resembles the woman warriors of the military romance in her pursuit of an unwilling man. Unlike the military romance, however, Hua

Bilian never fights Luo. Oddly, that trope is given to another woman warrior, Bao Jinhua, who is already married at the time she fights him. Her interest is piqued by her father's statement that had he not already married her off, he would have chosen Luo for her husband.[66] *Green Peony* plays on the situation, describing the match in suggestive terms, but continually thwarting the reader's expectations. The novel invokes both the military romance and the scholar-beauty romance, while misapplying and mixing the conventions. The trope that is played upon, of the woman warrior falling in love with the general by matching her martial skills with his,[67] clearly belongs to the military romance. While one chapter heading in *Green Peony* calls the scene a hero (*yingxiong*) meeting a heroine (*jienü*), the next chapter heading uses the terms of the romance: "A drunken beauty (*jiaren*) peeks at a talented man (*cailang*) in his study."[68] Thus the label "proper beauty" (*jiaren*) is applied to Bao Jinhua, the daughter of a notorious pirate, despite her blatant disregard for the rules of propriety—she talks back to her father and orders her husband around. The label simply does not fit.

Apart from the midnight tryst in the study, the episode also recalls the scholar-beauty romance in its use of descriptive poetry.[69] When Bao Jinhua looks Luo over, the poem describing him combines a hero's strength with a "refined appearance," declaring him a "handsome noble scion (*jia gongzi*)." Luo then looks Bao Jinhua over, and a poem describes her "Lightly painted pear-flower face / Supple willow waist / Her whole face wreathed in smiles / In all respects she's completely lovely." When they begin dueling, a couplet runs "An outstanding girl meets a marvelous man / A brilliant fellow fights a beauty under the moon."[70] The nouns and verbs in the second line are obviously mismatched: One would expect a "brilliant fellow" and "beauty" to meet, rather than fight.

Originally the sparring match between Luo and Bao Jinhua was more or less for show; indeed, Luo thinks to himself, *When will this act* (xi) *be over?*[71] But it becomes a fight in earnest when Luo unintentionally injures Bao Jinhua in trying to end the match.[72] At that point Bao Jinhua decides to kill him to preserve her undefeated reputation. Accordingly, the next chapter heading reflects the change in her perception of Luo's role from brilliant scholar (*caizi*) to "righteous man" (*yishi*). They fight on the rooftops until Luo jumps into the wilds outside Bao's fortress.

In Bao Jinhua's midnight duel with Luo Hongxun, the juxtaposition of genre codes raises the reader's expectations in order to expose the conventions it plays upon. Parody "first sets up the text to be parodied (by imitation or partial quotation, or by way of other such devices) so that the reader will expect it, and then produces another version of it which the reader does not expect and which sets up some incongruous contrast or comparison with the other work."[73] Both tropes invoked—the midnight tryst from the scholar-beauty romance, or the woman warrior matching skills with a young general from the military romance—lead to marriage. In this scene, however, the expected outcome becomes impossible. The reader knows that Bao Jinhua is already a married woman. Moreover, the misapplication of the discourse invoked rips it from its usual referent. Bao Jinhua is something of a shrew, but she is portrayed in the chapter headings and descriptive poetry as an ideal demure beauty. However, the "beauty" shows her true colors (and belies that label) when wounded pride makes her try to kill Luo Hongxun. When *Green Peony* uses genre codes to create an "impossible" situation, as in this scene, the conventions can no longer be taken seriously.

Just as the encounter between Bao Jinhua and Luo Hongxun seems created to play on the juxtaposition of roles, so, too, do Hua Bilian's encounters with Luo have a noticeably staged quality, especially when she is displaying her skills. Their first encounter, translated above, occurs when she and her family come into Dingxing County in the guise of entertainers. As we have seen, Luo and his friend Ren commission a performance and praise Hua Bilian's skill.[74] But the role of entertainer is a tricky one; the villain also watches her performance and misinterprets entertainer to mean prostitute. Even Luo and Ren do not realize that the skills being displayed are true martial skills rather than circus tricks until one of her uncles takes part. They praise his performance, which "can't be compared with the illusory spears of the rivers and lakes (*jianghu*)."[75] While the Hua gang is truly skilled, this suggests that those who are not can impersonate the role of hero. Performance always leaves open the relationship between performer and role, appearance and reality. The fact that Luo and Ren can see the worth of the Huas proves their own status, since it takes one to know one. In contrast, just three chapters later when Ren and Luo are trying to convince Wang not to lay siege to the Hua gang, they emphasize the role over the reality, telling Wang that the Hua gang are "just acrobatic performers of the rivers and lakes."[76] This statement need not be taken at face value. They may not think it necessary or proper to reveal the true identity of the Huas to Wang.

Hua Bilian's next encounter with Luo comes when she attempts to catch the monkey. Yu Qian's efforts to catch it have already drawn a huge crowd; there are so many people watching that the Huas cannot even pass by on the street. The crowd refuses to budge, saying, "We all got up early in the morning, ate something and came straight here; we didn't even go home to eat lunch. It wasn't easy to get this spot, so why do you think we'll yield to you?"[77] Having taken on the task and raised the public's expectations, Yu cannot quit without forfeiting his self-imposed role as hero. Besides helping out a hero who has gotten himself into a difficult situation, Hua Bilian's attempt to catch the monkey is commissioned primarily for the villain Luan's entertainment, as Luan explicitly tells his henchman. Her leap to the top of the pavilion is praised by the crowd as "seldom heard of from ancient times."[78] However, this performance is the turning point in her transformation from woman warrior to demure beauty; from the time she falls down and is taken into the women's quarters of Luo's home, the reader does not see her again until Luo arrives to marry her. Even then, she leaves the room as soon as he enters, in accordance with maidenly propriety.[79] After they are married, she is free to display her skills again.[80]

The special women's examinations mandated by Empress Wu prove to be more exhibition than competition. The examinations are held in two parts, covering both martial and literary skills. However, only the three women escorted by Bao Zi'an (Bao Jinhua, Hua Bilian, and Hu Saihua) are skilled in the martial arts. After Bao Jinhua hits the bull's-eye with all three arrows from horseback, "everyone in the place cheered."[81] The examiner is impressed and asks himself, if even women are so skilled at riding and archery, who knows how many heroes have been wrongly living in obscurity on the rivers and lakes? Even so, the competition is merely for show, since the outcome has already been determined by corrupt officials.

Even the real battles that Hua Bilian fights in *Green Peony* are couched in terms of exhibition. When she is tricked into going to Wang's house and forced to fight her way out, her objections are interpreted as staged; at first Wang thinks she is acting coy in order to seem more attractive.

> Mother and daughter saw there were no women in the parlor, so they stopped in their tracks. Wang Lun said, "Old He, why did the two of them stop?" He Shilai said, "Their kind is great at putting on airs. They're just that sort, but they want to act as if they're better. They're not really shy at all, but they twist and turn to be the picture of shyness, to make people love them. Now when they were walking along and suddenly stopped, they're putting on airs. They mean to make us go down to greet them. Why don't we go meet them then? Won't it be a happy occasion when you come back with her hand in hand?" Wang Lun happily said, "Fine, fine!"[82]

Since He Shilai believes Hua Bilian to be a prostitute, he explains her propriety as an act intended to win hearts. Accordingly, the villain Wang Lun steps into the role of the romantic hero, explicitly referring to himself as *xiaosheng*, "young student."

> Wang Lun said to Bilian, "Yesterday I saw you walking the tightrope at Peach Blossom Knoll, it was marvelous. Today I've especially invited you to my home to meet you, to comfort this young student in my longing for you." When Hua Bilian heard him call himself "young student" her powdered face blushed completely red. Mrs. Hua heard these flowery phrases and knew he was up to no good, so she already was a bit upset.[83]

From his discourse, Hua Bilian immediately "reads" the role Wang Lun is playing. His invocation of the *xiaosheng* of fiction and drama, the romantic young scholar, tells her what to expect, and she is offended. Hua Bilian refuses to play along; she and her mother fight their way out of the Wang manor, creating quite a spectacle. Hua Bilian's mother's main concern is also with appearances; she wants to get out quickly so that Ren and Luo will not hear of it, since it might be damaging to her daughter's reputation and future marriage prospects. When Hua Bilian participates in the climactic event of the novel, the battle to restore the ousted emperor, in her own mind the performance aspects outweigh any thought of the larger meaning of her actions. She is conscious of Luo watching her, and she kills her opponent in order to show off in front of her new husband.

This emphasis on battle as exhibition brings out an aspect of the woman warrior implicit even in *The Water Margin*. Nearly every time a woman warrior appears on the battlefield, the men watch the women fight and are either dazzled or lose their fighting skills. When Hu Sanniang fights Wang Aihu, this effect is clearly described; "Who would have thought after over ten rounds, from looking at her his hands shook and his feet went numb, so his swordplay deteriorated." After capturing Wang Aihu, Hu Sanniang takes on Ma Lin. Their skillful battle is aestheticized, compared to "jade chips floating on the wind, snow scattering on jeweled flowers."[84] Even Song Jiang is dazzled. The difference between the two works is that in *The Water Margin*, the "audience" inside the novel consists of the warrior's comrades-in-arms and battlefield opponents, whereas in *Green Peony* the emphasis on martial arts as performance means it is aimed primarily at crowds of onlookers who are presumably not skilled in martial arts themselves. In effect, the reader also becomes a spectator of the performance, probably visualizing it in terms of the theatricals that helped shape these martial conventions. This raises the possibility that the role of hero could be impersonated by mere circus performers without the requisite skills.

The Impossibility of Heroism

How are the heroes portrayed in *Green Peony*? How do they relate to the code of the martial hero (*haohan*) established in works like *The Water Margin*?

Hua Zhenfang invokes and also thwarts the reader's expectations of a bandit chief (fig. 3.5). No doubt, he is a *haohan* with a reputation that commands respect and fear. When he first appears, Ren and Luo confirm that he is truly skilled and lives up to his reputation.[85] Even Hua's enemies acknowledge his prowess; when begging to be released Wang's servant calls Hua a hero (*yingxiong*). This initial portrait of Hua as a powerful bandit chief is complicated by occasional indications of his literary learning and desire to serve in government. Hua's room at his inn befits a scholar: "Zither, chess, books and paintings, . . . everything was there, it didn't seem at all like an inn."[86] The revelation of this

Figure 3.5 The bandit Hua Zhenfang, from the 1800 edition of *Green Peony*

side of Hua makes the reader aware that initial appearances may be deceiving. These are not mere trappings; Hua can also recite Confucian teachings. While at the inn, he proceeds to give Luo a lecture on the relative importance of the five relationships, in which he states, in accordance with Confucian thinking, that the relationship between friends is the least important.[87] The lecture contrasts sharply with the views of the heroes in *The Water Margin*, who value friendship above all else. Immediately after the lecture, however, Hua shows the importance he attaches to friendship by rushing off to save Ren.

While Hua's willingness to save Ren might seem to confirm the reader's expectations of the selfless *haohan*, he also has an ulterior motive. He wants Ren to act as a matchmaker for his daughter Hua Bilian, and he believes saving Ren's life would oblige Ren to help him.[88] Hua also decides to bring along some of his gang so they can make some money on the trip. The delight in money and robbery, which is fitting for neither the *haohan* nor the scholar, further complicates Hua's character.[89] On several occasions his greed for money leads him to compromise a friend, and even his own daughter. Hua's first attempt to save Ren is sabotaged by his decision to make money.[90] Almost as soon as he sets out, Hua goes back on his promise to help Ren catch his wife with her lover. Instead, he escorts his gang back to their stronghold after they have robbed Wang Lun. When Hua considers whether he should go back on his word to Ren, the gang reminds him, "Look after yourself first, others come later" (*xian gu ji er hou you ren*).[91] This is in direct contrast to the characteristic altruism of the martial hero. Ironically, the trip that was intended to save Ren from danger leads to further peril: Ren is framed for the robbery, beaten and jailed.

Hua is not motivated solely by money; he does feel obligated to return, and in trying to redeem himself becomes embroiled in further misadventures. Seeing Ren's house boarded up, he asks a shopkeeper why. When the latter tries to get rid of him, Hua says, "I haven't killed anyone or burned anything down, I'm not a big-time bandit, how could I implicate anyone? So why are you trying to get rid of me?"[92] His protestation is distinctly ironic, since his gang has just burned down the temple, he is a bandit by trade, and he has just implicated Ren. After talking to the shopkeeper, Hua faces the consequences of his previous actions and thinks to himself:

> "I came here to save Ren, I never expected I would end up implicating him. Yesterday if they hadn't robbed Wang Lun, Ren Zhengqian would not be in trouble today. Now that they've all left, leaving me here alone without anyone to help me, how am I supposed to save him?" He wanted to go back to Shandong to get help, but to go there and back would take several days, and he was afraid that if Ren Zhengqian was interrogated again in court he might not survive. After hesitating a while, Hua said, "Since things have come to this, there's no other way. I'll just have to risk this old life of mine, wait until midnight, then sneak into the prison and carry him out."[93]

These heroics outdo anything that even the stalwarts in *The Water Margin* would attempt.[94]

In the prison that night, Hua murders two watchmen. The narrator explains, "It's not that he was bloodthirsty, but he feared that if he didn't kill them, they might wake up and look for the cymbals and drum, startling everyone around into action. He had no choice but to kill them."[95] By trying to explain away moral objections to the protagonists' actions, the narrator conversely ends up highlighting them, calling the heroic ideal into question. Similarly, Hua's promise to rebuild the temple that his gang burned down emphasizes the consequences of morally questionable behavior, especially since he plans to use some of the stolen money to do it.

By going "behind the scenes" like this to explore what lies beyond the story as told in other books, *Green Peony* parodies genre. This happens constantly, through too much explanation on the narrator's part or through telling part of the story not usually told. It implicitly poses new questions. What happens to the monks when the temple is burned down?[96] Are innocent people implicated when the heroes rob?[97] Addressing these issues makes the reader aware of both the selectivity of narrative and its effects on characterization. In Bakhtin's words, "the process of parodying forces us to experience those sides of the object that are not otherwise included in a given genre or a given style."[98] The heroes look less heroic when their actions are shown to have dire consequences for innocent people.

Green Peony not only plays on the moral limitations of its heroes; in the course of Hua Zhenfang's rescue attempt, even his capacity for heroic action is shown to have its limits. Once he breaks Ren out of jail, Hua is reduced to running away, and the narrator explains that even though he was a hero (*yingxiong*), he could not jump walls or scale roofs with Ren on his back. The emphasis on the limitations of Hua's martial capacity may be a reaction to the exaggeration of martial skills in the military romance, in which many a hero was portrayed as invincible.[99] Hua then leaves the injured Ren on the city wall, despite Ren's concerns about what will happen if he is found, and goes off to kill the adulterers. After he gets to Wang's estate he realizes that he does not know where to find them. He overhears a pair of illicit lovers talking, so he cuts off their heads and brings them back to Ren to prove the act of vengeance. It is only when Ren looks at the heads that Hua realizes he has killed the wrong pair! The narrator explains that since Hua had seen Madam He and Wang before, there was no excuse for the mistake; he was just in too much of a hurry. The end-of-chapter poem states, "After killing someone, the hero runs away."[100] However, despite his obvious limitations, Luo and Xu still praise Hua as a hero (*yingxiong*) when he recounts how he saved Ren.[101]

In this first incident the heroic gesture is a secondary priority, after money and family. When Hua Zhenfang is forced to choose between money and family, however, he chooses money. Before he orders Hua Bilian to catch a monkey in the incident described above, he haggles with the monkey's owner, Luan Yiwan. Luan's desire to see Hua Bilian perform prompts him to offer twice as much money if she can catch it, and Hua Zhenfang immediately agrees. His wife, understanding it could jeopardize Hua Bilian's chance to marry Luo, objects, but Hua Zhenfang insists he cannot go back on his word.[102] As before, his greed takes precedence over the original purpose of his trip. Greed triumphs again when he insists on payment after the monkey has fallen to its death. It is this insistence that causes Luan Yiwan to seek vengeance on Luo.

Not only does Hua's love of money nearly get Luo killed, but the assassin is the pirate Bao Zi'an's prospective son-in-law, Pu Tianpeng. Pu hires himself out to avenge Luan.[103] Luo defeats him and demands the truth from him. Pu explains that Bao has required him to earn a hundred taels before marrying his daughter. Luo's mother lectures Pu on morality, urges him to try a proper occupation, and gives him the money to get married. She may appear to be the embodiment of virtue, but comparison with a similar trope in an earlier scholar-beauty romance reveals that Mrs. Luo is simply erring in the other direction. If Hua Zhenfang and Bao Zi'an are at fault for their greed, Mrs. Luo becomes the victim of misplaced charity. In the scholar-beauty romance *Sheng hua meng*, a desperate thief is pardoned and given money by the man he has tried to rob; he uses the money to set himself up in an honorable profession, and later is able to save his benefactor's life.[104] In contrast, Pu Tianpeng, while grateful, does not change his ways, and his attempt to express his gratitude to Luo by having him kidnapped puts Luo in an even more difficult position. The narrator once more tries to explain Bao's demand for money as his natural desire to see Pu make something of himself.[105] However, the large bet Bao proposes at a martial arts contest suggests it may be greed that motivated the demand.[106]

The use of the master thief motif to describe both Hua and Bao further reinforces this emphasis on money. Before each attempt on Wang's life, the thief's outfit that Hua or Bao wears is described, an element also found in some of the early vernacular short stories.[107] This motif reinforces the ambivalent characterization of Hua and Bao. While the most memorable thieves in the short stories tend to play a positive role, their motivation for robbing and tricking people ranges from revenge to merely making a living. Moreover, in *The Water Margin* the heroes look down upon petty thieves.

Another of the traditional vices, drunkenness, is not only excusable but almost a virtue for heroes in *The Water Margin*. Lu Zhishen insists that he fights better when he is drunk.[108] Indeed, it seems that in *The Water Margin* the more physical heroes can be ranked by the prodigious amounts they eat and drink.[109] Seldom does drunkenness interfere with a hero's ability or his plans, with a few possible exceptions. Yang Xiong is drunk when he reveals to his wife his suspicions of her affair, which allows her to turn the accusation of infidelity around and frame Shi Xiu.[110] In another episode Li Kui is explicitly warned against drinking, but ignores the warning and is captured and tied up.[111] The most famous example of drunkenness leading to trouble in *The Water Margin* is the poem Song Jiang writes on the tavern wall when he is drunk.[112] Still, the scores of merry drinking scenes outweigh these examples, or at least convey an ambivalent attitude toward drinking in *The Water Margin*.

In *Green Peony*, drunkenness on the part of the heroes repeatedly renders them vulnerable to the villains' schemes. The first time Wang commits adultery with Ren's wife, he is able to do so because he conspired to get Ren and Luo drunk. When Yu Qian returns, also drunk, he puzzles out what is happening, but he does not barge in and kill the adulterers; he is afraid that if he enters Ren's wife's room he will get into trouble, and so he decides to wait outside for the culprit to come out. He is preoccupied with the separation of the sexes. This episode serves as a parodic echo of Guan Yu guarding Liu Bei's wives in *Three Kingdoms*. In that scene, Cao Cao quarters Guan Yu and Liu Bei's wives in same room "to confuse the relations between lord and minister . . . Lord Guan held a candle and stood outside the door; from night until morning, he showed no sign of weariness."[113] Although Yu Qian intends to guard the door as an expression of loyalty to his master, he is too drunk to live up to Guan Yu's model. He falls asleep, and Wang escapes. Realizing that he has allowed the adulterer to escape, Yu Qian wakes Luo up and lectures him on the perils of drunkenness![114] After this Luo vows to be careful. When he relates the incident to his cousin Xu, he says, "One cannot avoid drink, but one must not drink too much."[115]

But Yu Qian and Ren never learn. At one point Yu Qian comes back so drunk that he cannot walk a straight line. Drunkenness also affects his martial skills; he sees something on the roof and wants to jump up and go after it, but Luo advises him that it would be unwise.[116] More seriously, Ren's weakness for alcohol repeatedly leaves him vulnerable to manipulation by Wang. When Ren's wife follows their instructions and accuses Luo of flirting with her, Ren, drunk and angry, falls for the ploy and raises his sword against Luo.[117] Later, when Hua Zhenfang goes in the middle of the night to tip Ren off to his wife's adultery, Ren is drunk and asleep. Hua thinks, "No wonder his wife is having an affair and he still doesn't know; you could throw him in the river and he might not notice!"[118] Even after he is informed of his wife's affair, Ren continues to be undone by drink. Plotting with her brother to frame Ren, Madam He prepares wine to distract Ren until the police come. He Shilai "knew that Ren Zhengqian liked to drink, in fact that he never saw any wine that he did not drink, and so if they got him drunk, he would be easier to capture."[119] In *Green Peony* the consequences of drunkenness far outweigh its celebration.

In short, none of the characters in *Green Peony* lives up to the code of the martial hero (*haohan*). In this way *Green Peony* caricatures the values held by the heroes in *The Water Margin*, which continued to be problematic.[120]

Ritual "Acts": The Danger of Prescriptive Roles

Heroism is called into question in *Green Peony* by the characters' failure to live up to it, but more importantly it proves dangerous for those who try. Like any prescriptive role, it can be used by one character to manipulate another. Characters set up a ritual situation in which the other party has no choice but to fulfill a certain conventional role. For example, Wang uses the ceremony of brotherhood to render Ren vulnerable, Hua Zhenfang uses a mock funeral to try to convince Luo to marry his daughter, and Bao Zi'an uses a mock wedding to trap a powerful villain.

The villain Wang Lun subverts the ritual of swearing brotherhood in order to seduce Ren's wife. After Hua Bilian fights off Wang's unwanted advances, he lays siege to the inn in which the Hua gang is staying. Luo and Ren visit Wang to ask him to lift the siege, but are conned into swearing brotherhood with him.[121] It is not that Wang has had a change of heart. The reader sees Wang's henchman, He Shilai, suggesting the plot to Wang before he puts it in action. The henchman tells Wang that Ren is immune to the temptations of money and power, so an oath of brotherhood is the only way to gain access to the wife. The cardinal heroic virtue, loyalty to a sworn brother, is considered to be an exploitable weakness in Ren.[122]

Much of the obvious irony in the situation is due to the narrative method employed. The reader learns of the villain's plan before it is carried out, rather than merely learning that something was being planned and waiting in suspense until it happens. (In popular novels of the Ming and the Qing the details of such plans are often replaced by *ruci ruci*.) This produces dramatic irony, since the reader knows more than do Ren and Luo. The reader cannot take the ritual as a true expression of values, although Ren and Luo still do.

Wang is able to act the part of the straightforward hero in order to win Ren's trust, and Ren, *being* the straightforward hero himself, does not realize it is an act. Wang uses the language of admiration often used among *haohan* to greet Ren. His evocation of a meeting between heroes seems to signify a new relationship, since Wang goes on to ask Luo's name, even though he knew it a couple of chapters earlier. For their part, Ren and Luo "saw that Wang Lun's actions and words were reasonable and not inconsistent with those of a good person."[123] Thus even though they knew He Shilai for a rogue before, they still swear brotherhood with him. Both He Shilai's proposal and the ceremonial document explicitly invoke the paradigmatic oath of brotherhood in *Three*

Kingdoms. Afterward, when Wang suggests that He Shilai and Luo are in no position to play host, Ren takes his suggestion as the "words of an intimate friend (*zhi xin zhi yu*)."[124] The irony continues when Ren tells Wang to his face that he did not think much of him before, which goes to show one cannot believe what one hears. This comment is almost immediately followed by Yu Qian's reaction; he thinks to himself, "The two masters really are not very discerning. I've heard that Wang Lun has a human face but a beast's heart and that He Shilai will forget righteousness for profit; how could the two masters go and swear brotherhood with them?"[125]

This parody of the ceremony and bond of brotherhood in *Green Peony* may have been influenced by a similar parody of brotherhood in *Jin Ping Mei*. As Martin Huang points out, the swearing of brotherhood in *Jin Ping Mei*, although explicitly modeled on *Three Kingdoms*, is tainted by ulterior motives, and rather than ranking the brotherhood by age, they are ranked by wealth. Moreover, shortly after this oath of brotherhood Ximen Qing conspires to kill his sworn brother in order to marry his wife.[126] Still, the differences between *Green Peony* and *Jin Ping Mei* serve as a convenient example of parody's distinct functions in the two works. While both Ximen Qing and Wang Lun misuse the discourse of brotherhood, in *Jin Ping Mei* nobody participating in the ceremony believes in it; the brotherhood is actually an economic relationship, and the ceremony a hypocritical cover for their inglorious motives. In *Jin Ping Mei*, the empty discourse reflects the moral bankruptcy of those who employ it—their lack of belief is the problem. In *Green Peony*, on the other hand, the misappropriation of the discourse is useful precisely because some of the characters do believe in it. Moreover, Wang Lun explicitly swears brotherhood in order to commit adultery with Ren's wife, while Ximen Qing does not reveal that intent until well after the ceremony.[127] In *Green Peony* the real critique is of fools like Ren Zhengqian who, blindly believing in the discourse of brotherhood, act against their better judgment to fulfill the expectations of that model.

The parody is made explicit in *Green Peony* in a drinking game on the night Wang first commits adultery with Madam He; the poems composed prefigure each character's role in the incident by explicitly invoking his model. Wang and He Shilai's poems refer to *The Story of the Western Wing* (*Xixiang ji*), Wang casting himself as the romantic hero Scholar Zhang and He Shilai as the clever go-between Hong Niang.[128] These roles are in one sense appropriate, since Wang is lusting after a woman and He Shilai is acting as his go-between. However, the comedy of the scene derives from the incongruity between each of these roles and the unlikely person playing it. The villain plays the romantic hero, and his unscrupulous manservant plays the role of clever maid. Although Wang and He imagine themselves to be worthy of these roles, the reader sees the discrepancy between their literary models and their own actions. Likewise, when the scholar Luo Hongxun refers in his poem to Shi Xiu catching the adulterers in *The Water Margin*, he creates a discrepancy between his character and the role he wishes to play.[129] Because Luo invokes the example of Shi Xiu the reader expects he will thwart the adulterers and avenge his friend, but immobilized by his scholarly caution Luo is unable to act the hero.

Perceiving Luo's failure as a hero requires a fairly detailed knowledge of the Shi Xiu narrative. In *The Water Margin*, Shi Xiu is staying with a friend when he discovers that the friend's wife is having an affair. He reports this to the friend, but the wife discredits him by saying that Shi Xiu flirted with her. Shi Xiu is thrown out, but he stays in town and bides his time until he can prove her guilt to his friend, at which point they lure the wife up a mountain and kill her as a gruesome affirmation of the ties of brotherhood.

Green Peony explicitly imitates this episode from *The Water Margin*, but inverts many of the details. Unlike Shi Xiu, when Luo becomes aware that Ren's wife is committing adultery, he does not tell his friend, but just as in the Shi Xiu incident the wife learns of his suspicions and tells her husband that Luo flirted with her. Luo's reticence is what separates him from Shi Xiu, and marks Luo as a scholar at heart. While in *Green Peony* their friendship is eventually restored when the truth comes out, their revenge does not take the form it does in *The Water Margin*. Thus brotherhood, the central value of the hero, is undercut from the very beginning of the book. The heroes' attempts to live up to it expose both themselves and the values they hold to scrutiny.

Just as Wang uses the ceremony of brotherhood to manipulate Ren, Hua Zhenfang manipulates Luo by misinforming him that his mother and fiancée have died and arranging a fake funeral. The third time Hua Zhenfang proposes a match between Hua Bilian and Luo, Luo replies that he could only marry Hua Bilian if his original fiancée were dead.[130] This answer shows how Luo's attitude differs from that of a brilliant scholar; when the proper scholar in *Yu Jiao Li* is told that his prospective fiancée is dead, he swears to stay single all his life.[131] Luo's exasperated comment probably inspires the funeral ruse, the most outrageous episode in *Green Peony*. While preparing to leave Bao's stronghold to go and marry his original fiancée, Luo learns in a letter from his cousin that his mother has died in a fire and that his fiancée has been killed by bandits. Grief-stricken, he returns home to perform the last rites for his mother. Only afterward does he learn that both reports were hoaxes perpetrated by Hua Zhenfang, who has merely kidnapped the women to ensure that Luo will agree to marry Hua Bilian.

Upon examination, the funeral hoax in *Green Peony* reveals itself to be a comic reworking of the reported death of Song Jiang's father in *The Water Margin*.[132] A messenger comes with a letter from Song Jiang's brother to tell Song Jiang that their father has died and he must come home at once. Song Jiang leaves immediately, but when he arrives in his hometown the innkeeper tells him his father is alive and well. Suspicious, Song Jiang goes home and finds his younger brother not wearing mourning attire. It turns out that the whole episode was his father's idea to keep Song Jiang from joining the bandits and becoming a "disloyal, unfilial person," since an amnesty has been declared and Song Jiang need no longer hide from the law. However, that very night Song Jiang is arrested, tried, and exiled.

In *Green Peony*, the episode starts out in a similar manner. When Luo is in the company of outlaws, a letter arrives to inform him of his mother's death. But the letter serves a very different purpose. In *The Water Margin* the letter was his father's attempt to keep him from joining the bandits. In contrast, in *Green Peony* it is part of a plot by the bandits themselves to oblige Luo to join them (or at least to marry Hua Bilian). Even though the scheme is revealed to the reader in full just before it is acted out,[133] the ruse is taken much further than in *The Water Margin*. Rather than the truth being revealed upon arrival in his home town, it exploits the comic potential of the situation: for it tells of the enactment of a full funeral ritual, in which the grieving Luo gullibly kowtows to a stranger's bones.

In both cases the ruse is exposed by a breach of etiquette. When Song Jiang arrives home and sees his brother is not dressed in mourning, he is incensed (*da nu*) that his brother would trick him. In *Green Peony* a hint that the funeral is a ruse comes after everyone else at the funeral has kowtowed to "Mrs. Luo," and Luo and his cousin politely suggest that Pu need not kowtow. Pu takes them at their word and merely bows. Luo is secretly upset (*an nu*) by Pu's ingratitude, but Yu Qian becomes suspicious, investigates, and exposes the ruse. When he learns from a monk that the bones in the urn are not Mrs. Luo's, Yu Qian smashes the urn to bits, forcing Pu to confess to the hoax.[134] It takes a shocking act of impropriety to expose the falsity of the ritual.

The shadow of the death ruse from *The Water Margin* obviously looms large over this episode in *Green Peony*. But its reworking also incorporates tropes from two other genres: the plot against the hero's fiancée from the scholar-beauty romance, and the plot against the hero's mother from the historical novel. The fact that the ruse in *Green Peony* is premeditated sets it apart from the trope in the scholar-beauty romance novels. In *Yu Jiao Li*, the story that the hero's fiancée had died is made up by his rival on the spur of the moment. In *Gui lian meng* (Dream of returning lotus), it is pure coincidence that the hero's fiancée falls into the hands of a woman warrior who is in love with him; one of her underlings happens to capture the fiancée when out on another mission. So in this respect *Green Peony* is closer to *Three Kingdoms*, in which the kidnapped mother is a pawn. There may be faint echoes of the episode in which Cao Cao takes Xu Shu's mother hostage to win Xu's allegiance. The plot works, but Xu's mother lectures her son on his poor judgment, saying he should never serve an unworthy lord just to save her life, and commits suicide to reprimand him.[135] *Green Peony* also parallels the military romance *Yishuo Fan Tang quan zhuan* (Another tale of rebellion against the Tang) in that the hero puts himself in harm's way for the sake of filial duty;[136] Luo is already a wanted man and has an ongoing feud with Luan Yiwan when he returns to Yangzhou to attend his mother's funeral. But whereas in *Another Tale of Rebellion against the Tang* the hero's parents are truly dead, and in *The Water Margin* the reader knows only as much as Song Jiang, in *Green Peony* the situation is tempered with dramatic irony. That the reader knows that Luo's mother is not really dead makes the situation grimly comic.

The significance of ritual is seriously challenged when a stranger can be substituted for a mother without the son realizing the fact. Through intertextual reference, the novel contests Luo's status as a filial son.[137] While Song Jiang leaves immediately, despite the gang's protestations, Luo is persuaded to stay another night before departing. Similarly, Song Jiang refuses to eat or drink after he hears the news; Luo continues to eat and drink afterward. However, the greatest challenge is created by the novel *Green Peony*: how is it that Luo does not realize that a stranger had been substituted for his mother? A couplet underscores this: "A beggar woman masquerades as the wife of a former official / A true son cries for a false mother."[138] Once again, uncritical acceptance makes the character vulnerable. Ritual and punctilious etiquette are a double-edged sword, since they allow the hoax to be perpetrated but also lead to its exposure when one of the perpetrators is reluctant to perform his part. The mock funeral leaves the reader wondering whether the displays of filiality Luo has given elsewhere are true expressions of feeling, or whether his concern is simply to keep up appearances.

Which Side of the Story?

The implications of this episode extend beyond Luo's role to the characterization of the Hua family. It reveals a certain cold-heartedness or cruelty on Hua's part. The gang member who accompanies Luo to his mother's supposed funeral marvels to himself, *No wonder Mr. Hua has no sons.*[139] He means that it must be retribution for Hua having no compunction about toying with people's emotions in this way. As discussed above, the relentless pursuit of an unwilling, engaged scholar by another girl's parents, which provides the motivation behind the funeral hoax, is a classic villain's role in the scholar-beauty romance. In terms of these conventions, Hua Bilian's parents should be seen as villains. Indeed, some of their actions make this a plausible classification; they repeatedly endanger Luo and Ren.[140]

Hypothetically classifying the Huas as villains leads us to interpret the situation in the one way that the conventions of the scholar-beauty romance do not permit. One method of understanding a genre is to examine what cannot happen in it.[141] In the scholar-beauty romance, neither the hero nor the heroine can be forced into an unwanted match. Yet that is exactly what happens to Luo when he marries Hua Bilian.

Still, the juxtaposition of genres means these actions can also be read another way. In the funeral ruse from *Later Tang Third Collection* analyzed above, similar means are used for similar ends; the woman warrior, after proposing and being repulsed three times, fakes her own death to win the man she is pursuing.[142] Her actions are condoned by none other than the emperor, who is happy to see them married because he will gain her formidable skills for his cause. Thus the conventions of the military romance (*yingxiong chuanqi*) would excuse the ruse the Huas employ. The juxtaposition of these two sets of conflicting genre conventions creates ambiguity; it is up to the reader to decide how to evaluate the characters.

The conventions that form the core of the scholar-beauty romance are once again turned upside down when Bao Zi'an arranges a fake engagement and wedding in order to make a surprise attack on a corrupt clique. The pattern of events parodies the scholar-beauty romance: the boy and girl get engaged, she takes the examinations and wins first place, and the wedding is set for the following day. Besides the obvious gender inversion, the habitual connection in the scholar-beauty romance between the exams and marriage is also spoofed: In *Green Peony* the evil Prime Minister Zhang Tianzuo has arranged the women's exams as a way to choose a suitable bride for his son. Public institutions are being misused for private ends. Moreover, when Zhang Tianzuo hears of Bao Jinhua's beauty he intends to force the marriage whether or not she is already engaged to someone else. Thus the fake wedding may be seen as poetic justice. Bao Zi'an explains to his daughter that the wedding will provide the perfect opportunity for his gang to kill the corrupt officials.[143] This plot would be absolutely unthinkable in the scholar-beauty romances. Besides, Bao Jinhua is already a married woman!

The wedding exaggerates convention to the point of absurdity. The family of a girl being forced into an unwanted match often goes to great lengths to delay it, but in a parody of this trope, the bandits in *Green Peony* delay the groom's men from escorting the bride to his house by demanding money before they open the door. By evening, when they release the bride, they have collected a huge sum (800 taels).

The fake wedding brings to mind parallels in both *Three Kingdoms* and *The Water Margin*. The episode in *The Water Margin* in which Lu Zhishen saves a girl from a local bandit leader by taking her place as bride is the most obvious.[144] The play on expectations in *The Water Margin* is purely for shock value: Instead of a bride in the wedding chamber, the bandit finds a naked fat monk who starts to pummel him. There are several places where *The Water Margin* sets up expectations, then defuses or reverses them, as in this scene. But the use of roles to play on expectations is never carried beyond the isolated incident in *The Water Margin*. The situation is always resolved through recognition of friendship or sworn brotherhood, and the reader is brought back to the central story. While the inversion of expectations is used for entertainment value, it has little effect on the conventions or rituals being played upon.

The episode in *Green Peony* is even more extreme than Lu Zhishen's adventure; it is an orchestrated attack. The mock wedding may have been inspired by the scheme in *Three Kingdoms* in which a beauty is used to distract the enemy until he can be defeated; the prime minister in *Green Peony* is too caught up in the wedding preparations to notice that the restoration of the proper emperor is imminent. Once Bao Jinhua has killed Zhang, her "maid" signals to the others to attack, and all the wedding guests are slaughtered. This may play out the potential in another *Three Kingdoms* episode in which Liu Bei fears his martial bride; when he sees even the maids are armed, he thinks he has walked into a trap, although his fears are groundless.[145] Although appearances are similarly deceiving, *Green Peony* creates the opposite situation: The bridegroom is so consumed with desire that he does not notice the weapons his bride and her maid have concealed until it is too late.

The play on ritual in *Green Peony* suggests the question of legitimacy so prominent in *Three Kingdoms* and *The Water Margin*. With a role of authority, if others accept the performance of that role, the role can become reality. *Green Peony* explores the relationship between name and reality, or institution and action, in its variations on the role of the judge. The most striking example is the pirate who self-consciously plays the judge but decides each case justly, in contrast to corrupt or inept officials. The pirate has no official sanction, but he is more responsible with his self-declared powers than most of the men in official robes. The exception among officials is Judge Di, who, precisely because he is an upright official in an overwhelmingly corrupt regime, is circumscribed in his power and movements. In the end, the righteous outlaw and the upright official join forces to restore the emperor; once the pirate is enfeoffed, institution and practice are unified.

The sheer incongruity of a notorious outlaw holding a trial would be enough to render it comic. In *The Water Margin* there is a short episode in which Li Kui dresses as an official and holds a mock trial "just for fun," with *yamen* workers acting the parts of plaintiff and defendant.[146] Li Kui inverts expectations by punishing the plaintiff and releasing the defendant. His reasoning stems from his martial values—he lets the winner of the fight go as a "hero" and puts the loser in a cangue as an example. Paradoxically, this inversion of justice proves an accurate imitation of the real judges, who consistently punish the victims.

Li Kui acting the judge seems primarily a visual comedy. *The Water Margin* describes him wearing official robes in a court with underlings going through the ritual, bowing to him and doing his bidding. Still, his words, actions, and values are unchanged and do nothing to accommodate the expectations for the role of judge. Li Kui borrows the judge's robes, but not his "lines"; he cannot use the official discourse appropriate to a judge. Instead, his threats of violence if others do not play along serve as constant reminders of his "real" character. He dresses the part and goes on the "stage," but does not really try to play the role. The scene merely displays the contrast between character and role, while the "audience" within the novel—the townspeople watching from outside the *yamen*—laughs at the spectacle.[147]

Unlike Li Kui, however, when the outlaw plays the judge in *Green Peony*, he is dealing with actual cases. *Green Peony* neatly contrasts the official and the bandit worlds through two trials of the same incident: an official trial and the trial held by the pirate Bao Zi'an on board his ship (fig. 3.6). Bao spares no effort in mimicking the official trial, rendering the ritual aspects a total mockery. Bao Zi'an even can pass for an official to the widow on trial: "She saw an old man of sixty sitting upright there, and did not know what kind of official he was." She addresses him as "Master" (*laoye*), the same form of address she uses for the real official in court. Bao Zi'an also goes further in his role playing than Li Kui by appropriating official discourse during the trial. However, Bao is determined to learn the truth of the case and actually does a better job of investigating than his official counterpart. In some ways, then, the trial becomes a mirror image of a real trial, with the same methods but opposite results. Bao first suggests the trial as something to do "for fun."[148] In the example I used to open this chapter, Bao begins by pointing out the difference between his court and the official court to those on trial. He dismisses the charge that Widow Xiu committed adultery with Luo, considering it slander by her accuser, Mei Tao, but asks her to testify as to where her baby came from; his wording of the question is almost exactly that of the official judge.[149] When she says she does not know, he starts to sound more and more like the official judge, and even orders her tortured. Although the command he gives is the same as that given by an official judge, he does not have the official instruments of torture on the ship. Instead the finger press is imitated by two strong men crunching her fingers between their hands.[150]

As an outlaw, Bao even has some advantages over a real judge. Before he captures the adulterers, he hears them talking privately, and their conversation reveals their relationship and their intention to harm Widow Xiu. Thus when Bao questions Mei Tao, Mei cannot insist that Luo's story is untrue, as he did in the official court. Mei first reverts to the story he told Luo, but after being tortured, he quickly confesses the truth in almost the same words as the original explanation given by the narrator.[151]

The differences between the official and the bandit trials are not merely in investigative technique; they also concern the values to which the accused

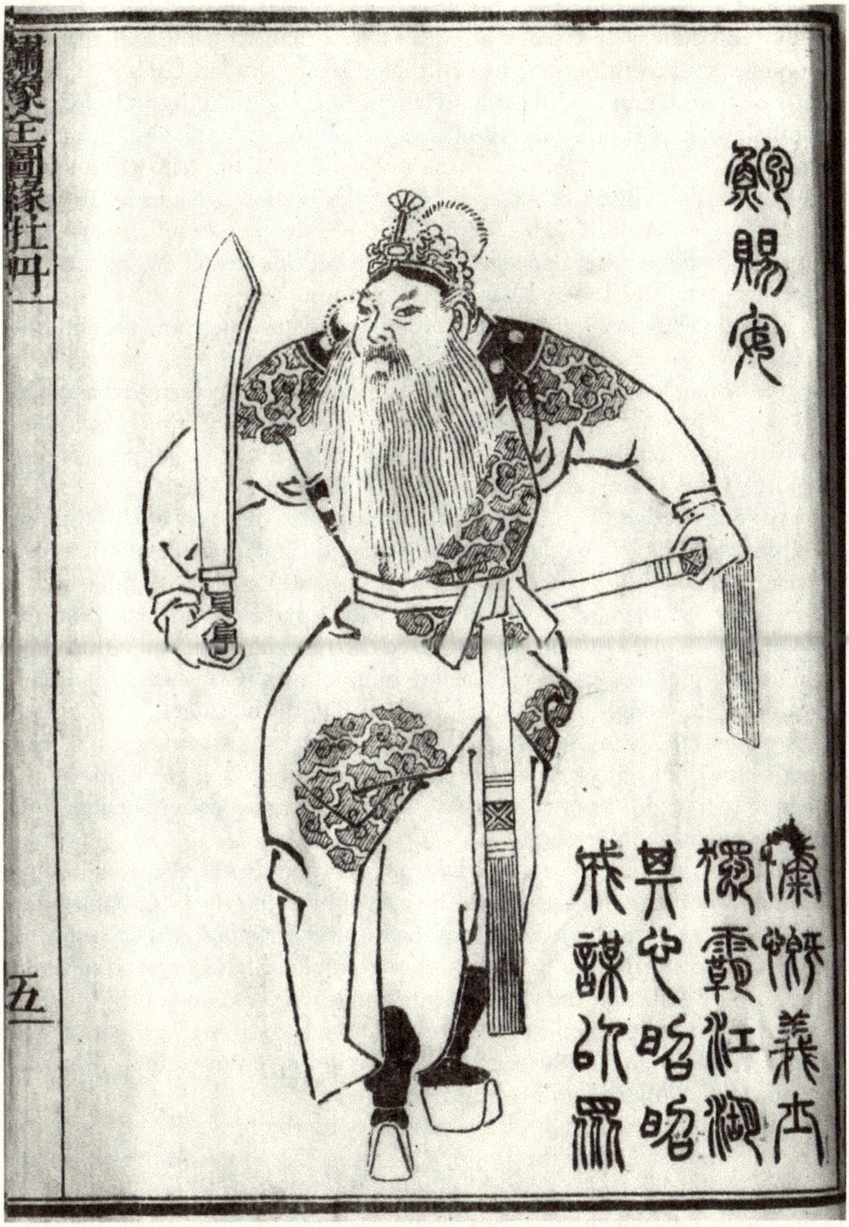

Figure 3.6 The pirate Bao Zi'an, from the 1892 edition of *Green Peony*

are held. Bao is less concerned with the fact that Mei Tao and Lao Mei have committed adultery or even an attempted rape than with the fact that they were ungrateful to those who helped them. Their crime in Bao's eyes is less their violation of proper Confucian relations (*mie lun*) than ingratitude (*wang en*); official values are secondary to the values of the martial hero. The price of ingratitude in *The Water Margin* is death; when Song Jiang releases Lin Gao's wife but she has him arrested as a bandit, he is soon avenged.[152] In *Green Peony*, however, even though Bao mimics the actions of an official judge, he does not assume any real power in this case yet. He keeps the baby as evidence, and puts Mei Tao and Lao Mei in custody.

Both dichotomies—public institutions versus private motives, and official values versus those of the martial hero—are intertwined in another court case. He Shilai violates both sets of values when he has Luo arrested as a bandit, since he is using his official position for private ends (*jie gong bao si*) and Luo is technically his sworn brother. It is at this point that Judge Di enters the novel, hears of the case, and has He Shilai arrested for slander.

Although Judge Di holds a high office and has the trust of the empress, he is rendered helpless by the corruption around him. Twice he presides over a court case, but he never actually passes judgment. He plays a similar role in the military romance, in which he works with Empress Wu to curb excesses and corruption and with others to restore the rightful emperor.[153] Instead of trying to settle the cases brought before him, he uses Luo's case as an excuse (*yi guan shi wei ming*) to get Luo, Hua, and Bao to the capital. He hopes to employ their talents in the restoration.[154] Judge Di can be seen as a symbol of imperial impotence because of the corruption surrounding the empress. All he has left is the position without the power, so he must coopt outsiders who have power without position.

The actual state of power is driven home by another comic situation, the plight of the runner entrusted with the task of bringing the formidable pirate Bao Zi'an to justice. Much is made of the runner's trepidation at each stage of the trip, but his fears prove to be another example of false expectations built up only to be deflated. The government cannot force Bao to appear in court, but Bao listens to the appeal from Judge Di and agrees to go to the capital after he takes care of "a matter that's been weighing on my mind"—the capture and trial of Wang and Madam He.[155]

The trial and execution of the adulterers by the pirate Bao Zi'an in his makeshift court contrast the frontier justice of *The Water Margin* with the fearless official justice of *Longtu's Court Cases*. Bao's role playing is again highlighted; Hua Zhenfang jokes about Bao's presumption when the latter announces that he will hear the adultery cases in his court the next day. Bao sits in the front with twenty men lined up on either side in imitation of official court. Hua, Luo, and the other gang members are seated at a banquet watching the proceedings, an arrangement more in keeping with justice in *The Water Margin*. The issue of status is brought into focus this time, with a righteous outlaw trying the case of a corrupt official. This clearly inverts the roles in previous court cases, when He Shilai tried Luo as a bandit in chapters 43 to 45, and Wang Lun ordered his capture in chapters 29 to 34. As an appointed official, He Shilai refuses to kneel to bandits. After Bao has him beaten until he is forced to kneel, he turns him over to Ren for questioning. Ren confronts He Shilai with his crimes, then cuts out his heart and eats it. But after this display, Bao tries to control Ren long enough to get a deposition out of Madam He; twice Ren comes at her with a knife, and twice Bao rebukes him for contempt of court. Ren still expects the private vengeance typical of *The Water Margin*, while Bao is play acting the "official" judge and must administer a more objective "public" justice. Although this time Bao exercises the power of judgment, he orders his underlings to execute the adulterers, instead of having them die gruesome deaths at the protagonists' hands.[156] Once again the conflation of genres creates ambiguity: Bao's choice to deny Ren personal vengeance on the adulterers seems wrong by the code of the hero, but right by the standards of the judge.

When Bao finally does present himself in the capital courthouse, Judge Di uses the pretext of hearing his case to determine Bao and Hua's loyalties. Neither he nor Bao concern themselves with the actual sentencing; Bao hopes to use the opportunity to join the restoration movement with Judge Di's help. When Di questions Bao about his life as a pirate, Bao reveals his lifelong battle against the corrupt factions in court. Judge Di acts enraged and orders Bao taken to the back chambers. Instead of an adversary, however, Bao finds an ally; Judge Di merely wanted to meet Bao in private so that they can talk freely.[157] The corrupt officials know that Judge Di intends to restore the emperor and have effectively isolated him inside the capital city, and so he cannot afford to let his partnership with Bao become common knowledge.

This whole sequence, including the show of courage by the prisoner and the fact that both parties repair to an inner chamber to reveal their true intentions, echoes Luo's first meeting with Bao Zi'an in chapter 23.[158] Both may have been influenced by another episode from *The Water Margin*, when Song Jiang shows his courage in jail by refusing to give the warden Dai Zong the customary bribe and mentioning the names of some mutual outlaw friends.[159] Whatever its origins, the scene in *Green Peony* merely gives the outlaws official sanction for the "treasonous" acts they are planning as gestures of loyalty to the ousted emperor. Judge Di's role, in the restoration as in the novel, is nominal; the planning and action are the outlaws' work. This confirms Chen Pingyuan's observations on the role of the judge in martial arts novels; the upright official serves simply to clear up any allegation of wrongdoing on the heroes' part and give them a good name.[160]

Any authority Judge Di might have in *Green Peony* is undercut not only by Bao's settling of the actual court cases, but also by an episode in which Bao smuggles Di out of the city disguised as his ailing father-in-law. Di is carried out on a stretcher, a plaster over his face, while Bao derides him as a nuisance who should have stayed home.[161] While dramatic irony and the contrast of Judge Di's assumed and actual positions makes it comic, it leaves him little dignity. Once again, he was not the architect of the plan. Bao had offered it to him.

Even when rendered isolated and powerless, Judge Di manages to serve as a mediator and accomplish the emperor's restoration by using the trust he has earned from Empress Wu, the ousted emperor, and others like the Hua and Bao gangs. Once the emperor is restored, he enfeoffs all those who helped him. In this way the gap between official position and actual power is eliminated.

Apart from the parody of rituals described above, certain inversions of social order are recounted in *Green Peony.* The novel is set during the reign of Empress Wu, and even though she is overthrown, she is portrayed fairly sympathetically.[162] This twists the conventions of the historical novel and military romance: The "evil" empress is cast in the conventional role of the good emperor who is the victim of corruption around him. The change in her characterization also contributes to the ambiguity of the novel's values; if she is portrayed as "good," the bandits are still "rebels" in a sense. The institution of exams for women and women's martial superiority also suggest an unconventional hierarchy. Yu Qian's promotion from Luo's servant to his brother further challenges the traditional class structure. Still, not all rituals in *Green Peony* are hoaxes or parodies: Luo's father's funeral, Luo's and Hua's wedding, and the outlaws' enfeoffment are not mocked, although the first two rituals are not given extended treatment.[163] In the end, the confusion of roles that the work has gone to such pains to create seems to be resolved and the conventional social order restored.

What does the manipulation of roles in *Green Peony* tell us about the genres it plays upon? The miscasting in *Green Peony* not only highlights the codes of behavior within these genres (the heroic code, the code of the "beauty and scholar"), but also points to the conflicts between these codes. While previous novels have upheld the codes distinguishing heroes from villains, or brilliant scholars from impostors, *Green Peony* foregrounds the characters' attempts to live by those codes, exposing them as arbitrary conventions.

The scholar-beauty romance and the military romance (*yingxiong chuanqi*) are both predicated on fundamental dichotomies based on status and adherence to codes of behavior. But the validity of these dichotomies is called into question in *Green Peony* by the collapsing of categories. This is best symbolized by the collapsing of the roof, which blurs the line between Hua Bilian's initial characterization as woman warrior and her role as beauty, and forces Luo into his role as hero (*haohan*). Later Hua Bilian marries Luo Hongxun and in that way attains the status of "beauty" to his "scholar." Marriage to Luo conversely frees her to become the woman warrior again when the restoration movement needs her. Similarly, Luo returns to his proper status as an official through his participation in the restoration of the emperor as planned by the outlaws. To return to my opening example, when the pirate Bao Zi'an finally meets the "real" judge, Judge Di, both men overcome their differences. The judge shows his faith in the pirate by allowing him to decide the cases he has brought in. The role that the outlaw took up "for fun" becomes reality.

As we have seen, the way *Green Peony* plays with previous conventions makes it impossible for those conventions to stand unquestioned. *Green Peony* tests the discourse of previous fiction through characters who try to live according to literature. Whenever roles from previous fiction are invoked, they are turned upside down. In several cases the characters explicitly play roles from other fiction. "Living according to literature" is also taken one step further in *Green Peony*, since characters can force other characters to play roles. This brings up the special function rituals play in exposing the values in *Green Peony*. Ritual functions as the performance of values, and so any parody of ritual calls the values themselves into question. Because ritual reduces values to set forms, the ability of the characters to use an alien discourse to manipulate other characters makes that discourse a mere tool. Ritual is performed correctly, but misapplied, so that it loses its meaning and is exposed as empty discourse.

In parody, the conventions carry two layers of meaning: the conventional meaning, and the meaning they acquire from being placed in a new context. The brotherhood ceremony, fake funeral, and fake wedding in *Green Peony* exemplify the methods of parody. The scheming character is like the author in that he knows what the response should be to a particular motif and can thus use it to his own ends. He plots against other characters who, like the naïve reader, recognize the reference and play along. Thus the victims still take this motif at face value. But the new context of the motif invests this role playing with a meaning totally different from the original being invoked. The fact that even the characters can recognize these conventions as such exposes the motifs to the reader's scrutiny. The strategic use of dramatic irony in *Green Peony* also makes the reader privy to the plan before it is carried out. On the simplest level this serves the same function as genre expectations. Because the reader already knows what will happen, his interest is in how the victims will react—how the prescriptive role shapes their actions. The performance of the expected role is "real" only to the victims of each ruse.[164] The reader of *Green Peony* cannot take the conventions at face value, since he is aware of the scheme behind the ritual. He knows they are being mis-used by the scheming character, and also by the novel as a whole. In realizing this, he is able to see the conventions as mere devices. He also is shown the dangers of naïve reading!

What implications does this kind of parody have for the Chinese novel? A comparison with previous uses of parody is instructive. Parody in the masterworks of the Ming novel results from the misapplication of epic conventions to a realm of action previously considered insignificant. Martin Huang argues that the masterworks of the Ming novel developed through the anxiety of precedent. As each great novel parodies and deflates the previous one, the scale of events becomes less historic and more individual, from the saga of a dynasty in *Three Kingdoms* to rebellion in *The Water Margin* to the infighting in a merchant family in *Jin Ping Mei*.[165] However mundane the events described in the four great Ming novels become, the standard to which they are held for judgment is still clear and unquestioned. Even though it centers on one household, *Jin Ping Mei* is still interpreted as the decline of a "bad last emperor."[166] Thus the characters' failure to live up to the standards does not undermine the standards themselves. Some episodes in *Green Peony* employ the method Huang observed: They elaborate on elements or episodes that are merely implicit in their predecessors. Still, most parody in *Green Peony* questions the values inherent in the conventions of previous fiction.

At first glance, parody in *Green Peony* seems to serve the same purpose as irony in the major Ming novels. In *The Four Masterworks of the Ming Novel*, Andrew Plaks argues that literati authors inserted irony to reflect their Confucian views and add formal complexity. If the great Ming novels are ironic, that irony deflates the characters portrayed, exposing them as less than "heroic." Nevertheless, even the most complex rhetoric in these novels is generally interpreted as presenting a set of values.[167] In their own day, the commentaries to the four masterworks read them as didactic and as conveying a moral message (even if indirectly).[168] Ellen Widmer notes that Jin Shengtan allows "only one correct way to read the text."[169] Therefore, although the irony pointed out in works like *The Water Margin* has the potential to foster indeterminacy,[170] Jin Shengtan uses it to undercut one reading in favor of another, "correct" reading. In this way irony in the commentaries to the Ming masterworks becomes, as Jonathan Culler suggests, "essentially, the replacement of an apparent meaning by a 'true' meaning, which we justify on the grounds that the text becomes more coherent thereby."[171] Read this way, irony in the Ming masterworks does not expose the relative nature of previous discourse in the same way *Green Peony* does. The following chapter will examine *Green Peony* as a self-conscious novel.

Chapter 4

Metafiction in *Green Peony*

CHAPTER 3 EXAMINED HOW *Green Peony* plays various roles against one another to expose those roles as conventions. The argument was inspired by Bakhtin's theory of the Second Line novel, which provides a good starting point for the issue of metafiction. Bakhtin calls the Second Line novel a "critique and trial of literary discourse."[1] What does he mean by literary discourse? Bakhtin's discussion is based on his interest in languages. He discusses the relationship of language to society, suggesting that each group or profession within society has its own language within the larger common language, and these languages reflect their specific status and interests. His view of literary languages is similar. Genres also develop their own languages to reflect their interests and values.

> Certain features of language take on the specific flavor of a given genre: they knit together with specific points of view, specific approaches, forms of thinking, nuances and accents characteristic of a given genre. . . .
>
> What is important to us here is the intentional dimensions, that is, the denotative and expressive dimension of the "shared" language's stratification. It is in fact not the neutral linguistic components of a language being stratified and differentiated, but rather a situation in which the intentional possibilities are being expropriated: these possibilities are realized in specific directions, filled with specific content, they are made concrete, particular, and are permeated with concrete value judgments; they knit together with specific objects and with the belief systems of certain genres of expression and points of view peculiar to particular professions.[2]

How do literary languages relate to the languages of society? The First Line novel attempts to unify all the languages of society into one style, "painstakingly . . . cleansed of all possible associations with crude real life."[3] The Second Line novel, on the other hand, derives its meaning from incorporating two or more languages.

> This interaction, this dialogic tension between two languages and two belief systems, permits authorial intentions to be realized in such a way that we can acutely sense their presence at every point in the work. . . . He makes use of this verbal give-and-take, this dialogue of languages at every point in his work, in order that he himself might remain as it were neutral with regard to language, a third party in a quarrel between two people (although he might be a *biased* third party).[4]

The interaction between the languages, whether they are the languages of society or languages of genre, exposes each as a code with its own conventions and values. The way the author employs those codes in the Second Line novel determines the novel's meaning. Thus the Second Line novel is characterized by the "*auto-criticism of discourse*," foregrounding a critique of novelistic discourse within the novel.[5] One of the things that sets Bakhtin apart from later theories of metafiction is his concern with the values that various genre codes convey and their relationship to society.

Bakhtin's ideas seem to have influenced the concept of metafiction.[6] Bakhtin recognizes three techniques for the criticism of discourse in the Second Line novel: "living according to literature," "a laying bare of the device" by methods like introducing the author inside the novel, or parody. Later theories of metafiction admit all of these methods. However, metafiction is broader than the Second Line novels both in terms of narrative techniques and the concerns those techniques address.

For the purposes of this chapter, metafiction means techniques that foreground the workings of the novel within the novel itself.[7] A fairly comprehensive definition of metafiction is works that "explore a *theory* of fiction through the *practice* of writing fiction."[8] Metafiction by definition adapts readily to a range of theoretical approaches. How to translate the concept to Chinese fiction requires consideration. In Western theory, metafiction is often defined in opposition to realism, and discussion centers on how the novels call attention to the relationship between fiction and reality. It is also used to discuss the relationship between production and reception and how the novel foregrounds this process through intertextuality, parody, and insistence on the active participation of the reader. As critics grapple with its implications, they identify an ever-expanding array of techniques of metafiction, from "self-consciousness" to covert metafiction. Contemporary theorists like Linda Hutcheon have argued that metafiction can be overt or covert. The novel can state its views overtly on how novels are written, or it can covertly assume familiarity with a popular genre and play on those expectations to expose them. In contrast to works that are explicitly self-referential, Hutcheon suggests that the stylization inherent in popular genres like detective fiction or fantasy in the West allows the metafictional author to "*assume* that his reader already knows the story-making rules," and thus "when either parodied overtly or covertly used as structural principles . . . [they can be] employed to point to the text in its existence as literature, as patterned, ordered art."[9]

As we will see, in *Green Peony* metafiction takes both forms. *Green Peony* reflects on the workings of fiction by engaging the literary criticism of the masterworks of the Chinese novel and by foregrounding the conflicting discourses of thematic fiction. Hutcheon's concept of covert metafiction translates well to traditional Chinese fiction because China also had well-established thematic genres. Since the fictional genres *Green Peony* plays upon were some of the most popular formulae of the preceding century, their "rules" would be widely known. Thus the patterning in *Green Peony* that foregrounds the conflicting conventions of these thematic genres does serve as metafiction in Hutcheon's sense. The more overt metafiction in *Green Peony*, on the other hand, must be understood in relation to Chinese critical practices. Much of the discussion of the novel and how it should be written in Ming and Qing China was conducted not through separate works of "theory," but in the kind of peritextual commentary that Jin Shengtan pioneered. Therefore the internalization of such commentary within the novel *Green Peony* should be understood as a special kind of metafiction related to Chinese critical practices, even if it takes a form different from Western metafiction.

Green Peony's Self-conscious Relationship to Other Fiction

Let us first consider how *Green Peony* exposes genre. Genre expectations grow out of previous experiences with similar narratives. These experiences provide a set of rules, often called a "generic contract," for both reader and author. The text orients the reader as to which set of rules to use through signals like its title, beginning, character types, and motifs. Thus even before a reader opens a book, he often has a good idea of the character types, plot, and style he will encounter in it. These cues usually operate at an unconscious level; thus "fiction, in general, depends upon a body of generally accepted popular assumptions and attitudes which commands immediate, emotional, and inarticulate assent among the audience."[10] As we will see, *Green Peony* takes on each of these signals to expose its conventionality and question the values implicitly offered as a "model for life."

As a Second Line novel, *Green Peony* allows the value systems it incorporates to represent themselves. The dialogue between these value systems means the reader can see the argument from either side and support either side. A given action may be both valid by one system and wrong by the other. This suggests that the ultimate interpretation of *Green Peony* has to be ambiguous. For example, the clash between the values of the scholar and the martial hero is exposed when Hua comments on Luo's decision not to tell Ren of his wife's adultery. At first Hua categorizes Luo's action as proper for a gentleman. He immediately criticizes that decision, however, implicitly invoking the values of the martial hero in pointing out the danger to Ren. When Luo feels caught in a quandary as to what to do about it, Hua spouts Confucian discourse to justify Luo's current course of action, then returns to the discourse of the martial hero and promises to go himself to save Ren and clear Luo's name. How should the reader interpret the juxtaposition of these two value systems? Luo is told in the same breath that what he did was both right and wrong, depending on which value system is invoked. When the martial hero employs Confucian rhetoric, is the effect to make his characterization more complex, or to defamiliarize the discourse? It certainly is the last thing the reader would expect from the martial hero. Such conflict between values is inevitable when discourses are represented on their own terms.

The dialogue between genres in *Green Peony* extends beyond particular episodes; it is built into the structure of the entire novel. Unlike most previous fiction, which incorporated material from other thematic genres piecemeal, *Green Peony* relentlessly juxtaposes genres to allow each to comment dialogically on the others. The frame to *Green Peony* allows it to be interpreted in light of each of the three genres of popular fiction it draws upon, without any one genre being sufficient in itself. *Green Peony* actually has three beginnings and endings, nested inside each other. The novel starts and ends as a military romance (*yingxiong chuanqi*); within that it starts and ends as a scholar-beauty romance; and within that it starts and ends as court-case fiction.[11] These beginnings are distinguished not only by the narrative disjunction between them but by the values and conventional language they employ.

Green Peony begins with a poem on history.[12] David Rolston observes that even the early popularized history narratives (*pinghua*), the forerunners of the historical novel and military romance, "almost always begin with a poem that sets the scene for the narrative to come by summarizing all prior history."[13] *Green Peony* then adds poems and comments about the hero and the age he lives in. Fate is the ultimate authority appealed to in order to explain events. From the first pages of the novel, the "historical" ending is a foregone conclusion. Since the novel is set in Wu Zetian's reign and begins with the Xue Family Generals saga, the reader expects a tale of revenge and the restoration of dynasty. But this tale is preempted by prolepsis: "Later the Prince of Luling summoned them to Fangzhou, and when the dynasty had been restored, enfeoffed Xue Gang as Supreme Commander, and Xue Yong as a vanguard. But that comes later, so I will put it aside for now."[14] The ending is told at the beginning, then suppressed. Part of what makes this acceptable is the fact that at least in some editions, the novel presents itself as a sequel to the military romance *Yishuo Fan Tang quan zhuan* (Another tale of rebellion against the Tang). This saga serves as the context within which the main story can be developed.[15]

When this first beginning is abruptly laid aside, a second beginning invokes the conventions of the scholar-beauty romance to introduce our protagonist, Luo Hongxun. After a storyteller's tag indicates a break in the narrative, his family background is given in biography format. As we have seen in chapter 3, this first glimpse of Luo Hongxun portrays him as a romantic hero.[16]

The third beginning is in the style of court-case fiction. After another narrative leap, the character Ren Zhengqian is introduced. Notice that his biography immediately mentions a problem.

> Now there is a person from a wealthy family in this county, named Ren Zhengqian, whose style name is Weiyuan. This person has a swarthy face and bulgy eyes; he looks really ferocious. When he was fourteen his mother and father both died, and he had no brothers or sisters. Luckily, an old servant managed the household and hired a teacher to teach the young master how to read. But ever since he was born, he was only interested in riding and archery, swords and daggers, and never paid much attention to literature; he wandered from teacher to friend, studying martial arts. When he got to be twenty or so, he had grown a little beard which was bright red, so he was black-faced and red-bearded. Since he was so repulsive, even uglier than Lord Yuchi,[17] he was nicknamed "Yuchi's rival." Because his appearance was strange, no proper girl would agree to marry him. He set his ambition to just spend his time and effort on martial arts, and did not care much about this, so even though he was over twenty, he was still single. During the day when he was discussing punches and clubs with people, he had a great time, but when night came and he slept all alone, he couldn't help but be a bit lonely. Truly:
>
> Full and warm you think of sex,
> Cold and hungry you want to steal.
>
> So he often went with some friends to the brothel, and not just for one day.[18]

Court-case fiction often centers on how a character's weakness or poor judgment leads to his undoing. Ren Zhengqian's weakness is loneliness. Predictably, Ren meets a prostitute and marries her. She is a capable housekeeper; and all seems well until she convinces Ren Zhengqian to hire her brother to help out. Her brother gambles and begins stealing from the household to pay his losses, until eventually Ren catches him in the act and throws him out. His sister does not defend him, but she is also upset with how Ren Zhengqian handled it. As a result, the brother swears revenge. He later convinces his sister to sleep with the villain Wang Lun, which begins the feud between Wang Lun and Ren Zhengqian.

Not only is the motif in general typical of court-case fiction, some of the verse traces back to previous court-case stories. For instance, the couplet quoted above is used in two court-case stories.[19] Moreover, the trope of the good man who falls afoul of his own desires also figures in the novel *Qing Feng Zha* (Clear Wind Sluice), which is based on another court-case story.[20] A widower gives in to his desires and marries a wicked woman who kills him and nearly destroys his family. The widower's quandary is described in terms very similar to the passage in *Green Peony* quoted above. Though he is aware of the dangers of remarrying, and tries to resist, his desires overcome his judgment.

> Every day he went out and entered the yamen, working very diligently; it's just when he came back at night, he felt the bitterness of being alone. Even though he could talk with his daughter, father and daughter slept in separate rooms. So when the old father went to his room he couldn't help that half the bed was ice cold, and in his heart wanted to take another wife. Tossing back and forth, it was hard to sleep at night.[21]

In both cases, the characters' problems primarily stem from their own folly.

These three beginnings to *Green Peony* signal the novel's self-consciousness. The kind of popular fiction *Green Peony* drew upon, like the military romance and the scholar-beauty romance, generally went without prologues of any kind.[22] Such novels sometimes begin with a poem, but then introduce the main character, who promptly launches into his adventures. Since the title and opening of a novel usually set up a "generic contract" between the author and the reader providing clues to how it should be read,[23] the use of multiple beginnings in *Green Peony* calls attention to the question of genre. Instead of providing the reader with a single framework, it offers three different sets of genre conventions.

The novel also includes three endings to match its three beginnings: the resolution of the court cases, the marriage of Hua Bilian and Luo Hongxun, and the restoration of the emperor. In this way, the plot lines are each resolved separately, in the reverse order from that in which they were introduced. However, none of the endings is completely satisfying. As we have seen, the resolution of the court case falls somewhere between the usual practice of the bandits and that of the officials. The court-case plot line escalates to the point at which it is brought to Judge Di's attention. He issues a summons for the bandits. This prompts them to take matters into their own hands; they capture, try, and kill Wang Lun, thereby bringing the court-case plot to an end. Contrary to the conventions of court-case fiction, the judge has almost no role in dispensing justice. Similarly, Luo Hongxun's wedding to Hua Bilian seems almost a marriage of convenience rather than the fitting ending to a romance. No explanation is given for why Luo changes his mind and agrees to the match. As for the third ending, in contrast to the military romances it invokes, in *Green Peony* the heroes we have followed throughout the novel play a negligible role in the actual restoration of the emperor. First of all, the reader is faced with another abrupt about-face: the outlaws, who have spent the whole book trying to get Luo to join them, suddenly resolve to give up their lawless ways and become respectable for posterity's sake. They decide the best way to do this would be to join the movement to restore the proper emperor. The summons from Judge Di provides them with the opportunity to join the loyalists. However, the heroes' own attempts to oust corruption in the capital essentially serve as a prelude to the Xue Generals' successful restoration of the emperor. The main characters play a negligible role; it is not their accomplishment, although they are rewarded for being in the right place at the right time. The combination of three beginnings with three unsatisfying endings suggests that it is not sufficient to interpret this novel in light of any one genre. Each provides just one perspective. The play with form also serves as a subtle "laying bare of the device," reminding the reader of the importance of beginnings and endings to the generic contract.

Alternate titles under which *Green Peony* appeared confirm its generic indeterminacy, showing different ways the novel was read. While the titles *Xu fan Tang zhuan* (Sequel to tale of rebellion against the Tang) and *Fan Tang hou zhuan* (Later tale of rebellion against the Tang) emphasize *Green Peony*'s debt to the military romances on the Tang, *Hong Bi yuan* (The destiny of Luo Hongxun and Hua Bilian) and to a lesser extent *Si Wang Ting* (The Four Gazes Pavilion) emphasize the romantic aspect. Each title suggests a different emphasis for reading *Green Peony,* but the text of the novel itself undermines any single reading. The disparate groupings and labels under which *Green Peony* appears corroborate this sense of generic ambiguity. *Moral Heroes and Heroines* depicts the novel *Green Peony* lying on a table with other court-case fiction like *Cases of Judge Shi*,[24] while a late edition of *Rulin waishi* (The unofficial history of the scholars) adds a reference to *Green Peony* as one of many historical novels.[25] When the novel *Green Peony* appeared under the title *The Destiny of Luo Hongxun and Hua Bilian* in the early twentieth century, it was labeled a martial love story (*xiaqing xiaoshuo*).[26]

The three beginnings and endings serve as cues to the meticulous patterning of the novel *Green Peony.* As we will see, the juxtaposition of genres apparent in the beginnings and endings carries through the entire novel. Traditional Chinese fiction criticism emphasizes the importance of the beginning of a novel to the understanding of the work, since the opening sets up in miniature the principles and relations that will govern the rest of the novel.[27] In the discussion to follow, I will explore how the structure and patterning of *Green Peony* relate to traditional literary criticism of the Chinese novel.

Defining Metafiction in Chinese Literature

The nature of literary criticism in China must be considered in analyzing metafiction. One could hardly expect the expression of metafiction in China to be the same as in the West, since China had its own kind of criticism and conventions. For example, Western metafiction deals largely with the relationship between fiction and reality, since it is often a reaction to realism, the dominant set of conventions for the nineteenth-century novel in the West. In the traditional Chinese novel, however, the narrative conventions are quite different. Chinese fiction critics praised realistic description, but "realism" never became *the* defining critical concern.[28] To establish the concerns of literary criticism in traditional China, I will focus on *The Water Margin* and Jin Shengtan's commentary on that novel. The poetics established by Jin Shengtan and his followers through their fiction commentary served the function of a "theory" of fiction in the Qing, as the paradigmatic statements of how fiction was written and how it should be read.[29] Most scholars agree that it set the standards by which traditional Chinese fiction was valued. As Plaks notes, the work of Jin Shengtan and other major fiction commentators established

> the outlines of a more or less dominant set of aesthetic norms and compositional techniques governing the genres of extended vernacular prose fiction in late imperial China. In the prefatory and textual comments of the best of the critics . . .—Chin Sheng-t'an, Mao Tsung-kang, and Chang Chu-p'o—we do in fact have something that comes close to a systematic poetics of the Chinese novel.[30]

The fact that this commentary set critical standards for Chinese fiction would be sufficient to justify my focus on it here,[31] but *The Water Margin* also epitomizes much of the thematic material against which *Green Peony* and other early martial romance novels react. Through his commentary, Jin Shengtan valorizes the repetition of conventional motifs, emphasizes characterization, and establishes new ways of analyzing the structure of the novel.

Traditional Chinese fiction criticism as practiced by Jin Shengtan emphasizes the structure of the text; it concerns itself as much with how the novel means as with what it means. In so doing, Jin Shengtan draws on traditional Chinese aesthetics, which early on distinguished art from non-art on the basis of its "intrinsic patterned structure."[32] Nearly all of Jin Shengtan's terms of analysis (*wenfa*) as set forth in "How to Read the Fifth Work of Genius" are related to structure, and about half are related to repetition (including recurrence, prolepsis, and analepsis).[33] Some techniques unobtrusively build up the reader's expectations through frequent repetition of a word before a central event.[34] Others refer to an incident after it has happened; an example is Wu Song's retelling of how he killed the tiger to the hunters he meets on his way down from the ridge.[35] Still other instances of repetition are broken up by the insertion of a separate plot line. One example is the diversion between the second and third attacks on the Zhu family village.[36] All of these forms of repetition are credited with contributing to the structure of *The Water Margin*.

Many of the elements canonized by Jin Shengtan as examples of *The Water Margin*'s superior artistry were produced by phenomena common to the composition of popular fiction in its time. In "The Composition of the *P'ing yao chuan*," Patrick Hanan demonstrates that the same motif is found in a number of works of a similar period. He shows that *Ping yao zhuan* is "to a large extent, made of other works" and suggests that this sharing of motifs between and within works was a common mode of composition at the time.

> The *Shui-hu chuan* [*The Water Margin*] shares material with several other works, including a number of short stories. Indeed, it even repeats the same material within itself. . . . If we look closely at the *Shui-hu* in the light of the *P'ing yao chuan*'s patchwork composition, it begins to appear as a mass of variations on familiar themes.[37]

Hanan gives the example of the role of the street vendor, which appears in both Song Jiang's murder of Yan Poxi and Wu Song's murder of Pan Jinlian. In these patterns events are repeated, substituting different characters. Hanan explains:

> The process of composition probably consisted of first associating one character with another, and then transferring the material attached to him. . . . Duplication of material within one work, as in the *Shui-hu*, occurs because the various elements eventually combined in that work have influenced each other like separate stories.[38]

Jin Shengtan attributed the entire novel *The Water Margin* to Shi Naian's genius; he never admitted the possibility that anything in the novel came from popular origins. But Jin Shengtan's critical influence ensured that such use of repetition would be regarded as a conscious strategy to add meaning to the novel. In Rolston's words:

> Repetition is not only allowed but encouraged, both as a structural technique . . . and as a technique for obtaining subtler characterization. Although the repetition in early novels such as *Shuihu zhuan* is probably

> not there by design, Jin Shengtan and other commentators promoted this type of (partial) repetition as a marvelous technique, and later novelists consciously employed it.[39]

Jin Shengtan explains his appreciation of repetition in the chapter commentary at the beginning of chapter 11:

> I see writers today always say "I have a trick for avoiding repetition." That is so, but I know those are not works of genius. In a work of genius, how could it be as simple as just not avoiding repetition? It must also deliberately violate the rule against repetition in those places where originally there was no violation, and later go on to avoid it. . . . If you violate the rule against repetition and then avoid repetition, then there is something that you are avoiding. If you are not able to violate the rule against repetition and only wish to avoid repetition, then what is being avoided? Thus in creating literature being able to avoid it is not difficult, truly it is being able to violate the rule against repetition which is difficult. . . . Thus if I violate the rule against repetition and reach the point that it cannot be avoided, then later all those under heaven who read my writing will see in this my genius, my writing. . . . For this reason, shortly after this book relates Lin Chong buying the sword, it relates Yang Zhi selling a sword. This is truly what is called a work of genius, one must first violate the rules against repetition, in order to make me enjoy and slowly observe how it is avoided.[40]

Rolston asserts that Jin Shengtan "often used 'formalist' criteria as a cover to justify problematic aspects of his texts."[41] Jin Shengtan considers this kind of repetition to be a tour de force, showing off the author's skill. In the interlinear commentary on an instance of "partial repetition" (*lüe fan*, literally "partial violation"), Jin Shengtan states that the major episodes of the book are never repetitious, only minor portions are repeated. "Like Zhang Sengyao painting the dragon, if he painted every scale and claw, it would break the wall and fly away . . . thus the author intentionally did not want perfection, but this is not something ordinary mortals understand."[42] Jin Shengtan interprets repetition as an intentional device on the part of the author even when he does not point out how it contributes to meaning. This valorization of repetition is one of Jin Shengtan's contributions to the aesthetic of the novel.

Repetition of incident contributes to structure by encouraging comparison of similar episodes in different parts of the novel. Jin Shengtan valorizes "direct repetition" (*zheng fan*)[43] by calling attention to its effect on characterization. For instance, the commentary at the beginning of chapter 45 states that the apparent repetition of events in the killing of Pan Jinlian by Wu Song and the killing of Pan Qiaoyun by Shi Xiu is "not the same" because of the differences in motivation of the two heroes. Wu Song is completely within his role, avenging his brother's death, while Shi Xiu is actually bringing his own grievance to light. Even a phrase repeated verbatim can take on a different meaning in a new context. Jin Shengtan points out that when Wu Song uses a particular phrase, one feels his magnanimity; when Shi Xiu says the same words, one sees his sharp dealing.[44]

Jin Shengtan's critical terminology was imitated in commentaries on other masterworks of the Chinese novel, thereby assuring repetition a prime position in the panoply of structural techniques of the novel. The interpretation of the masterworks in their respective commentaries would largely agree with E. M. Forster's view, in which the function of plot is to portray the motivations of the characters in such a way as to lead the audience from mere curiosity into a consideration of values. "It can teach us to ask 'Why?' instead of the untutored response of 'And then?'"[45] Even with episodes classified as direct repetition, Jin Shengtan focuses on the differences in the repetition, which he attributes largely to differences in motivation.[46] As Andrew Plaks noted in an essay on the terminology of traditional fiction commentary, "[t]he problem of whether later men will understand the true motives behind personal action is, of course, fundamental to the whole enterprise of writing commentaries on works of fiction."[47] Jin Shengtan calls attention to narrative technique in order to build a case for his vision of the underlying meaning. He approaches that meaning by reading significance into the patterns of repetition in the novel and showing readers new ways to use its structure as a tool in interpretation.

Besides pushing the reader to look beyond the plot to meaning, Jin Shengtan believed that the patterning achieved by these devices served to give the work unity. Even repetition of words creates coherence: "Read in haste, there seems to be nothing there, but a closer look reveals a connecting thread which, if pulled, draws the whole sequence together."[48] He insisted that one must read the novel as an organic whole. In his own words, "if you take them at a single glance, the seventy chapters of the *Shuihu chuan* [*The Water Margin*], which cover more than two thousand pages, really constitute a single composition."[49] The repetition of elements, big and small, creates resonance between the parts and gives the work unity.[50] Jin Shengtan sees the genius of the author precisely in the patterning of the work; such patterning makes the work "literary" and much of its value lies therein.[51] Indeed, for Jin Shengtan, repetition serves as "a highly conscious manipulation of narrative materials on the part of the author," which leads the reader to notice the techniques shaping it; the commentary on these elements turns the reader from a consideration of story to discourse.[52]

In *Traditional Chinese Fiction and Fiction Commentary*, David Rolston argues that such commentary influenced the development of the Chinese novel. Authors not only wrote novels to conform to the principles set forth in previous commentaries; they also gradually incorporated commentary into the novel in various forms. As a result of the influence of commentary, he sees an increasing self-consciousness in the novel, a more explicitly fictional stance, the incorporation of criticism by the authors themselves,[53] and increasing demands by the author on the reader. Rolston's argument largely supports the idea of a trend toward metafiction in the Chinese novel around the mid-eighteenth to the mid-nineteenth century.

Literary Criticism within the Novel *Green Peony*

How does *Green Peony* reflect on this tradition of literary criticism? At one point, the narrator in *Green Peony* uses the terminology of fiction commentary and calls attention to the text as a text. "Gentle reader, at this point you must be saying that the person who wrote this text did not make what came before and what came later resonate (*qian hou bu zhaoying).*"[54] Not only does the narrator refer to the text as a text, but he refers to the author in the third person. Moreover, the narrator invokes a key term of fiction criticism, *zhaoying* (resonance or cross reflection), in order to head off a possible objection by the reader. The implied reader has expectations shaped by the demands of fiction commentary. This raises Jin Shengtan's ideal of the text as an organic whole, which *Green Peony* both provides, through satisfying linkage, and thwarts, through juxtaposition of genre and the unsatisfying endings discussed above. Elsewhere, the narrator explicitly refers to the text by chapter:

> Gentle readers, in the previous chapter you said again that I'm forgetting what I'm writing. In a household like that, how could they have no stable boys? And how could it be so easy for Xiao Ji to set fire to the place, without alerting anyone? It's just because the Zhu brothers despised Luo Hongxun and intended to fry his heart and liver to go with wine. This is an event rarely seen in life, so all the stable boys threw some hay down and went to the kitchen to see it; thus there was no one in the stable. Also, Luo Hongxun would later have the honor of escorting the emperor back to power, and serve as a Regional Commander,[55] a position arranged by Heaven. Otherwise, that day there were 50–60 escorts, and Luo was in a cage cart. Even if there were a few more people they could kill them all, how could they mind one more? But they just happened to decide to bring him home and dispose of him later, so as to wait for Xiao Ji and Yu Qian to come.[56]

Besides referring to the text as writing, this passage also calls attention to the improbability of the events just described. Although it is part of the traditional narrator's role to explain improbable or incongruous events, this explanation goes farther than most. The reason Luo survived is overdetermined. It is due partially to the stable boys' curiosity regarding the spectacle of eating one's enemy's heart and liver, the "fictionality" of which is suggested by the phrasing—"an event rarely seen in life." It is also attributable to his enemies' consuming hatred, which denied him an easy death, and to Luo's own destiny to help the emperor. The profusion of rhetorical questions in the narrator's explanation emphasize how unlikely it is. Elsewhere, in a move similar to one of the standard techniques of Western metafiction, the "author" appears briefly in *Green Peony* to expose the text as a text. The novel begins with a poem followed by a disquisition on the hero meeting his time, written in a parallel, almost classical style distinct from the rest of the novel. At the end of the discussion, the author inside the novel explicitly refers to his work as a story to be written down.

> Today I heard a story, in which flatterers got their way and controlled the workings of government, while heroes' aspirations were crushed as they wandered about the rivers and lakes. It agrees with this poem, to the tune of "West River and Moon." You say, in which dynasty and which reign period did this story occur? Gentle reader, don't be impatient, let me gradually write it out.[57]

Overall, however, the narrator in *Green Peony* is quite conventional; he hardly can be considered the self-conscious narrator often found in Western metafiction.

Instead of focusing on the narrator, *Green Peony* internalizes fiction commentary by having the characters point out elements of structure and comment on characterization. Sometimes the character's comments suggest they know they are part of a story. When Hua Bilian revives after her fall and hears she is in Luo's arms, she thinks "How could there be such a coincidence? When I fell today, how could he happen to be here to save me?"[58] This calls to mind a phrase often used by the narrator of vernacular fiction, "without coincidence there is no story," but coming from a character instead of the narrator it takes on a whole new force. Earlier in the same scene, the audience praises Hua Bilian's feat as "something rarely heard of since ancient times," a phrase that resembles a commentator's praise of a particularly ingenious scene.[59] Again, the audience inside the novel watching events unfold speaks almost as if they know it is a story.

In fact, the characters consistently comment on the pattern of the plot. *Green Peony* is carefully structured into regularly alternating plot lines, each built of escalating repetitions of incident. One plot line develops the courtcase beginnings into a feud over Ren Zhengqian's wife with the villain Wang Lun. Another plot line takes its cues from the scholar-beauty romance in a series of proposals to Luo Hongxun from a bandit chief on behalf of his daughter, Hua Bilian. The third plot line is a series of tournaments to avenge the pride of another villain, Luan Yiwan. Every time the novel returns to one of the three plot lines, one of the characters will summarize what has happened before. The characters are not only able to recognize the pattern of events, but they can even use that knowledge to their own advantage, for example, to win a fight.

The pattern of repetition becomes increasingly explicit as the plot line progresses. At first, the narrative implicitly points out the repetition of incident through repeated phrases. This kind of verbal repetition is similar to some of the structural techniques praised by Jin Shengtan. The tournament motif begins when Pu Tianpeng provokes Yu Qian to a contest of skills by challenging his ability and accusing him of having an "empty reputation."[60] Outclassed, Pu Tianpeng is soundly defeated. "He fell outside the circle. Yu Qian came forward and used his foot to hold him down."[61] This pattern repeats throughout the entire feud, at the level of plot and also the level of language. For example, when Pu Tianpeng attempts to avenge his loss he fails again; "With a thump he fell to the ground . . . [Luo Hongxun] used his foot to hold him down."[62] The language calls attention to the repetition. Like the verbal repetition Jin Shengtan notes, this repetition in *Green Peony* provides unity and sets up expectations.

This begins a series of tournaments that lasts for six chapters and includes four different stagings.[63] Not only does the narrative implicitly point out the repetition of incident through certain repeated phrases, but even the characters explicitly refer to previous fights in discussing the current fight. Moreover, analepsis doubles as prolepsis: when retold by the characters, what has happened predicts what will happen.

When Luo Hongxun returns to Yangzhou, Luan Yiwan is waiting for him. Luo Hongxun's cousin Xu Songpeng recounts how he was provoked into fighting Luan's men by being accused of having an "empty reputation." Note that the challenge once again centers around the same words. Xu Songpeng explains to Luo and Yu that he accepted the challenge because "not even the most restrained person can stand it if he is being cursed by name!"[64] Xu fell and broke his leg in the course of the fight. His retelling of the incident compels his listeners, Yu Qian and Luo Hongxun, to take up his role in the next repetition.

Yu Qian defeats two of Luan's men using very similar moves. The first man is actually surprised. "He [Zhu Long] didn't expect Yu Qian to raise his left leg and strike at Zhu Long's right ribs. With a thump Zhu Long fell down from the stage."[65] "[Yu Qian] lifted his right leg, and kicked Zhu Hu right in the gut, with an 'Aiya!' Zhu Hu also fell down from the stage."[66] However, the third man, Zhu Biao, seems able to use the previous pattern of Yu Qian's movements to his advantage, breaking Yu Qian's leg. "Yu Qian used his leg to kick as before, but Zhu Biao used his hand to strike at Yu Qian's knee. With a yell Yu Qian fell on the stage, then tumbled down . . .

On the ground he tumbled about five yards."[67] The very pattern that brought Yu Qian success in the first two fights is his undoing in the third, and the narrator subtly notes the pattern with the words "as before." Zhu Biao then challenges Luo Hongxun in language very similar to the challenge made to Xu Songpeng; "'If you don't dare come up, you're no hero (*haohan*)!' . . . When he was being cursed by name, how could he just stand there and take it?"[68] Zhu Biao again uses the predictive power of previous events to his own advantage. "Zhu Biao intentionally left himself open; as Luo Hongxun kicked with one leg, Zhu Biao struck under Luo Hongxun's knee as before. Luo Hongxun with a great yell also fell down from the stage, and he, like Yu Qian, tumbled on the ground for about five yards."[69] The same action yields the same results; Zhu Biao breaks Luo Hongxun's leg. In recognizing and using the pattern of moves within the incident to his advantage, Zhu Biao also brings the incident to the anticipated conclusion. Ever since Xu Songpeng told Yu Qian and Luo Hongxun his story, part of which is quoted above, they were bound to play his role and repeat it.

In the next iteration, the characters not only recognize the pattern of events, they even comment on it. When told of their plight, Bao Zi'an and Bao Jinhua travel to Yangzhou to avenge Yu Qian and Luo Hongxun. The tournament proceeds on the same pattern, even using some of the same words. Bao Zi'an soundly defeats Zhu Biao. "Zhu Biao with an 'Aiya!' fell down from the stage. Poor Zhu Biao tumbled on the ground for about ten yards," to which Bao Zi'an's reaction is, "'That ought to make up for the tumble they took the other day!"[70] The relationship of repetition with exaggeration between the two fights is typical of the popular novel; what is interesting is that in this case Bao Zi'an seems to aim for exactly that effect. Again, the characters themselves call attention to the pattern of repetition. Bao Jinhua even recognizes the pattern of falls that indicate defeat and fakes a fall to catch her opponent off guard. She then kicks his eyes out, and he falls down from the stage.[71] Throughout, characters on both sides actively take advantage of the pattern of repeated moves.

This constant emphasis on the pattern of the plot resembles a running structural commentary. It begins by noting repetition through repeated words, then becomes slightly more explicit as the narrator notes it in his description or the character's indirect thoughts, and finally the characters comment openly on the repetition. Notice that each iteration is initiated by one of the characters retelling what happened to them. The retelling of previous events by characters who participated in them is a convention of the traditional Chinese novel. While in the masterworks such retelling simply reprises previous actions, in *Green Peony* these retellings are significant in several ways.[72] First, they nearly always pass the role of "hero" along to the narratee—when the next iteration occurs the role of "hero" will be played by the person hearing the story.[73] Second, they double as analepsis and prolepsis: what has happened predicts what will happen. Third, as I will demonstrate, for the reader certain retellings revisit previous incidents critically, turning from plot to other issues such as structure, characterization, and motivation.

For example, in the feud between Wang Lun and Ren Zhengqian over Ren's wife, the general pattern is: The adultery is exposed, and the hero attempts to catch the adulterers, but fails. This allows the adulterers to frame a victim whom the hero must return to set free. In this plot line, nearly every retelling passes the hero's role to the listener. In the first instance, Yu Qian discovers the adultery and reports it to Luo Hongxun, who is then framed. After he is freed, Luo Hongxun tells Hua Zhenfang. Hua Zhenfang promises to go back to Yangzhou in order to save Ren Zhengqian and kill the adulterers. Luo's story not only reminds the reader of the first attempt but sets the second attempt in motion. In the second iteration, it is Hua Zhenfang who tries to capture them and Ren Zhengqian who is framed.[74] The characters who fill the roles of "hero" and "victim" do not remain constant from one incident to the next.

The retelling also serves to "modify the meaning of past occurrences of the event"[75] by offering a new interpretation. For example, the story of how Hua rescued Ren is told three times—first by the narrator, then by Hua to Luo and Xu, and finally by Hua to Bao Zi'an. The second telling shows the reaction of a naïve audience. As Hua retells his efforts to save Ren, the narrator points out: "He didn't mention the Ba brothers stealing Wang Lun's property and his breaking his promise in order to escort them. He was afraid that Luo Hongxun would loathe him and it would be difficult for the marriage proposal to succeed."[76] This comment shows not only ironic undercutting of the "hero" but the selectivity of his narrative—which has the intended effect. Luo and Xu praise Hua, "If you weren't such a hero, who else could pull off a single-handed jailbreak?" However, Hua's omission shows his own awareness that those actions do not jibe with his desired image as a "hero." Hua wishes to preserve his heroic image; he knows that the "behind the scenes" peek the novel has afforded the reader (in contrast with the general conventions of the genre) casts him in an unflattering light, so he omits these events. This undercutting makes the reader begin to reevaluate Hua's actions.

The most noteworthy aspect of such repetition in *Green Peony* is its self-consciousness. When Hua recounts his exploits again it is not the narrator but another character who critiques it; the "audience" for his story also becomes its critic and future protagonist. Bao Zi'an criticizes the narrative:

> "According to your fascinating telling, the single-handed jailbreak is something rare in ancient and modern times. But in my critical estimation (*ping*), I would say it has a head but no tail, a beginning but no ending, and you should be slapped a hundred times!"

Hua Zhenfang said, "What do you mean I 'have a head but no tail, a beginning but no ending'?"

Bao Zi'an said, "Just stand aside, and listen to an old man's lecture. If you say you killed the wrong adulterers, because you were in a hurry, I don't blame you for that. But since you knew you killed the wrong ones, you still should have gone back to kill the right adulterers."

Hua Zhenfang said, "You know some of it, but you don't know all of it. When I hung the heads on the gate, it was already getting light; if I went back to kill again, how could the Wangs not notice? I had nothing to fear, but Master Ren was badly wounded and lying at the bottom of the city wall, and if I were captured, he would surely be harmed."

Bao Zi'an said, "Bullshit and nonsense! It sounds as if you think waiting until dawn was the important thing, and killing the adulterers was not important. For the last six months, have you been rushed? You should have gone back to Dingxing and killed the right adulterers; only then would Master Ren's grievance have been avenged. Then it would have a beginning and an ending. After you broke him out of jail, of course Dingxing sent people to catch you, and since you had no guts, you didn't dare go back to Dingxing county. What do you say, am I right or not?"

Hua Zhenfang thought to himself, "At the time I was in a hurry; later I should have gone back again, so it's no wonder he's reprimanding me today." He said, "I truly didn't think of this, so I don't blame you for reprimanding me."

Bao Zi'an laughed and said, "Since you've learned your lesson, that's fine. You and Master Ren are friends; now that I've met him today, we're more than passing acquaintances. Since the first half has been your responsibility, it's my turn to be in charge of the second half. Tomorrow I'll stroll up to Dingxing, and not only will I kill the adulterer and adulteress, I'll also steal all of Wang Lun's possessions, to pay Master Ren back for his losses."[77]

Once again the hero's role is passed on by recounting previous attempts. But Bao Zi'an is not content simply to repeat the incident. He takes a more critical stance, examining this tale as a narrative and commenting on both its form and characterization. He guesses at the motivation of the character, Hua Zhenfang, and calls the tale itself unsatisfying since it has not reached its promised conclusion in which the villain would be properly punished. Bao explicitly frames his tirade as his "critical estimation" (*ping*), the same term used to refer to the comments of literary critics.[78] Thus a character within the novel figures the narrative's reception and interpretation and promises to "rewrite" it through his own actions.

By commenting on Hua's retelling from inside the novel, Bao seems to be in a position to put the story right.[79] Instead, the pattern of repetition proves too strong to change. In both cases, the first attempt to capture Wang is sidetracked. The second attempt is then undertaken to save the victim of the failed first attempt. Just as Hua Zhenfang gets news of Ren Zhengqian's plight and whereabouts from a shopkeeper, news that allows him to rescue Ren Zhengqian in Dingxing, Bao Zi'an gets news from a monk, news that allows him to effect a rescue in Jiaxing.[80] Even though he has men available, whereas Hua Zhenfang did not, Bao Zi'an insists on going alone to capture Wang.[81] In both cases, Hua Zhenfang and Bao Zi'an fail to capture Wang and endure close calls in their escape; each vows to return later when things are calmer.

By comparing different characters in similar situations, the traditional fiction commentator promises to reveal the characters' true motives and to expose the subtleties of characterization. The characters themselves take on this function in *Green Peony.* In one instance, Yu Qian sees the monk Xiao Ji bury his begging bowl before a fight and thinks how careful he is, remembering how Xiao An's begging bowl got "stolen" in a similar situation. Here the character Yu Qian takes on the role of a fiction commentator, initiating the comparison of repeated incidents often found in Jin Shengtan's fiction criticism.[82] To return to our previous example, after Bao has criticized Hua, he also fails to capture the adulterers the first time. His daughter Bao Jinhua urges him to try again immediately, arguing that otherwise he would be open to his own criticism of Hua.

> Bao Jinhua laughed "La!" behind the door, and said, "You're afraid yourself, but you deride others." Bao Zi'an said, "Why do you say I'm afraid?" Jinhua said, "When Uncle Hua from Shandong couldn't go back to Dingxing to catch and kill the adulterers, you laughed at him as a coward. Why don't you dare go back today? Now you talk of putting it off a little, or of making others go again. Are you the only one who's worth anything around here? Everyone else is just fit to die?" Bao Zi'an said, " . . . If even you are already laughing at me, tomorrow Hua Zhenfang will laugh at me even more."[83]

Bao Jinhua explicitly compares the way the two men handled the situation. By being in some sense both inside and outside the plot, as critic and protagonist, Bao Zi'an falls prey to his own criticism.

Retelling serves another function in *Green Peony* as well. Since the pattern of repetition is so strong, each time another character offers to take on the previous hero's role the analepsis also serves as a kind of prolepsis. It creates an expectation in the reader that the new hero will repeat the action they just heard about, which runs counter to his promise to make good on his critique (and catch the adulterers). It thereby highlights repetition's role in shaping narratives. Umberto Eco suggests that in genres like the detective story, "there is no variation of deeds, but rather the repetition of a habitual scheme in which the reader can recognise something he has already seen and of which he has grown fond."[84]

It is worth remembering that Jin Shengtan valorized "techniques" that were actually vestiges of *The Water Margin*'s popular origins. Prime among these are the various kinds of repetition in *The Water Margin*. In much of traditional Chinese fiction, actions originally performed by one hero would become associated with another, so that eventually both heroes' stories would include them. Hanan comments on this phenomenon to account for repetition of motifs within *The Water Margin*, and C. T. Hsia sees something comparable happening in the military romance.[85] Even if the process is different—oral association versus written composition—the result is similar. Indeed, once character types and motifs become established, one largely predicts the other. Robert Hegel notes that from the initial characterization of a warrior hero "a reader could anticipate the hero's ideals and probable range of behavior."[86] Thus, for example, in the military romances *Another Tale of Rebellion against the Tang* and its predecessor, *Another Tale of the Later Tang, Third Collection*, the appearance of a young woman warrior on the battlefield will inevitably call up expectations of romance, and the ensuing scene sometimes corresponds down to the phrasing of the dialogue. However, such connections are not pointed out by the text, so the reader recognizes the repetition largely unconsciously. Repetition in popular fiction may look forward and backward at the same time, predicting the events at hand in light of the prior conventions they draw upon, but it does so only implicitly. In *Green Peony*, on the other hand, as one incident is related, the retelling itself sets up its recurrence, often with a new set of characters. Moreover, retelling often provokes explicit criticism by the character listening to the tale. The way a particular motif is passed along from hero to hero and reenacted exposes the mechanism behind this common practice. In effect, each character in *Green Peony* parodies the previous character's actions.

Parody's special power is due to its foregrounding of its relationship to other literary works. Margaret Rose argues, "the complexity of the production and reception of the text is one of the basic themes of metafiction,"[87] and parody is a particularly appropriate means to explore those themes.

> Though metafictional parody may, as a higher-order action, be unable to describe itself "completely", it can, as an archaeology of the text, foreground its own origins in commenting critically on the pre-formed language of other works or discourses. In evoking the expectations of the audience for a certain text, or discourse, it also foregrounds both the epistemological and material conditions for the reception of literary texts, which will also affect its own reception and "realisation" by the reader. But the parodist's reflexion on his text is both "hindered" and expanded by the appearance of these

> other conditions, for here his text is shown to be both object (and victim) and subject (and initiator) of other interpretations.[88]

This description of the workings of parody also explains why analepsis doubling as prolepsis is such an interesting phenomenon. It explicitly links two instances of repetition in the kind of double relationship Margaret Rose describes. "New" narratives are created as reactions to the existing ones. Thus the audience listening to a narrative within *Green Peony* becomes the protagonist of the next iteration, highlighting the way narratives become models for their audiences. When analepsis doubles as prolepsis in *Green Peony,* the repetition serves to make the reader aware of how expectations form through previous experience with a trope. Since each instance tries to change what it repeats, the combination of retelling and criticism sets up conflicting expectations. The interest of each new iteration lies in whether it will be able to change the pattern. In *Green Peony* what begins as critical imitation, a way to set things right, soon becomes merely repetitive because the conventional plot is too hard to change.[89] Even with different actors playing the role, for most of the novel the outcome stays largely the same.

The invocation of terms from fiction commentary inside the novel *Green Peony* serves the same function as commentary, to turn the reader's attention from story to discourse. The terms that appear inside *Green Peony* point toward meaningful patterns in the text of the novel. *Green Peony* employs repetition to create a self-conscious, carefully patterned and structured text. It delights in repetition, ranging from the recurrence of similar events to verbal echoes. Its three regularly alternating plot lines, each built of escalating repetitions of incident, make isolated, unrepeated episodes the exception rather than the norm.[90] Beyond providing the characters with ample opportunities to compare actions and characterization, the carefully alternating pattern of the three plot lines also calls attention to the form of the novel. Structure is constantly foregrounded. The insistent consistency of the patterning reminds the reader of the text's status as a text. In this way *Green Peony* resembles Linda Hutcheon's category of covert metafiction.[91] The pattern itself calls attention to the novel's fictionality.

> Patterns betray the hand of a pattern-maker, who pulls all the bits and pieces of his artefact into their pre-ordained places. They also reveal the whole as the pattern-maker's fabrication, as a contrived, artificial construct. Moreover, patterns lay bare that it is the author, not the logic of events which is said to inform the conventional plot, who decides what comes next.[92]

Rather than relying on the narrator's asides to reveal its metafictional ambitions, *Green Peony* builds self-consciousness into the structure of the novel. Moreover, the nature of traditional commentary in China would condition the reader to understand these cues.

While *Green Peony* also borrows terms from fiction criticism, unlike most commentaries *Green Peony* often uses those terms not as praise of the work, but to handle instances of perceived failure to fulfill these expectations. Thus, just as inconsistencies of characterization and double coding point to the conventions of genre, these "critiques" of the novel's structure point to the operative conventions of the form. However, *Green Peony* does not seem to be reflecting back on fiction criticism so much as acknowledging those conventions. Its main critical thrust targets thematic genres, rather than the form of the novel. Throughout the novel, the places where the characters fail to fulfill expectations serve as the most telling exposure of generic conventions and values. Similarly, it is precisely the tight structure of this novel that allows for the full dialogization of genres. *Green Peony* uses recurrence to engender cross reflection, but it employs dialogization to turn the focus to genre.

The Aesthetics of the Novel versus the Drum Ballad

These patterns and terms are not in the novel by accident. Many of the changes the novel *Green Peony* made to its drum ballad source serve to emphasize the novel's status as a text. The novel incorporated techniques and terms from fiction criticism, calling attention to patterns and referring to the novel as writing. The overt references to patterns in the novel serve to "activate" that kind of reading, and by extension one quickly sees that the patterns extend throughout the novel. These changes introduced by the novel suggest a particular kind of reading familiar to nineteenth-century Chinese readers, informed by fiction criticism and focused on structure and characterization. The emphasis traditional fiction criticism places on hidden meanings of the text also influenced the novel *Green Peony*, which engages in ironic undercutting of characters. In addition, through patterning and play with roles, the novel *Green Peony* juxtaposes and exposes the genre conventions on which it draws. These differences distinguish the aesthetic of the novel *Green Peony* from its drum ballad source.

The explicit positioning of *Green Peony* as a written text occurs only a few times in the novel, but it points to one of the special characteristics of this novel. Many of the features introduced by the novel in the process of adapting the drum ballad emphasize its textuality. The patterning requires a textual approach that stops and looks back across the novel, a spatial reading rather than simply a linear reading. In cases like Yu Qian's comparison of Xiao Ji and Xiao An, the character serves the role of commentator, comparing similar incidents and using the contrast for characterization. This creates the same kind of spatial reading required by Jin Shengtan in his commentary to *The Water Margin*. Irony is also introduced by the novel *Green Peony*. The critiques that other characters or the narrator provide of the "retellings" within the novel occur only in the novel.

Parody sometimes appears in the *Green Peony Drum Ballad*, but the novel intensifies it and makes the play on genres consistent. For example, the novel invents most instances of the juxtaposition of roles that engender multiple expectations. Thus, for example, Luo wanting to hide from the Hua gang rather than entertain another marriage proposal, and his cousin's critique of his impulse invoking the values of the hero, appears only in the novel. Similarly, the novel creates the most striking elements of the midnight duel between Bao Jinhua and Luo Hongxun, which juxtaposes the martial with the romantic.[93] In addition, the novel creates or heightens the misappropriation of roles and rituals. The novel inserts the fake funeral, drawing on intertextual models to display and question Luo's filiality. Indeed, most of the dialogization discussed in chapter 3 is original to the novel.

Even when a similar scene appears in the drum ballad, the novel intensifies its implications. For example, in both the drum ballad and the novel, the villain Wang Lun subverts the ritual of swearing brotherhood in order to seduce Ren's wife. However, each form frames and interprets the episode differently. In both cases the reader sees Wang's henchman, He Shilai, suggesting the plot to Wang before he puts it in action. When he suggests the scheme in the novel, the henchman He Shilai tells Wang that Ren is immune to the temptations of money and, being "one of the top heroes in the world," cannot be intimidated, so an oath of brotherhood is the only way to gain access to the wife. His heroism suggests the means by which he can be deceived. In contrast, heroism does not figure in the initial scheming in the drum ballad; there He simply suggests that Wang entertain Ren and Luo because they have had nothing to do with each other before, and being on friendly terms would make access to Ren's wife easier.[94]

Throughout this scene in the drum ballad, the narrator's comments frame it in clear ethical terms. They emphasize Wang Lun's deceit, calling him a "scoundrel" (*zeizi*) or "crafty" (*zei*), and point out the difference between him and the "heroes just and straightforward," Ren and Luo. In contrast, the narrator of the novel lets the actions speak for themselves. This shifts the focus from a simple right and wrong to the more complex relationship between the roles enacted and the realities behind them. The novel also adds material to underscore Ren's misplaced faith in these roles. While the drum ballad largely focuses on Wang Lun's trickery, the novel makes it more of a give-and-take. The novel adds Ren's enthusiastic acceptance of Wang Lun as an "intimate friend" and his explicit rejection of what he already has heard of Wang's shady character. Ren's willingness to play the role of hero and use the language of brotherhood is also played up. While the drum ballad shows Ren and Luo want to refuse the oath, the novel omits this. The novel also makes Ren respond in kind when Wang Lun uses the language of brotherhood. Each of these additions emphasizes Ren's role; none are present in the drum ballad. Thus the treatment of this scene in the novel shifts the focus from Wang's underhandedness to Ren's gullibility. In addition, whereas the drum ballad relies on the narrator for evaluation, the novel generally leaves any evaluation up to the other characters.

Overall, the novel seems to have picked up on the conflict of roles and genres which remains mostly latent in the drum ballad and expanded it into a central principle. Comparison of *Green Peony* and the drum ballad it draws on suggests that each calls for a different kind of reading. Under the widespread influence of fiction criticism, the novel invites a more critical reading, creating a game of catching the gaps between what is said and what is meant. *Green Peony* also delights in displaying and questioning the genre conventions. By dialogizing these conventions, the novel *Green Peony* fosters ironies and ambiguity. Still, the ambiguity in *Green Peony* would not make it meaningless to its readers. Rather, like some of the fiction in the *Bibliothèque bleue* studied by historian Roger Chartier, it allows for a range of possible readings, including sophisticated readings which recognize the self-conscious criticism of previous fiction.[95] The reader can choose to see it as a novel of adventure, romance, or justice, although the disruption of expectations would make simple reading in a genre less satisfying. More likely, the comic scenes would make the reader appreciate the parody of these well-known characters, roles, and conventions.

Metafiction, Popular and Elite

While finer examples of metafiction can be found in Chinese literature, the presence of metafictional moments in *Green Peony* is significant on two counts. First, the presence of these patterns and terms is no coincidence. Rather, the self-referential elements are some of the only consistent changes the novelist made in adapting the drum ballad.[96] This suggests that metafiction may have become part of the genre definition of the novel by the turn of the nineteenth century. I am not claiming that this is due to *Green Peony*; earlier examples of metafiction in the Chinese novel exist. What *Green Peony* shows is that at the time of its creation, these metafictional elements were an expected part of the novel's aesthetic, something with which it had to conform when adapting the drum ballad.[97] Second, the presence of metafiction in a popular novel like *Green Peony* questions common conceptions of popular and elite literature. The reflexive ruminations on the art of the novel in *Story of the Stone* and *Jinghua yuan* (Flowers in the mirror) generally have been considered anomalies attributed to the genius of their well-educated authors.[98] However, *Green Peony* shows that by this time even popular fiction calls attention to the novel's conventions.

Metafiction takes different guises in *Green Peony* and *The Story of the Stone*. *Green Peony* thematizes genre, exposing previous conventions through parody and juxtaposition. Its multiple beginnings and endings thwart the expectations they raise, resulting in ambiguity. Similarly, discussions of genre in *The Story of the Stone* "subvert conventions by using the text to declare its own uniqueness—while identifying several quite conventional elements therein."[99] Besides explicit discussion of fictional genres, within *Story of the Stone* the characters sometimes read events in their own lives in light of the conventions of the scholar-beauty romance. Thus, for example, the parallels between Baoyu's jade and Baochai's locket, or his gold kylin and Shi Xiangyun's, upset Daiyu, because in the scholar-beauty romances such matching objects prove marriage destiny.[100] However, *Story of the Stone*'s allegorical and autobiographical frameworks complicate and undermine such reading by genre. Moreover, while both *Story of the Stone* and *Green Peony* use genre and multiple frameworks to produce ambiguity and multiple readings, *Story of the Stone* goes much further. It is concerned not only with genre but also with narrative as a whole. Many passages throughout the work "suggest a reading process while at the same time discounting the validity of any one reading—or perhaps of reading altogether."[101] Although the differences between the two novels might seem to argue against any significance for literary history, the fact that metafiction took different forms in different works should not obscure the presence of this kind of self-consciousness. Its target is less important than the impulse.

Despite their differences, *Green Peony* and *The Story of the Stone* converge in influencing a number of later novels, most notably *Flowers in the Mirror* and *Moral Heroes and Heroines*. While *Story of the Stone*'s influence on these works is well known, their debt to *Green Peony* is less widely acknowledged.[102]

In his study of *Flowers in the Mirror*, Stephen Roddy suggests that *Green Peony* may have served as its model.

> This slightly earlier work [*Green Peony*] is also set during Wu Zetian's reign, and its plot shares many elements with Li Ruzhen's work, including the prominence of talented young girls, a special female examination, and the banding together of Tang loyalists to fight for the restoration. . . . Indeed, it seems quite possible that Li Ruzhen may have used this . . . novel as a source or even a blueprint for his work, "transposing" the former, so to speak, into the medium of the scholarly novel.[103]

The two novels share more than just the time period of Wu Zetian's reign; *Flowers in the Mirror* is set in a similar world with related characters. For example, in *Green Peony* the character Luo Long is Luo Hongxun's father and Luo Binwang's uncle; he is Luo Binwang's father and Luo Hongqu's grandfather in *Flowers in the Mirror*.[104] Both novels present Empress Wu as a supernatural being (either a female dragon or a fox spirit) sent to earth to throw the Tang dynasty into chaos—even the phrasing is similar.[105] She sends Zhongzong away. Those who oppose her are sentenced to execution, but the scions of generals escape into hiding and later lead the restoration of Zhongzong. After a brief section at the beginning, both novels turn abruptly away from the restoration narrative to other narrative threads. The two novels also end in a similar fashion with a sudden turn to the restoration movement after some of the main characters are married off. In each case they divide into male and female armies to take one or more strategic passes and kill the treacherous officials but spare Empress Wu, who abdicates in Zhongzong's favor.

Not only do both novels include the women's examinations, they present the impetus for it in strikingly similar fashion. In *Green Peony*, Hua Zhenfang is told by one of his informants that Wu Sansi went abroad to look for medicinal plants and came back with an extraordinary flower, the green peony (whence the novel's title). As it blooms, Empress Wu says this flower is something China "has never had since antiquity," so it is auspicious. She thereupon invites all talented women regardless of rank or class to come to her garden to enjoy the flower, and take civil and military examinations. The rationale is that flowers are female, and such an extraordinary flower must mean there are extraordinary girls in the world who are living in obscurity in their maidenly chambers. Thus this exam will select the best to exemplify China's thriving civilization.[106]

The rationale in *Flowers in the Mirror* runs along the same lines. After Empress Wu orders all the flowers to bloom, in the garden Shangguan Waner explains to her "all these famous flowers are rare treasures; today they promptly obeyed your order to bloom, this is truly accomplished by your majesty's fortune equal to heaven. It can be called a grand event that has never been since antiquity, and a lovely story for a thousand autumns."[107] A princess notes that many of the flowers are double, which codes them as female, and suggests that the omen means Empress Wu should broadly receive talented females. Empress Wu thinks it over and decides that interpretation is reasonable.[108] Years later Tang Ao recounts to Lin Zhiyang that the hundred flowers poetry party inspired Wu Zetian to start a nationwide search for female talent; because of this all girls, whether from eminent or humble families, are studying.[109] The resemblance between the two novels is particularly striking here; even some of the phrasing is quite similar.

In contrast, the seventeenth-century historical novel *Romance of the Sui and Tang* frames the episode where Empress Wu orders the flowers to bloom simply as an example of her overweening arrogance and ambition. No mention is made of the women's exams. Indeed, the whole idea of the women's exams would be out of place in *Romance of the Sui and Tang*. The novel portrays Empress Wu as lascivious, frivolous, and vindictive. Thus the end-of-chapter comment on Empress Wu begins with the common tack, "It has always been the case that a woman with no talent will be virtuous (*nuzi wu cai bian shi de*); those with talent will inevitably commit ugly acts." It goes on, however, to say her talent was unparalleled and list her accomplishments.[110] While the novel's narrative paints Empress Wu as largely evil, the commentary starts to open up space for a reevaluation of Empress Wu. However, exploring that possibility in narrative would wait until *Green Peony*. The eighteenth-century series of novels on the Tang simply elaborate on Empress Wu's lasciviousness and poor judgment.

Green Peony and *Flowers in the Mirror* depart from the standard depiction of Empress Wu by painting her in a largely positive light. *Green Peony* portrays her as a capable ruler with one weakness: lust. Unlike the notoriously explicit portrayal of Empress Wu's liaisons in the erotic novels, however, *Green Peony* offers no description, just two sentences explaining that the evil ministers gained power by spending time with Empress Wu day and night. *Green Peony* carefully whitewashes most of the "crimes" of her administration, placing the blame on the treacherous ministers surrounding her rather than on Empress Wu herself. She acts as regent simply because Zhongzong is too young to rule and then exiles Zhongzong out of shame, hoping in this way to prevent him from finding out about her love affairs. Unlike other versions of the story, in *Green Peony* Empress Wu summons Judge Di of her own accord to request his help in restoring Zhongzong. Similarly, although in the end she gives the order to send troops against the restoration army, the narrator takes pains to explain that, due to a false report, she thought it was a bandit revolt. In a sense, the "false" report is true—they are bandits and it is an uprising. However, on another level this explanation serves to make the new version of events in *Green Peony* compatible with the standard version, despite the change in Empress Wu's characterization. In order to have the well-known battles she orders to defend the Zhou, even in *Green Peony* she has to send reinforcements, so the narrator tries to smooth over the contradictions.

The ambiguity of Empress Wu's characterization in *Green Peony* invokes expectations from two kinds of military romances, each of which requires different responses. If the white-washing succeeds in presenting her as basically good but surrounded by treacherous officials, she is playing the same role as the ruler in most military romances; in such a case the generals must show undying loyalty at any cost. However, the military romances on the "restoration of the dynasty after disturbances" view Empress Wu's reign as an aberration;[111] in that case the restoration serves to throw her out and the heroes owe loyalty only to Zhongzong. In *Green Peony* and to some extent in *Flowers in the Mirror*, the ambiguity of Empress Wu's portrayal conflates these two sets of expectations, each positing different obligations of loyalty, thereby complicating the significance of the frame story.

Unlike the military romance, *Green Peony* pays little attention to the issue of loyalty. It appears almost exclusively in the opening and closing chapters. Luo Hongxun's mourning period for his father conveniently excuses him from obligations to government service, thereby allowing most of the narrative to sidestep the question of loyalty. However, the case of the pirate Bao Zi'an poses more problems. When he wishes to join the restoration, he coopts the rhetoric of reclusion to cover his past, claiming that he is an outlaw only because, in an age without the Way, his talents could not find their proper outlet. Judge Di calls his bluff, however, pointing out that the sages' idea of reclusion did not involve killing and banditry. Bao then returns to his stance of righteous bandit, claiming to harm only treacherous government ministers.[112] Even this stance is undermined by his actions: he has on numerous occasions refused summons and killed government soldiers sent to capture him. Indeed, Judge Di's own messenger nearly met the same fate.[113]

Green Peony invokes the rhetoric of reclusion opportunistically to smooth over sudden shifts like the outlaws coming to serve Emperor Zhongzong. In contrast, *Flowers in the Mirror* builds it into the structure of the novel, so it becomes a serious alternative to the rhetoric of loyalty central to the military romance. *Flowers in the Mirror* fleshes out the alternative of reclusion in the quest to become a Daoist immortal, first by Tang Ao and then by his daughter Tang Guichen. Granted, the military romance often incorporates the motif of reclusion—some of the Yang Family Generals retire to the mountains after winning great victories, and Fan Lihua goes off after her triumphs in battles of magic. Still, by changing the usual order and removing central characters before the battle, *Flowers in the Mirror* foregrounds the inherent contradictions between the two sets of values. Stephen Roddy and Maram Epstein both point out how this narrative curiously allows Tang Ao to avoid government service, and both note that the value of loyalty seems to be undermined in *Flowers in the Mirror*.[114]

As we have seen, *Green Peony* empties the military romance of content. It uses the structure of the military romance as a frame, beginning with Empress Wu's ascent and ending with Emperor Zhongzong's restoration. Because of dialogization, however, in *Green Peony* the frame story does not set the tone for the work. Instead it is undermined by multiple beginnings and endings and alternating plot lines. Similarities between the overall structure of *Flowers in the Mirror* and *Green Peony* suggest that *Flowers in the Mirror* also juxtaposes thematic material in a way that undermines the force of the values of the military romance. *Flowers in the Mirror* has two frame stories: the dispute among immortals in heaven that sets the novel in motion, and the tale of Empress Wu. While *Flowers in the Mirror* also concludes with Zhongzong's restoration, like *Green Peony* it undercuts the force of the military romance ending. The best-developed characters play only minor roles in the restoration in *Green Peony*; they play almost no role in the restoration in *Flowers in the Mirror.* As in *Green Peony, Flowers in the Mirror* relegates most of the work of restoration to characters who were briefly mentioned, then largely ignored for the bulk of the novel. *Flowers in the Mirror* even takes this one step further. Whereas in *Green Peony* it seems the main characters accept subsidiary roles in the restoration in deference to the superior fighting skills of Xue Gang, in *Flowers in the Mirror* the central characters have already chosen other pursuits. Tang Guichen and her father have retired to become immortals before the restoration is accomplished, essentially refusing to participate in it. Thus the elements *Flowers in the Mirror* shares with *Green Peony* serve a similar function, to undermine genre conventions and their attendant values, creating ambiguity.

If *Green Peony*'s play on the military romance may have provided inspiration to *Flowers in the Mirror*, its juxtaposition of the martial with the scholar-beauty romance anticipates *Moral Heroes and Heroines.* In both novels a match is forced upon the scholar at the initiative of a martial heroine. In fact, in *Moral Heroes and Heroines* the motif appears twice; in the second instance the martial heroine herself is forced into marriage.[115] Neither *Green Peony* nor *Moral Heroes and Heroines* is truly a "romance"; both preserve a structure emptied of its content in order to focus on values. These values become both more and less problematic in *Moral Heroes and Heroines.* According to the prologue, *Moral Heroes and Heroines* is intended to show how "feelings of boys and girls" (*ernü*, or dutiful love) and heroism (*yingxiong*, or the will to act) are not contradictory but actually inseparable.[116] In this it reverses the critique implicit in *Green Peony*, which shows the incompatibility of the codes of love and heroism. Still, even though *Green Peony* revolves around the clash of the values of the scholar and the swordsman (or swordswoman), it does not force a choice between them. Hua Bilian can marry Luo Hongxun but still use her martial skills when called for. In contrast, while *Moral Heroes and Heroines* states the fundamental compatibility and indivisibility of these two value systems, if one views it from the vantage point of the genres it draws upon, it does force He Yufeng to choose between them. Indeed, it devotes whole chapters to explicit discourse leading to her "conversion" from swordswoman to wife. The title couplet of the most crucial chapter in this process even states that Zhang Jinfeng's words must "dispel [He Yufeng's] gallant spirit" (*xiao xiaqi*) before she can "realize a good match." [117] While *Green Peony* plays with exposing the conflict between the values inherent in each genre and their prescriptive power over behavior, in *Moral Heroes and Heroines* Wen Kang's "goal is nothing less than to reconcile separate and incommensurate worlds."[118] *Green Peony* may have proposed some of the central issues in *Moral Heroes and Heroines*; Wen Kang certainly knew of the novel *Green Peony*, as a reference in chapter 39 of *Moral Heroes and Heroines* shows.[119]

Flowers in the Mirror and *Moral Heroes and Heroines* both foreground issues surrounding received genres and their values. Whether they ultimately critique or uphold them, they no longer simply assume their validity. In this way they serve as Second Line novels.

Whether or not the narrative techniques in *Flowers in the Mirror* and *Moral Heroes and Heroines* show the influence of *Green Peony*, these two novels almost certainly "read" and elaborate on elements of the earlier novel. We have seen how *Green Peony* engages with models ranging from its drum ballad predecessor to thematic fiction and the masterworks of the novel, traversing the conventional boundaries of genre in the process. The final chapter will explore *Green Peony*'s place in the range of fictional practice in nineteenth-century China.

Chapter 5

Placing the "Popular" Novel in the Qing

THE STUDY OF POPULAR FICTION is fraught with difficulties. As Roger Chartier has observed, popular culture is all too often defined in terms of what it is not.[1] He offers two approaches to a better understanding of the relationship between popular texts and their social context.

> The first, reversing ordinarily recognized causalities, suggests an interpretation of "popular literature" as a repertoire of models of comportment, as an ensemble of representations of imitatable and possibly imitated norms. The second centers on the variety and instability of meanings assigned to the same texts by different audiences.[2]

I have attempted in the preceeding chapters to explore the value systems *Green Peony* exposes from previous fiction. While the paucity of sources makes it difficult to examine in any detail how the novel *Green Peony* was appropriated by different audiences, that challenge suggests a way to approach its social and literary context.

Who read *Green Peony*? How does its audience and aesthetic relate to each of the genres it draws on, and how did they relate to each other in the nineteenth century?

Our view of the audience for traditional Chinese fiction is largely shaped by the masterworks *The Water Margin*, *Three Kingdoms*, *Journey to the West*, and *Jin Ping Mei*. When the educated elite in China first took notice of the novel as a genre, they elevated these four novels to the status of "art," works by and for geniuses (*caizi shu*), by publishing fine editions and writing commentaries on them. We tend to forget that at the same time, different texts of these novels were being published for other, wider audiences.[3] Similarly, when we think about readership in the Qing dynasty, we might envision *Story of the Stone* being circulated in manuscript among the author's friends and relatives, people of similar education and social station. To an even greater extent, *Rulin waishi* (The unoffical history of the scholars) and *Flowers in the Mirror* are read as vehicles for elite concerns.[4]

While there was of course other fiction being produced, we imagine a huge gap between these "masterworks" and run-of-the-mill "chapbook" fiction.[5] Such different works, we reason, must have attracted different audiences. But the evidence paints another picture. By the nineteenth century the martial romance and the masterworks shared a common audience.

Most of the novels we cherish for their artistry were also read and enjoyed as popular fiction. Research on the publication of fiction shows that by the Qing, commodification allowed the "masterworks" to be widely read. Even though the limitations of our sources make it extremely difficult to ascertain the actual audience for a work in the Qing, the editions themselves and the publishing houses that printed them offer some clues to their reading publics. Based on her work on popular publishing, Cynthia Brokaw argues for a "common core" of reading material that extended socially across all literate levels and geographically across the Chinese empire. These were the "bestsellers" of their day, read by the entire literate public, from literati down to shopkeepers and peasants. They were printed not only in the major urban printing centers, but also in remote rural print shops like those in Sibao, Fujian Province.[6] In fiction, Brokaw's "common core" overlaps significantly with Robert Hegel's tabulation of the novels most frequently reprinted during the Ming and Qing. Indeed, only three novels on Hegel's list, including *The Unofficial History of the Scholars*, apparently were not produced in Sibao. The works in common include military romances, the "masterworks" *Three Kingdoms, The Water Margin, Journey to the West, Jin Ping Mei, Story of the Stone,* and *Flowers in the Mirror*, scholar-beauty romances, and martial arts novels like *Green Peony.*[7] Moreover, from the finest to the crudest imprints, publishers in the Qing were reproducing commentary editions of *The Water Margin* and *Three Kingdoms.*[8] Unlike the late Ming when many different editions of the masterworks targeted different segments of the reading public, by the mid-Qing these novels were read by all levels of readers in commentary editions.[9] As fiction becomes a commodity, one observes a convergence of texts.

The constant reprinting of *Green Peony* in commercial editions, even in rural areas, argues for a wide audience. While the availability of *Green Peony* means that "elites" could have read it, what evidence is there that they did? *Green Peony* is mentioned in *Moral Heroes and Heroines*, whose author was from a prominent Manchu family and served as an official. It is also mentioned in a later revised version of *The Unoffical History of the Scholars*.[10] Moreover, *Green Peony* was appreciated by nobility. The 1831 preface for the novel *Green Peony* is signed Ailian jushi, the pen name for one of the most famous authors of the Manchu performance form *zidishu*, Yi Geng, also known as He Lü. Born a Manchu nobleman, he attained a first-rank title through his father's hereditary privilege, but this title was revoked when his father was stripped of office. As an adult, Yi Geng served as a third-rank official, but left office after about five years and never returned to officialdom. The date of the preface to *Green Peony* corresponds to Yi Geng's first year in office, so at the time he would unquestionably be counted among the legally privileged educated elite.[11] However, since it seems he had not yet begun writing *zidishu*, he probably would not be famous enough to warrant forging his name on the preface.[12]

Thus the audience of *Green Peony* ran the gamut of Qing society. *Green Peony* not only attracted a wide range of readers socially; publishing data also suggests a geographically diverse national audience. While the location of the first printing is as yet unknown, the novel was printed in Xiamen (1829), Beijing (1831), and Nanjing (1831) within a few years of each other, and eventually was reprinted in Chengdu (1858), Shanghai (1892), and rural Sibao, Fujian.[13]

Indeed, the publishers of some of the other martial romances imagine a universal reading public.[14] The preface to *The Chart of Good and Evil* states it was printed because "the print-shop owner wished to record it to morally influence the age, and not minding the cost, had it carved [on printing blocks] and made into volumes,"[15] while *Yun, Zhong, and Yan Stir up a Ruckus Three Times in Taiping Zhuang* is aimed at "ignorant men and women."[16] The inclusion of women in the reading public may not have been merely rhetorical; the preface to *The Picture of Tianbao* is signed by a woman.[17] The preface to the court-case novel *Qing Feng Zha* (Clear Wind Sluice) specifies its reading public in even more detail:

> Everyone who sees (*lan*) this book says wow in admiration. . . . Because this book is widely praised, and can reverse the trend toward decadence, I regretted that there had never been a printed edition, so it could not be passed down or go far. Today, with no regard to the cost, I sent it to be carved [on printing blocks], hoping to make it so in poor areas and remote places, seashores and mountainsides, there is no one who cannot buy a copy.[18]

In this preface, the publisher imagines a rural, geographically diverse, and not necessarily affluent audience for this book. The remark that the work was "widely praised" before it was printed is also suggestive. We might surmise that it circulated in manuscript before being published. Since we know from

Yangzhou huafang lu that the story was performed by the Yangzhou storyteller Pu Lin, it is tempting to speculate that it may have gained popularity through oral storytelling and been recorded from memory. However, the preface makes no reference to storytelling.[19] In another instance, the preface to the military romance *The Tale of the Tang* imagines its audience as those who read it, those who hear it, and those who tell it.[20] Thus it presumes a significant audience for auditory reading or retelling, beyond those who read it themselves. This would suggest that even the illiterate might have some access to novels through the practice of reading aloud.

Despite the convergence of texts the "bestsellers" represent, there were, of course, still differences between reading audiences in the Qing. Brokaw cautions that a given text could be experienced in different ways, thus ameliorating to some degree the unity imposed by this common core of texts. Moreover, the "bestsellers" were only one part of a spectrum of texts. Brokaw differentiates between an "elite" strata of specialized texts aimed at the small segment of highly educated men throughout the empire; the "core" of bestsellers already discussed; and texts largely of "local" interest. The latter included cheap songbooks (*changben*) printed in local dialect and intended for vocalization. Brokaw is quick to note that "local" does not necessarily mean non-elite; songbooks could be appreciated by local elite.[21]

An example from my own research illustrates the social elite's interest in songbooks. A manuscript copy of a drum ballad version of *Green Peony* survives in the the Palace Museum in Beijing, in the collection of the office responsible for dramatic entertainment for the Qing palace from the Kangxi period on.[22] In the same city but at the other end of the social spectrum, another drum ballad version of *Green Peony* (fig. 5.1) was rented out at a corner shop, Xing Long Zhai, which also sold steamed buns. The audience for that version appears to have included women.[23]

Even within the "core" there were differences between audiences for fiction. For example, *Story of the Stone* went through more editions than any other novel in the Qing and inspired fifty-five sequels, but in rural Sibao it seems to have been outsold by military romances.[24] This may reflect the influence of local performance traditions such as storytelling and drama. Many of the novels with the broadest circulation also appear in locally printed performance genres.[25] A survey of the Academica Sinica collection of performance-related texts from local genres across China shows the most widespread subjects are *Three Kingdoms, The Water Margin*, *Story of the Stone*, and Judge Bao—in approximately that order. Texts about Judge Bao outnumber those about particular military romances, but grouped together the military romances rank second only to *Three Kingdoms*. Some individual military romances (like the Yang Family Generals saga) outnumber *Journey to the West*.[26] While this can only be a rough estimate of the prevalence of

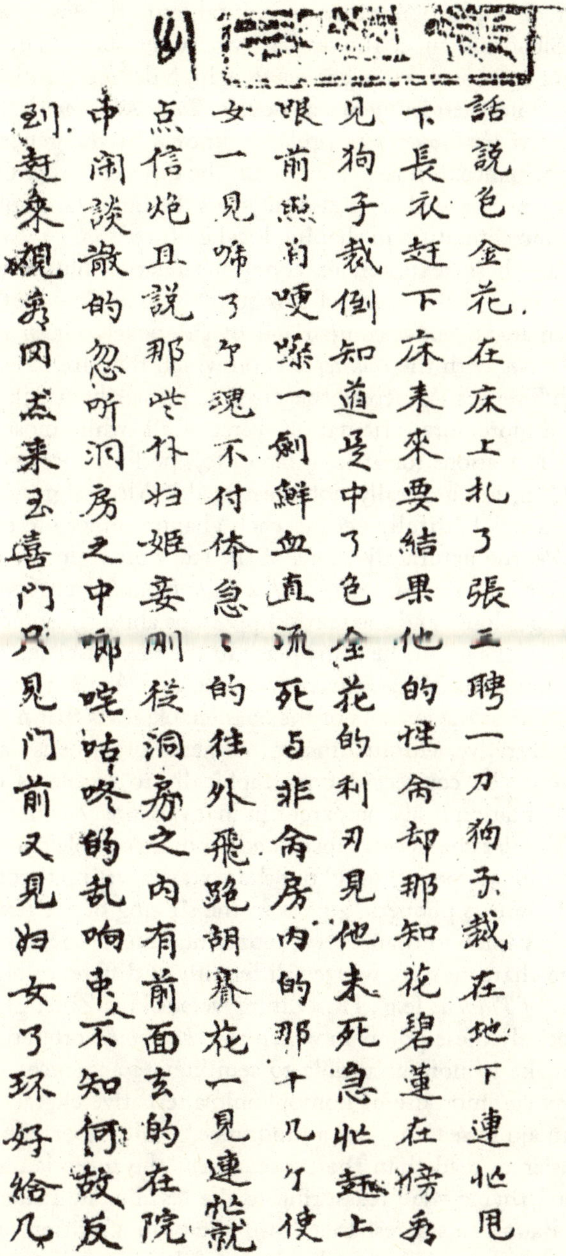

話說色金花在床上扎了張正聘一刀狗子栽在地下連忙甩
下長衣赶下床未來要結果他的性命却那知花碧蓮在傍看
見狗子栽倒知道是中了色金花的利刃見他未死急忙趕上
跟前照看嗖嗾一劍鮮血直流死与非命房內的那十几个使
女一見唬了个魂不付体急急的往外飛跑胡賽花一見連忙就
点信炮且說那些朴归姬妾剛從洞房之內有前面去的在院
中閑談散的忽所洞房之中唧咤咕咚的乱响众人不知何故反
到赶來觀看因為来至喜门只見门前又見妇女了环好給几

Figure 5.1 A page from the Xinglong Zhai manuscript
Green Peony Drum Ballad 51

these subjects in performance literature, it tallies fairly closely with the tastes of the rural Sibao audience. The similarity between subjects in core and local entertainment texts once again argues for a high degree of unity of culture in the Qing: Beyond their influence as novels, *Three Kingdoms, The Water Margin*, and *Story of the Stone* were probably known by the general population through performance. On the other hand, the different order of frequency of these performance-related texts also suggests the importance of performance and performance literature in shaping local culture.[27]

What can these texts tell us about the relationship between the two milieus? It is beyond the scope of this study to assess most of these performance-related texts, but a comparison of the novels *Green Peony* and *The Picture of Tianbao* with the *chantefables* on which they are based shows some important differences. Whereas the novel is primarily visual, many *chantefables* reveal a more aural orientation. First of all, while most novels would carry some illustrations (or at least claim to), performance-related *chantefables* in the Qing are generally not illustrated.[28] More significantly, in contrast to the novels faithfully ending each chapter on a note of suspense, in the *chantefables* the natural divisions of the story often do not correlate with textual divisions. In the case of *Tianbao Lute Ballad*, each fascicle is exactly ten double-pages long, and the text simply stops abruptly, sometimes in mid-sentence, and picks up in the same place in the next fascicle. The same phenomenon is found in Ming *chantefable* texts, and Anne McLaren explains, "It did not occur to the authors of the chantefable texts that natural divisions of the sung narrative, culminating in moments of suspense and storyteller questions, could be connected typographically to segments of the text."[29] This aural orientation is also apparent in many *chantefables* in the widespread practice of "simpler characters substituted for more complex homophones. . . . Such substitutions appear throughout the text, suggesting that the songbooks . . . are used more as phonetic guides to the singing of the text (the story of which is widely known) than as real representations of meaning."[30] Even the names of the characters are written differently at different points in the text of *The Picture of Tianbao* (e.g., Hua Zining versus Hua Zineng).

It is precisely these points in which the *chantefable* often differs from the novel that make it more accessible to semiliterate audiences. "As a text for chanting, the common use of homophonic alternative characters in chantefables was an aid to reading, not a hindrance."[31] Moreover, the verse sections could be easier to read than the prose, since "the formulaic repetition and persistent end-rhyme were reassuring to the less literate reader."[32] McLaren cites Franz Baüml to suggest that "formulicity in a written text . . . 'conditions reading' in that the sheer redundancy of the material renders a text more accessible to a reader of limited literacy and easier to fix in the memory. For a reader familiar with the performing arts, the repetitions and formulae refer continually to the formulaic configurations of the oral tradition."[33] Thus even if it cannot be proven that these songbook texts were actually performed, their format may have made them more accessible to the marginally literate. It is also interesting to note that the *Tianbao Lute Ballad* does not take literacy for granted. The narrator makes a point of explaining why the servant can read, a point that the novel simply assumes.[34]

Indeed, some of these songbooks might be a closer parallel to Western "chapbooks" than the Chinese novels to which scholars have applied that label. The physical format and circulation of the Chinese songbooks resembles the cheapest literature in Europe. Many Chinese songbooks in the Qing dynasty were produced in cheap, short booklets.[35] For example, the surviving volume of the Xing Long Zhai drum ballad on *Green Peony* is typical at twenty-six pages in manuscript, and in the Guangxu era a volume like it would have rented for about nine cash (*wen*) or sold for around 100 cash.[36] The fact that the songbooks circulated in parts also resembles Western chapbooks. We know Xing Long Zhai and other such shops in Beijing rented long works by dividing them into independent volumes intended as daily installments. Similarly, each of the volumes comprising *Tianbao Lute Ballad* runs only ten printed pages, and each carries an independent title page, with a separate title in the center indicating the events of that volume and the title of whole work across the top (fig. 5.2). This suggests the volumes may also have been sold or circulated separately. The same format appears in the songbooks on *The Gathering of Heroes* from Guangdong.[37]

Although format would make many *chantefables* more accessible to the marginally literate, one cannot automatically assume that was their target audience.[38] Each type of *chantefable* discussed here encompasses a range of texts, from those closely related to performance to texts more conducive for reading. While this is an underexplored area, a quick look at the presentation of three martial *chantefables* demonstrates how the format suggests reading practices. The *Tianbao Lute Ballad* published by Feichun ge, the *Green Peony Drum Ballad 51* rented by Xing Long Zhai, and the *Green Peony Drum Ballad* in the Nan Fu office of the palace differ markedly in the presence or absence of dialogue markers like "he said" or "she thought." If one interprets these dialogue markers as a guide to the reader, serving a function analogous to punctuation, then one would expect to find them less often in texts closely related to performance, and more often in texts that are primarily for reading.[39] In other words, since such tags are unnecessary in performance, a reader familiar with the conventions of performance would not need the tags.[40] I would suggest that as the *chantefables* become texts for reading, however, this kind of assistance becomes increasingly necessary.

Tianbao Lute Ballad generally omits dialogue markers altogether. The full title of this text, *Xinke zhenben tanci changkou Tianbao tu quan zhuan*

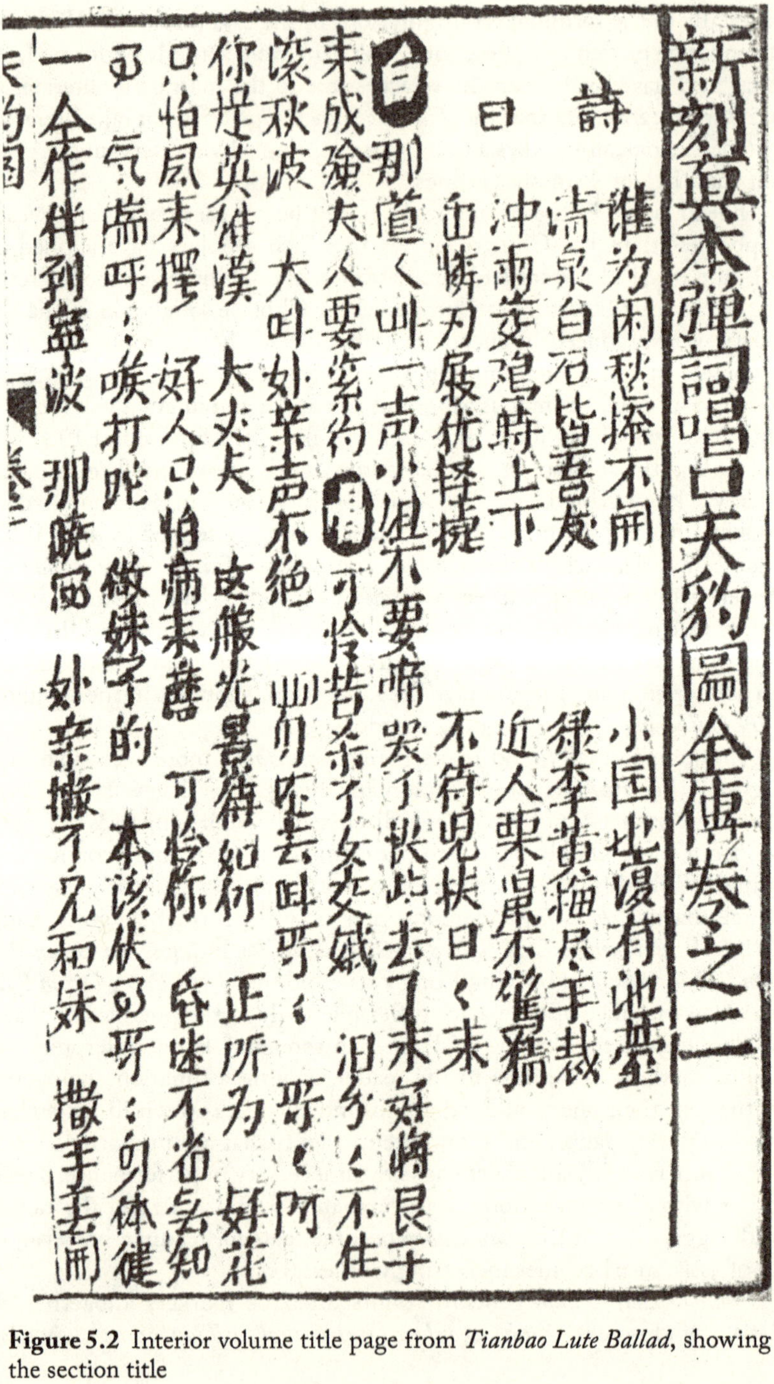

Figure 5.2 Interior volume title page from *Tianbao Lute Ballad*, showing the section title

真本天豹圖

賽專宗施仁濟困　二集

鬻霞報主

淨街王仗霸凌貧　飛春閣梓

(Newly carved authentic lute ballad for singing the whole story of the picture of Tianbao), suggests a close relationship between this text and amateur performance. In contrast, the Xing Long Zhai *Green Peony Drum Ballad 51* regularly employs dialogue markers. The Nan Fu *Green Peony Drum Ballad* approaches the conventions of the novel; it uses tags like "she said" in the prose to introduce speech and consistently indicates any change of speaker in the dialogue. This suggests it may have been primarily intended for reading. While drum ballad verse often includes a number of formulae to introduce speech, the anomalous inclusion of such tags in the prose may serve to orient the reader less familiar with the tradition of drum ballads. Based on this criterion, the three ballad texts suggest different reading practices or different degrees of familiarity with performance. The *Tianbao Lute Ballad* relies the most on knowledge of the performance tradition; it shows little visual orientation and few concessions to reading. The Xing Long Zhai *Green Peony Drum Ballad 51* falls in the middle. Its regular use of dialogue markers indicates a more visual orientation, but its widespread employment of homophonic substitution and non-standard characters would appeal to the ear rather than the eye. The Nan Fu *Green Peony Drum Ballad* shows the most tailoring for reading. Homophonic substitution is rare in *Green Peony Drum Ballad*, and three-quarters of its chapters use end-of-chapter formulae, although several end-of-chapter formulae appear in the middle of chapters. Thus while *Green Peony Drum Ballad* is not perfectly visually oriented, it is much more so than *Tianbao Lute Ballad*. The Nan Fu *Green Peony Drum Ballad* also shows no signs of circulating in parts. The visual format of this drum ballad, except for the extensive use of verse, comes close to a conventional novel.

Why translate from a *chantefable* text to a novel? To appeal to different audiences, or to create different effects? Possibly both. In the process of translation, the novel *The Picture of Tianbao* eliminates most of the dialect in the lute ballad, making the novel understandable to those outside the Wu dialect area. In other words, it translated the story from a local form to one with a potentially national audience. Despite this, *The Picture of Tianbao* never took off as a novel, but continued to be reprinted frequently as a lute ballad text. The failure of *The Picture of Tianbao*'s minimal case of genre translation, in contrast with the success of the more comprehensive changes in the novel *Green Peony*, suggests that the distinction between the novel and the *chantefable* goes beyond a simple matter of form.

The novel and the *chantefable* approach their literary heritage differently. *Green Peony Drum Ballad* uses many allusions, often piling them up in verse passages,[41] but only assumes general knowledge of *Three Kingdoms*, *The Water Margin*, *Journey to the West*, some historical novels, and some major drama. Usually these allusions are used to characterize by comparison, establishing characters as standard types like the warrior or the beauty. Thus, the allusions in *Green Peony Drum Ballad* describing Hua Bilian in terms of "Wang Zhaojun who went out of the passes" and "a face that could topple a city or a country" carry little significance beyond being legendary beauties.[42] By invoking several well-known roles from fiction and drama, the drum ballad limits the force of the reference to a general sense of type. Occasionally allusions in the drum ballad parody well-known episodes of fiction. In contrast, the novel engages with both the "masterworks" and the commentary on them.

References to other works within the novel *Green Peony* suggest its readership cut across the range of available fiction. It assumes knowledge of scholar-beauty romances, military romances, court-case stories, and also the masterworks *The Water Margin*, *Journey to the West,* and *Three Kingdoms.* The depth of knowledge demanded by these allusions varies. References generally involve genre conventions rather than a particular work. One exception is *Green Peony*'s frame story, which refers to the Xue Family Generals saga from the military romance *Another Tale of Rebellion against the Tang.* While allusions to the famous drama *The Story of the Western Wing* are more specific, they require only general knowledge of the characters and their roles; the same is true of allusions to *Journey to the West.* References to *Three Kingdoms* and *The Water Margin*, on the other hand, assume familiarity with the details of specific plot episodes. Much of the meaning of the novel *Green Peony*, and much of its humor, comes from its play on previous fiction. Thus its audience must have been familiar with the works it parodies, at least to the degree suggested above.[43]

Green Peony also playfully alludes to the Confucian classics. For example, when Wang Lun is smitten with Madam He, he starts blowing kisses to her. Luo Hongxun "raised his head and saw Wang Lun '*miming it with his hands and dancing it with his feet*' to flirt with Madam He, and was enraged." The quote in italics is from the "Great Preface" to the *Book of Songs.* By placing it in a radically different context, *Green Peony* plays games with it, investing it with incongruous sexual overtones, just as the masterworks *Jin Ping Mei* and *The Water Margin* do with this same quote.[44] In the masterworks this is certainly a textual game, creating "the most elegant parody . . . a quote deflected from its meaning or simply from its context, or demoted from its dignified status."[45] For the novel *Green Peony*, however, the immediate source of this playful quotation is the drum ballad, in which only the first phrase, "miming it with their hands," appears. By expanding the reference to include the second phrase, the novel *Green Peony* makes the misappropriation of the classics more obvious. Does it suggest that the audience would be familiar with the original reference in the classics? By the time of *Green Peony* would it retain its force, or would it have become proverbial in the centuries between *Jin Ping Mei* and *Green Peony*, as many phrases from Shakespeare have for us?

In the same scene, *Green Peony* appropriates a quotation from the *Analects of Confucius*. He Shilai warns Wang Lun that he is lucky that Madam He's husband did not notice, since "If Ren Zhengqian had seen through it, at this moment he would have already turned over our table and beat us 'is it not delightful' (*bu yi le hu*)." Once again, the novel borrows the quotation from the drum ballad, although the drum ballad varies it to "Is it not fortunate" (*bu yi xing hu*). The novel "corrects" the quotation. Frequent use suggests in this case the phrase has become clichéd. It is used in *Jin Ping Mei* to describe the monks' excitement at overhearing lovemaking,[46] but it also appears in two of the eighteenth-century military romances, *Later Tang Third Collection* and *Another Tale of Rebellion against the Tang*, to refer to sex and battle, respectively.[47]

In these two cases, the same technique (or at least the same phrase) appears across the range of fictional practice, from the Ming masterworks to the drum ballad and then the novel *Green Peony*. Still, the way the novel *Green Peony* expands or corrects the quotations from the drum ballad reveals a more textual or intertextual orientation. In addition, while adapting the drum ballad the novel *Green Peony* added most of the clearly textual references, including allusions to the *Chuci* (Songs of Chu) and *The Water Margin*.

Besides a more textual orientation, the novel *Green Peony* differs from the drum ballad in its more critical take on received culture. Andrew Plaks argues that the novel, in contrast to the material it drew on, introduced ironic reflection on the characters, their motives, and their actions. I have found this to be the case with *Green Peony*. Although the drum ballad exhibits many of the aesthetic traits of the "literati" novel, it does not generate ironic reflection, but rather tends toward parody. Indeed, *Green Peony Drum Ballad* created the conflicts between contrasting role types that appear in many of the same scenes in the novel. For example, the parody of the Shi Xiu episode from *The Water Margin* I analyzed in chapter 3 is based closely on the *Green Peony Drum Ballad*. Much of the playing with roles that makes the novel humorous originated in the drum ballad.

That the parody originated in the *chantefable* is not surprising. Bakhtin suggests that parody developed first in the "low" forms, and then worked its way into the novel.[48] An unexpected juxtaposition of roles was entertaining. In the case of *Green Peony*, the novel's contribution was twofold: To develop the occasional parody of roles into systematic dialogization of a genre, and to deftly add or subtract details to produce a more complicated picture of the characters than did the drum ballad.

Chapter 4 demonstrated how the novel alters the characterization in the scene in which Wang tricks Ren and Luo into swearing brotherhood. Another example of the change in characterization occurs in the funeral ruse in *Green Peony.* Since much of the episode is absent in the drum ballad, the novel is exploiting the comic potential of a scene in *The Water Margin* through intertextual reference. As I argued in chapter 3, the intertextual reference to *The Water Margin* in the novel *Green Peony* seriously challenges Luo's stature as a filial son. In contrast, *Green Peony Drum Ballad* unambiguously portrays Luo as filial.[49] In the drum ballad, Luo behaves appropriately at each of the points where the novel undercuts his filial piety. Thus in the drum ballad, the letter tells Luo his mother disappeared after their house burned down and no one was certain whether she was dead or alive. Luo faints away at the news, and when he is revived he leaves for home immediately. Once he arrives in his hometown he cannot eat or sleep until he learns his mother was "rescued" by the bandit gang.

Most of the systematic changes made in the process of translating material from the drum ballad make the novel *Green Peony* more self-conscious than the drum ballad. While *Green Peony* exposes genre codes and the constructedness of roles, it does not question narrative as a construction of language, nor does it directly challenge the relationship between fiction and reality. Compared to works like *Don Quixote* that inspired the theoretical models I am using, the most striking parallel in *Green Peony* is the mixing of genres. In *Green Peony,* characters reject their normal lives to try to live by other models from fiction.

Green Peony and *Don Quixote* play upon their models in similar ways. Each could be considered an "antinovel" or "antiromance," to use Genette's term. Instead of primarily parodying individual texts, the antinovel takes on an entire genre—the chivalric romance and to a lesser extent the pastoral in the case of *Don Quixote*; the military romance (*yingxiong chuanqi*), court-case story, and scholar-beauty romance for *Green Peony.* To do this it employs, among other methods, hoaxes that play upon the hero's assumed identity (the flying horse in *Don Quixote*), or

> Conscious and (nearly) lucid imitation . . . where, for example, Don Quixote does not at first *believe* himself to be a knight but seeks to *become* one, and cannot hold himself to be one until he has been knighted by an innkeeper whom he mistakes for a lord of the manor. He deliberately *simulates* madness in Sierra Morena, not because his thinks himself to be Amadis but simply to do as his hero would have done.[50]

In *Green Peony* these two methods are often combined: The false oath of brotherhood plays on the values of the heroes Luo and Ren believe themselves to be, but in order to carry it off Wang Lun also must consciously act the part of the hero himself. Thus, significantly, while the hero in *Green Peony* may not explicitly voice his model, the antagonist recognizes the model and plays on it.

Green Peony differs from *Don Quixote*, however, in that it exposes these generic conventions through contrast with other genres of fiction rather than through contrast with "reality." This contrast of genres in *Green Peony* is more than a game. Besides blazing a trail toward the new genre of the martial romance,[51] the juxtaposition of incompatible genres reflects back onto the values each genre espouses. They are exposed as conventions rather than truths.[52] More significantly, the conventions or forms these values take can be misappropriated by the insincere to manipulate believers.

The genres are presented on their own terms, so the reader can insist on reading in a genre if he wishes, although since the novel undermines each genre he would find such a reading unsatisfying. For the thoughtful reader—and in many cases the parody is so obvious that the humor is unmistakable—this dialogization of genres functions as "the ironic discrepancy between several angles of perspective," one of the defining characteristics of the novel.[53]

Still, although the reader may become disillusioned with the genre codes that are juxtaposed and relativized, the characters do not. Even if the characters in *Green Peony* attempt to escape into roles from literature, the result is different from Don Quixote's realization that he has been imagining reality to be something more heroic than it could be in his age. In *Green Peony* the characters are allowed to go back and forth between two generic worlds, although the gaps between them are exposed: Hua Bilian is both (and neither) beauty and woman warrior, Luo Hongxun is both (and neither) scholar and hero, and Bao Zi'an is both (and neither) outlaw and judge. Openly figuring the disillusionment of the characters with these genres or values within the narrative would have to wait for other works.[54]

Green Peony exemplifies the martial romance in the material it borrows from previous genres and, more importantly, in the way it puts them together. Its particularly tight structure and self-consciousness intensifies awareness of the clash of genres that exists in all of the martial romances. The martial romance appeared in China at a time when most genres of popular fiction were well established and had had long, successful runs. Although the martial romance employed familiar tropes and role types, rarely would they mean what they did before. The play with genre we have seen in *Green Peony* appears to varying degrees in the other martial romances.[55] Like Bakhtin's conception of the novel as a whole, the artistry of the martial romance lies in how it "orchestrates" existing materials and makes them speak to each other, reflect on each other, and criticize each other. Each of the martial romances pits conflicting genres against each other. In so doing it opens up a space for a new genre.

The juxtaposition in the martial romance of roles, structures, and motifs from different genres of thematic fiction dissociates established roles from classic situations. For example, the scholar appearing in the martial romance generally does not take the civil service exams; he does not exchange love poems with the beauty. These omissions raise significant issues for characterization. Like Bakhtin's First Line novels, the classic scholar-beauty romances work well as novels of trial, testing the lovers' talent, faithfulness, and virtue before uniting them.[56] The scholar-beauty romance makes the standards of excellence clear through two central fixtures of the genre: the test of poetic skill to win love, and the civil service examinations to prove both virtue and talent. The protagonists embody this excellence, while the villains represent its opposite. In this light, the invalidation of the "test" in the martial romance *A Gathering of Heroes*—where the evil servant does as well as his virtuous master on the examinations—seems particularly significant. When skill and virtue are decoupled, the test itself largely loses its meaning.[57]

Instead, the martial romance often pushes the scholar into situations appropriate to the martial hero. Most of the time this does not go as far as the "miscasting" in *Green Peony*—the scholar does not think of himself as a hero or try to be one. But when the scholar appears in a situation requiring a hero, such as a bandit attack, he seems pitiful or even useless. In *Garden of Competing Beauties* this occurs twice to comic effect. The first time, one retired scholar reasons with the bandits and tries to talk them out of robbing him. He believes he has succeeded and is quite pleased with himself; in fact, while he was making speeches the bandits have kidnapped his daughter without him realizing it. Another scholar meets with a robber. Being a "weakling student," fear and poor riding makes him fall off his horse; after the robber makes off with his money, horse, and clothes he just lies there, frightened half to death. The next time he appears he is starving and about to commit suicide.[58] This is the man whose "rare talent" impressed the emperor enough to choose him for his son-in-law! In these images of impractical, sheltered scholars it is tempting to see similarities to roughly contemporary ideas on the importance of a man's martial training that appeared in "erudite" novels like *Flowers in the Mirror*.[59] The helpless scholar also anticipates the comic side of An Ji in *Moral Heroes and Heroines*.

This raises the question: Is the juxtaposition of values in *Green Peony* essentially literary—a critique of the popular genres that preceded it, or a reflection of the influence of literary criticism of the novel—or is it tied to a broader questioning of values in society or intellectual circles? In other words, is this the "literature of exhaustion"? An extension of self-conscious literary trends in the novel? Or is it a product of the Qing debates over ritualism and evidential scholarship?

The shift toward self-consciousness in ordinary novels may be due in part to the ubiquity of fiction criticism. As mentioned above, by the mid-Qing the major novels were primarily available in commentary editions. We have seen the influence of this criticism in chapter 4, and how *Green Peony* engages it within the novel. With few exceptions, the most frequently printed novels in the Qing show the influence of Jin Shengtan and fiction commentary, through their use of titles, commentary, or within the novel proper.[60] As early as the eighteenth century, popular novels such as the scholar-beauty romances appeared under titles declaring them "works of genius" (*caizi shu*). Thus in the Qianlong era, editions of *San caizi shu Yu Jiao Li* (The third work of genius Yu Jiao Li) and *Si caizi shu Ping Shan Leng Yan* (The fourth work of genius Ping Shan Leng Yan) appeared, as well as a combined edition entitled *Qi caizi shu* (The seventh work of genius, or The book of seven geniuses). Similarly, fiction commentary appears in—or was claimed on the title pages of—works ranging from historical novels to supernatural novels. Almost no genre of fiction escaped this influence.[61] Indeed, even Cantonese songbooks use the designation "work of genius" in their titles, and some have prefaces and commentary justifying their claim.[62]

By the nineteenth century Jin Shengtan's rhetoric, which was originally designed to elevate the novel, is commercialized. Five of the martial romances invoke his rhetoric in prefaces, titles, within the novel, or through end-of-chapter comments. Three martial romances use "Book of Genius" (*caizi shu*) or "Extraordinary Book" (*qi shu*) in their titles: *San he jian: Xiuxiang di shi caizi shu* (Three united swords: The illustrated tenth book of genius), *Qun Ying Jie hou Song qi shu* (The gathering of heroes extraordinary book on the Later Song), and *Green Peony* as *Longtan Bao Luo qi shu* (The extraordinary book of Bao and Luo at Dragon Pool).[63] In addition, the preface to *The Garden of Competing Beauties* imitates Jin Shengtan's rhetoric, emphasizing the "extraordinariness" (*qi*) of the events, characters, and writing in the novel.[64] In *Green Peony*, the narrator and the characters themselves use key terms from fiction criticism to discuss structure and characterization. *The Pavilion of Myriad Flowers* even sports end-of-chapter comments.

If the use of Jin Shengtan's rhetoric by these works was a marketing ploy, it looks like it worked. The most "successful" martial romances—those that were the most widely reprinted—engaged Jin Shengtan (table 5.1). *Green Peony* had over twenty-eight Qing editions; *The Pavilion of Myriad Flowers* at least fifteen Qing editions; and *The Garden of Competing Beauties* was a steady seller, reprinted almost every decade, with at least sixteen Qing editions. As I argue in chapter 2, these three novels helped to set the formula for the martial romance as a genre. In contrast, martial romances that merely used terms from fiction criticism in their titles each produced around ten editions, and those that did not obviously engage fiction criticism went through fewer than ten editions apiece.[65]

Had Jin Shengtan's rhetoric become simply a marketing tool by this point? Perhaps in some cases. If it appears only in the title, as is the case with

The Gathering of Heroes, for example, it could be just a marketing ploy.[66] For the most successful martial romances, however, I would argue that besides helping to sell books, the appropriation or engagement of Jin Shengtan's rhetoric also suggested particular ways to read these novels, ways that fit with the reading practices of the general audience for novels.

The commentary to *The Pavilion of Myriad Flowers* not only demonstrates engagement of Jin Shengtan-style fiction criticism, it shows how the commentator applies them to a martial romance as a model for future readers. Chapter 4 discussed the influence of Jin Shengtan on *Green Peony* and its interest in unity, structure, and characterization. Similar interests figure in the chapter commentary to *The Pavilion of Myriad Flowers*, which analyzes it in terms reminiscent of Jin Shengtan. Thus the terminology of cross-reflection appears frequently, and the commentary finds significance in patterns of foreshadowing, even in the use of seemingly insignificant words.[67] It also pays special attention to differences within similarity when plot elements are repeated.[68] Discussions of characterization include the terms "host" (*zhu*) and "guest" (*bin*) to indicate the relative importance of characters in a particular chapter, or "padding" (*chen*) to indicate contrast between them.[69] The commentary also deals

Table 5.1 The martial romance and its appropriation of Jin Shengtan's rhetoric

NOVEL	ENGAGES JIN SHENGTAN'S RHETORIC?	NUMBER OF QING EDITIONS
Green Peony	Within novel; Title: *Longtan Bao Luo qi shu*, 1892	28
Garden of Competing Beauties	Preface	16
Pavilion of Myriad Flowers	Commentary	15
Yun, Zhong, and Yan	Title: *Da Ming qi xia zhuan*, 1895; Preface to 1895 edition	11
Gathering of Heroes	Title: *Xiuxiang Qun Ying Jie quan zhuan: Hou Song qi shu*, Qianlong-Jiaqing?, 1894	10
Three United Swords	Title: *San he jian: Xiuxiang di shi caizi shu*, 1848	10
Picture of Tianbao	No	7
Chart of Good and Evil	No	4
Embroidered Ball	No	4
Sword and Vase	No	2

with irony insofar as it points out hidden meanings and causes, for example where a "good" character causes harm.[70] While it occasionally critiques episodes it finds implausible, on the whole the commentary tends toward praise of the novel's technique with exclamations like "Extraordinary!" (*qi zai*).[71] In one case, the commentator commends the author's use of suspense in hiding key information. "Why doesn't he reveal it? It prepares for the text later on. Otherwise the next forty or so chapters would be boring (*wuwei*). Those who carefully savor books must certainly know this."[72] This appeals to the skilled reader, or at least promises to reveal the secrets that will make the reader of the commentary able to carefully savor books.

The preface to *The Garden of Competing Beauties* uses the terminology of traditional fiction criticism to appeal to the artistry of the novel as it highlights its adventurous content. The preface revolves around the term "extraordinary" (*qi*), which it uses to describe the events, people, and writing. "Extraordinary" was an important term in traditional Chinese fiction criticism.[73] It was widely used, but some of the specific phrasing in this preface echoes the preface to *Three Kingdoms* signed "Jin Shengtan." This preface, which appeared on most popular editions of the novel with commentary in the Qing, adapts an earlier preface that is signed "Li Yu" and may actually have been written by him.[74] In both versions, this preface to *Three Kingdoms* uses the term "extraordinary" (*qi*) to praise the novel, its writing, and the events upon which it was based. The basis for excellence here is not didactic value but the pleasure (*kuai*) the novel affords the reader. The *Three Kingdoms* preface explicitly says this book's extraordinariness (*qi*) will give pleasure to the learned and unlearned, heroes and commoners alike. This makes *qi* an accessible aesthetics, and may help explain why it was picked up as a "marketable" attribute.[75]

The preface to *The Garden of Competing Beauties* considers both the aesthetics and ethics of the novel, though it leans more toward aesthetics. Being "loyal to their lord and trustworthy to their friends" may be what makes the characters "extraordinary," but instead of a moral lesson the preface gives a structural outline of the novel. It briefly identifies the major characters and presents a glimpse of the novel's structure. Significantly, it identifies these keys to the novel in the terms provided by fiction criticism, implicitly claiming for this novel of adventure the status of "art" as an extraordinary piece of writing. This suggests a particular way to read the novel, informed by the tradition of fiction criticism. At the same time, the preface uses the superlative "number one" not for the novel itself, but for its protagonist, who it claims is the greatest martial hero that ever was. The explicit association of the novel with martial heroes in the preface serves as a sign of a new consciousness of that tradition.[76]

Besides the pervasive influence of traditional fiction criticism, I would suggest current intellectual trends, evidential scholarship and ritualism, also inspired self-consciousness in the novel. Evidential scholarship (*kaozheng*) arose in the Qing as a reaction to the "anything goes" attitudes inspired by Wang Yangming in the late Ming. Scholars in the Qing advocated a return to the texts of the classics. However, they soon realized the texts themselves were problematic. Ironically, the more they searched for the "true" meanings of particular words, the more they realized the original meaning was beyond recovery.[77]

The Qing also saw a renewed interest in ritualism. Before evidential scholarship, rituals were largely taken for granted. True, in the Song dynasty, when Zhu Xi prepared his ritual guide, he updated the rituals to bring them in line with the social conditions and practices of his time. In so doing, he distinguished inconsequential details from central ideas. Since he no longer relied on a literal reading of the classics, he potentially opened up the disjunction of act and meaning, and text and idea. However, since most scholars simply relied on Zhu Xi's ritual handbook, assuming it to be a digest of the classics, the implications of his changes did not surface until the Qing.[78] In the wake of the fall of the Ming, the seventeenth century witnessed a "strong return to punctilious traditionalism . . . the search for external and objective sources of authority that would establish for people how to act."[79] This return to the texts exposed Zhu Xi's agency and opened up debates over the proper forms of ritual and what was practical. While some still tried to follow the classics to the letter, others felt free to modify the forms. The relationship between text, prescription, and practice became a matter of debate.

To some extent these trends are mirrored in the world of fiction. The elevation of fiction was originally tied up with moral education. In the late Ming, intellectuals' interest in fiction was in showing how the text of a novel worked and using it to teach reading strategies (including the kind of subtle moral evaluation necessary to read the histories).[80] The text itself was not openly questioned.[81] In their own time, the commentaries to the four masterworks read them as didactic, and as obliquely presenting values.[82] An even more direct sense of fiction as models for life emerges from the early scholar-beauty romances, the plots of which center around propriety.

From the mid-eighteenth century on, however, the skepticism toward texts in intellectual circles is also reflected in fiction. The best example, *Story of the Stone*, shows an awareness of and play on text and its limits, engendering multiple interpretations.

It may not be surprising that the novels with known literati authors or commentators were concerned with contemporary intellectual trends. But *Green Peony* also shows an engagement with "elite" concerns like ritualism.[83] The primary points of tension in *Green Peony* center on rituals and roles. Many of these result from superimposing the expectations of different genres of fiction, for example, making a woman warrior the leading lady in a scholar-beauty romance. Often, though, a character gets into trouble because he follows a model too closely. For example, when Luo Hongxun remains doggedly faithful to his fiancée, his refusal of repeated proposals of marriage drive the spurned bandits to desperate measures. In the logic of the novel, his careful observation of propriety—including respecting the period of mourning for his father and insisting on his mother's approval of a match—is made ridiculous. Similarly, the villain Wang Lun is able to entrap Ren Zhengqian because Ren predictably follows the expectations for a hero too closely without considering the incongruous context. As a result, *Green Peony* seems to relativize most of the values it portrays.

Green Peony diverges most markedly from the Ming masterworks in this respect. The juxtaposition of conflicting discourses in *Green Peony* emphasizes ambiguity. As I have demonstrated, the dialogization of genres in *Green Peony* means that many scenes can be interpreted in two or more different lights. Once the comedy reveals such unlikely superimpositions, it profoundly affects how the reader understands the work. As Margaret Rose notes, referring to the famous drawing that can be seen as either a rabbit or a duck,

> the literary parody . . . may—like the rabbit which can also be seen as a duck, or vice versa—be viewed by another to be two things at once. It is obvious that the parallel between Jastrow's duck/rabbit and parody cannot be stretched too far, as we do not—in most cases of parody—have two complete works (or "representations") before us, but only the indication, or suggestion, of two. Yet the parallel between the parody text and our perception of the duck/rabbit can suggest that it is not in verifying which of the two images is "true," or if our perception of them is "valid," but in perceiving the contingency of these two things, and the effect of this on our normal processes of perception and validation of knowledge, that we pass through the stages of recognition which lead to laughter, to shock, to the destruction of expectations, and to a possible change in our knowledge of the thing observed and in our manner of observing it—to the knowledge of "how" characteristic of parody and the critically imaginative writing of texts.[84]

In other words, the double coding in parody creates a structure where the text can be two things at once. In recognizing the parody, the reader sees both the convention being drawn upon and the critique imposed by the new text. Parody exposes but does not destroy the previous conventions, which still "talk back" to the current text they helped shape. The reader can take sides, or stand back and appreciate the doubled "image" as a literary technique. In the dialogical text any "truth" is rendered partial and represents only one side of the picture. Ambiguity is inherent and irresolvable. Moreover, with *Green Peony*, no interlinear or marginal commentary (*pingdian*) intercedes to shut down alternate readings.

This suggests that, by the early nineteenth century, at least certain works of fiction were intended as entertainment, rather than models of morality or behavior. The earliest preface to *Green Peony* claims it serves simply to "please the eye and comfort the heart, and pass the time on long nights." In contrast to the standard apologia for the novel as a more accessible way to convey history's moral lessons, this preface dissociates *Green Peony* from history: "Although it does not follow the example of history, it is still worth looking at."[85] Entertainment becomes an end in itself. While some novels acknowledge this (as does *Story of the Stone*), many continue to claim the role of supplements to history in encouraging good behavior.[86]

Either way, the values at the core of thematic genres are no longer taken for granted, whether they are parodied as in *Green Peony* or explicitly debated and justified as in *Moral Heroes and Heroines*. The examination of literary and social conventions appears in different guises across much of the range of fictional practice in nineteenth-century China. Some works may still choose to uphold the conventions, but it becomes a conscious decision foregrounded in the discourse of those novels rather than simply being assumed and unstated.

The martial romance as a Second Line novel distances the reader from the values it portrays. They have become the values associated with particular literary roles. Perhaps the modern martial arts novel does the same thing in a different way. John Christopher Hamm argues convincingly that the appeal of the mid-twentieth century New School martial arts novel (epitomized by the works of Jin Yong) lies in its "nostalgic recreation of a Chinese culture envisioned as a whole and unchallenged."[87] The contrast between this often utopian vision of the martial arts as the "cultural tradition's consummate manifestation" and the modern world of colonial Hong Kong in which they were created is obvious. Indeed, that contrast created a collision of worlds in "comedies of displacement" appearing in the 1950s and 1960s, in which the heroes of traditional narratives like *The Water Margin* confront life in contemporary Hong Kong. Whereas the clash between the values of *The Water Margin* and modern life is made explicit in these comedies, allowing each to critique the other, in the New School martial arts novels the contrast with modern life is implicit, known "through the fervency of its disavowal."[88] The display of these martial tales through the lens of nostalgia, with their setting in the Chinese past and the marginal world of the *jianghu*, preserves a distance between the models and values represented in the modern martial arts novel and the reader consuming them.

Nostalgic distance may even be present in some of the late Qing martial arts novels. Paize Keulemans sees the Kangxi and Qianlong settings of many of the late Qing martial arts novels as a look back to a time when the Qing dynasty was still great and strong. For their original Beijing-centered readership, these novels might have had a double quality; in addition to nostalgia, their local Beijing settings may have allowed readers to imagine the emperors and heroes of the novels acting in the spaces of their own daily lives, thereby investing the present with the greatness of which they told. This immediacy would fade, however, as the novels reached audiences in other areas of China through lithographic editions from Shanghai.[89]

As already noted, the relationship between the heroes and the court, and the inherent tensions between them, vexed the late Qing martial arts novel. With the proliferation of these novels, however, a trend similar to what we have seen with the martial romance appeared. As the martial deeds take center stage, the judge's role becomes less central and eventually serves merely as a structural device. The sequels to *Cases of Judge Shi* and *The Three Heroes and Five Sworn Brothers* bear this trend out; the judges fade into the background and the heroes take over. However, the ideology of these novels is still exercised by the conflict between loyalty to the state and the righteousness or brotherhood demanded by the martial world of the *jianghu*. Here *Green Peony's* differences from Qing court-case adventure novels seem to prefigure the modern martial arts novel. In many twentieth-century works, the hero is firmly situated in the *jianghu* and often openly opposed to the court. The undermining of the importance of loyalty in *Green Peony* and its setting in the anomalous reign of Wu Zeitan means much of the novel focuses on the *jianghu* world of largely sympathetic outlaws. Similarly, the importance of romance to the structure of *Green Peony* presaged the central role romance would play in the structure of "countless" modern martial arts novels.[90] Thus, in martial romances like *Green Peony* we can see the seeds of the later martial arts novel.

Whether we approach *Green Peony* in terms of its aesthetic or its audience, we find that it shares a great deal with the "masterworks" of Ming-Qing fiction. Indeed, *Green Peony* lies at the center of a web of literary relations that connects many of the significant genres of fiction in its day. The wealth of surviving texts for martial arts novels and their corollaries in local printed performance genres allows us to better understand the relationship between cultural spheres both socially and geographically. We can conceptualize the relationship between *chantefables*, most novels, and the masterworks as a continuum. It is worth remembering that all three were considered *xiaoshuo*.[91] While significant differences in form and aesthetics remain, it would be fruitful to recognize the considerable interchange and influence among them. Within and across these three types of fiction we see a range of audiences; most of the masterworks were read even by rural audiences and some of the *chantefables* were read by the educated elite. Aesthetics vary from an aural orientation to an emphasis on textual complexity and unity. However, where each text falls is no foregone conclusion. Certain literary techniques can be found across the whole range of narrative from the "masterworks" to ordinary novels and drum ballads. On the other hand, not every *chantefable* has the same aesthetic orientation; some are more textually oriented or literary than others. Some "popular" fiction plays with its literary heritage and engages Jin Shengtan. We cannot simply assign a particular genre to one spot on any of these spectra.

Genre is a tool that helps to put works back into the context in which they would have been read in their own day. Rather than conceiving of genre as a set of rigid boxes in which to pigeonhole texts, Bakhtin's idea of genre as "preformed linguistic material" that carries with it a particular point of view or set of values may be more productive. A genre encapsulates a set of norms and values, or a horizon of expectations. How a fictional work uses its literary heritage determines to a large extent its possible meanings. In order to understand the text, then, one must know its context and the particular choices that it has made to invoke one set of predecessors and reject or ignore others. The fluidity of the boundaries between genres of Chinese fiction by the nineteenth century makes classification difficult,[92] but if one uses genre not merely to label works but to trace relationships to established conventions, it rewards the effort with critical insight. Reading *Green Peony* demonstrates the relevance of genre to literary criticism. Full appreciation of the novel depends on the reader recognizing the works and conventions it plays upon. Otherwise, the parody crucial to its aesthetic is lost.[93] Parody insists on reading in context, pointing out its debts to previous literature at the same time as it critiques the works to which it is indebted, in "a single dialectical gesture of recapitulation and repudiation, imitation and disillusion, continuity and rupture."[94] It provides us with another perspective on the corpus it invokes, and suggests its own literary history and criticism, if we follow its lead.

Appendix: Performance Genre Texts Grouped by Relationship to Novels

Lü mudan 綠牡丹 (Green peony)

Guban Bao Zi'an Lü mudan quan ge 古版鮑自安綠牡丹全歌 (Ancient edition of the complete song of Bao Zi'an and green peony). Ruiwen tang 瑞文堂. 28 fascicles. In the Chinese Academy of Social Sciences and Shoudu Tushuguan.

Guci chaoben Lü mudan 鼓詞抄本綠牡丹 (Green peony drum ballad manuscript). Reprint. Vol. 712, Gugong zhenben congkan: Qing dai Nan Fu yu Sheng Ping Shu juben yu dang'an. Haikou: Hainan Chubanshe, 2001. Reprint of manuscript in *Nan Fu* 南府 collection of Palace Museum entitled *Chaoben Lü mudan* 抄本綠牡丹.

Lü mudan 綠牡丹 (Green peony). Manuscript. 1 fascicle. In Beijing Library Rare Books Department.

Lü mudan 綠牡丹 (Green peony). Four episodes: Tao Hua Wu 桃花塢 (Peach Blossom Hollow), Si Wang Ting 四望亭 (The Pavilion for Gazing in Four Directions), 張王府: 四傑村下集 Zhang Wang Fu: Si Jie Cun xia ji (Zhang Wang Manor: Four Heroes Village, final episode), Da Nao Jiaxing Fu 大鬧嘉興府 (A Big Ruckus in Jiaxing County). Identified as Fujian songbooks by index. Harvard-Yenching Library microfilm of Academica Sinica collection of performance texts (中央研究院歷史語言研究所所藏俗曲). Reprinted in Wang Fansen 王汎森 et al, eds. *Su wenxue congkan* 俗文學叢刊, 368:333–406. Taibei: Zhongyang yanjiu lishi yuyan yanjiusuo, 2004.

Lü mudan guci 綠牡丹鼓詞 (Green peony drum ballad). Manuscript. 1 fascicle. Beijing: Xinglong Zhai, Guangxu period (1875–1911). In Beijing Normal University Library.

Lü mudan guci 綠牡丹鼓詞 (Green peony drum ballad). Shanghai: Jinshang tushu, 1905. In Dartmouth library and the Drama Research Academy of the Chinese Academy of Arts. Largely the same as the Nan Fu drum ballad. Completely different from the drum ballad text in Beijing Normal University.

Lü mudan quan ge 綠牡丹全歌 (Green peony complete song). Reprint. Chaozhou: Ruiwen tang, 1956.

Qun Ying Jie 群英傑 (The gathering of heroes)

The three editions below are reprints of the same text, in 4 volumes (*ji*) of 4 *juan* each (total 16 *juan*). None of them are clearly dated, though the Art Deco cover art on the Fudan University edition (published by Wu Gui Tang) suggests a Republican date.

Chu ji Qun Ying Jie 初集群英傑 (The first volume of the gathering of heroes). Guangzhou: Wu Gui Tang 五桂堂. In Fudan University library.

Erxu Qun Ying Jie quan ben nanyin 二續群英傑全本南音 (The nanyin complete edition of the second sequel to the gathering of heroes). Also includes the third sequel *San xu Qun Ying Jie quan ben nanyin* 三續群英傑全本南音 and fourth sequel *Si xu Qun Ying Jie quan ben nanyin* 四續群英傑全本南音. 11 fascicles total. In Beijing Normal University library.

Xinke qingchang da nanyin quan ben chu ji Qun Ying Jie 新刻清唱大南音全本初集群英傑 (The newly carved acapella giant nanyin complete edition of the first volume of the gathering of heroes). Also includes the second through fourth sequels. Foshan: Qin Xiang Ge. 16 fascicles total. In Shoudu Tushuguan.

Tianbao tu 天豹圖 (The Picture of Tianbao)

Da zi Tianbao tu zu ben quan zhuan 大字天寶圖足本全傳 (Large print original edition complete story of the picture of Tianbao). Shanghai: Daguan shuju. 10 fascicles, 57 chapters. In Shanghai Municipal Library.

Huitu Yingxiong qi yuan zhuan 繪圖英雄奇緣傳 (The illustrated story of the heroes' marvelous marriage destiny). Shanghai: Shi Wan Juan Lou, Guangxu (1875–1908). In Shanghai Municipal Library.

Shi Bixian 施必顯. 3 volumes. The second volume is titled *Tianbao tu* 天 豹 圖 (The picture of Tianbao), the third titled *Yingxiong hui* 英雄會 (The meeting of heroes). Identified as Fujian songbooks by index. Harvard microfilm of Academica Sinica collection of performance texts (中央研究院歷史語言研究所所藏俗曲).

Tianbao tu 天寶圖 (The picture of Tianbao). Daoguang 10 (1830). 10 volumes. Printed lute ballad. In Shoudu Tushuguan.

Tianbao tu tanci 天寶圖彈詞 (Tianbao lute ballad). Manuscript. Originally 6 fascicles, 50 chapters, of which 5 fascicles exist in 5 volumes. In Ma collection of Peking University Library.

Xinke tianbao tu 新刻天寶圖 (Newly carved picture of Tianbao). Jiezi yuan edition. Daoguang 26 (1846). 10 fascicles, 57 chapters. In Shanghai Municipal Library.

Xinke tianbao tu 新刻天寶圖 (Newly carved Picture of Tianbao). Tongzhi 8 (1869). 57 chapters. In the Drama Research Academy of the Chinese Academy of Arts.

Xinke zhenben tanci changkou Tianbao tu quan zhuan 新刻真本唱口天 豹 圖全傳 (Newly carved authentic lute ballad for singing the whole story of the picture of

Tianbao). Feichun Ge 飛春閣, Qianlong 41 (1776). 35 fascicles, 35 volumes. In Shoudu Tushuguan.

Xiuxiang Tianbao tu 繡像天寶圖 (*The Illustrated Picture of Tianbao*). Fan Chuan Wen Cheng Tang, Tongzhi 4 (1865). 10 fascicles, 57 chapters. In Shanghai Municipal Library.

Wanhua Lou 萬花樓 (*The Pavilion of Myriad Flowers*)

Guben Wanhua Lou quan ge 古本萬花樓全歌 (The original edition complete ballad of the Pavilion of Myriad Flowers). Chaozhou: Li Wanli. 12 fascicles.

Xinke Wanhua Lou Di Qing chushen quan ben 新刻萬花樓狄青出身全本 (Newly carved Pavilion of Myriad Flowers the complete story of Di Qing's background). Wu Gui Tang 五桂堂. *Nanyin* 南音 adaptation of novel. In Fudan University Humanities Library.

Notes

Chapter 1. Introduction

1. For the martial arts novel in the twentieth century, see John Christopher Hamm, *Paper Swordsmen: Jin Yong and the Modern Chinese Martial Arts Novel.*

2. Tong Shuozhi (Liang Yusheng), "Jin Yong Liang Yusheng he lun," 96.

3. While scholars agree that the ideals of the martial hero formed in antiquity, exactly which schools they owe their ideals to, or the relative proportions each school's philosophies play, is under dispute. See, for example, Tuo Bafeng, "Wuxia xiaoshuo yuanxing liubian de lunli jiyin," 58–64; and Chen Pingyuan, "Wuxia xiaoshuo yu zhongguo wenhua," 69–75. Luo Lichun presents a class-based argument, suggesting that the martial heroes, inspired by Moism, came from the lower classes and offered resistance to the three teachings (Confucianism, Buddhism, and Daoism) of the upper classes. See Luo Lichun, "Wuxia xiaoshuo yu minzu wenhua," 395–400.

4. James J. Y. Liu, *The Chinese Knight-errant*, 4–6.

5. Both Western knights and Chinese *xia* "uphold justice and unselfishly protect the poor and weak;" "preferring death to dishonour," stressing generosity, and insisting on "mutual faith and truthfulness." For more on similarities and differences, see ibid., 195–97.

6. Tuo Bafeng, "Wuxia xiaoshuo yuanxing liubian de lunli jiyin," 59–61.

7. Chen Pingyuan criticizes James J. Y. Liu's study and the thematic approach in general by suggesting that it is interested more in the cultural significance of martial arts in literature than in literary history. See Chen Pingyuan, *Qiangu wenren xiake meng*, 186. He also notes that any listing of attributes will necessarily be partial, colored by the concerns of the study and the period covered. Ibid., 1–2.

8. Idem, *Xiaoshuo shi: Lilun yu shijian*, 217.

9. Andrew H. Plaks, "Full-length Hsiao-Shuo and the Western Novel: A Generic Reappraisal," *Xin ya xueshu jikan. New Asia Academic Bulletin* 1 (1978): 170. See also Patrick Hanan, "The Early Chinese Short Story: A Critical Theory in Outline," *Harvard Journal of Asiatic Studies* 27 (1967): 176–77. As in the West, using the standard of realism for Chinese novels is not without problems. Whole categories of long fiction in China do not fit the definitions by their subject or style or both. This

causes critics to reassign novels not dealing with the normal sphere of human experience to other generic types (romance, allegory, or the fantastic), "thus reserving the term novel for 'domestic fiction' such as Chin P'ing Mei and Hung-lou meng." Plaks, "Full-length Hsiao-Shuo and the Western Novel," 169. Even the canonical Chinese novels present challenges to being understood through the lens of realism. C. T. Hsia holds six of the masterworks up to this standard in turn, and finds most wanting. Hsia says that in the absence of tradition of literary realism, *Shuihu zhuan* fails from historical undernourishment, and the heteroglossia in *Jin Ping Mei* strikes him as tampering with realism. See *The Classic Chinese Novel,* 75–76, 82–85, 166, 170. Of course, one could take the opposite tack and see in these novels a new space for fiction and a realization of the novel's dialogic potential. See Martin Weizong Huang, "Dehistoricization and Intertextualization," especially 55–56; and David Tod Roy's introduction to his translation of *The Plum in the Golden Vase or, Chin P'ing Mei,* I:xliii-xlv.

10. Ban Gu, "Yi wen zhi," translated by Laura Hua Wu in "From Xiaoshuo to Fiction: Hu Yinglin's Genre Study of Xiaoshuo," 340.

11. Laura Hua Wu, "From *Xiaoshuo* to Fiction," 342.

12. Martin Huang, "Dehistoricization and Intertextualization," 51.

13. Y. W. Ma, "The Chinese Historical Novel: An Outline of Themes and Contexts," 278.

14. C. T. Hsia, "The Military Romance: A Genre of Chinese Fiction," 339. The seminal work for this genre was the Yang Family Generals saga *Yang Jia Fu yanyi,* a version of which was published in the mid-sixteenth century. Ibid., 350–51.

15. Martin Huang, "Dehistoricization and Intertextualization," 45–68.

16. Indeed, C. T. Hsia argues that both tendencies are apparent even in *pinghua,* "plain tales" that are often seen as the forerunner of the novel in China. See "The Military Romance," 346.

17. See, for example, Mao Zonggang's comments on the superiority of *Sanguo yanyi* to ordinary novels (*baiguan*) in Chen Xizhong et al., ed., *Sanguo yanyi huiping ben,* 7; for an English translation see David Rolston, ed., *How to Read the Chinese Novel,* 162. The most influential commentator on *Jin Ping Mei,* Zhang Zhupo, explicitly notes this tendency to elevate one work by deriding others; see ibid., 221.

18. The definition of *xiaoshuo* that concerned bibliographers, even in the late Ming, excluded the vernacular novels. See Laura Hua Wu, "From Xiaoshuo to Fiction," 367–69.

19. See Chen Pingyuan, *Xiaoshuo shi: Lilun yu shijian,* 188–89. The term *wuxia* also appears in the title of a collection published in 1916, *Wuxia congtan.*

20. Xue Baokun, introduction to Wang Hailin, *Zhongguo wuxia xiaoshuo shilüe,* 1. Indeed, Lu Xun may have been the first literary critic to use the term "martial arts" (*wuxia*). It appeared in a lecture by Lu Xun entitled "Shanghai wenyi zhi yi pi," Aug. 12, 1931, at the Shehui Kexue Yanjiuhui. See *Lu Xun quanji,* 4:303.

21. Lu Xun, *Zhongguo xiaoshuo shilüe,* 216. The neat parallel between the "bifurcation" Lu Xun notes and that which Roger Chartier critiques in Western scholarship on other cultures calls Lu Xun's model into question. See Roger Chartier, *Forms and Meanings,*

85–87. In addition, culture before Lu Xun's posited bifurcation was hardly unified. For example, Anne E. McLaren's work on *Three Kingdoms* shows that in the Ming the "same" text reached different audiences in different versions. See "Ming Audiences and Vernacular Hermeneutics: The Uses of the 'Romance of the Three Kingdoms,'" 51–80.

22. Lu Xun, *Zhongguo xiaoshuo shilüe*, 225, 219.

23. Liu dates *Shi Gong an* to 1798, the date of the preface; the earliest dated edition listed in Ōtsuka is from 1820. However, the date proves to be a copying error for 1830. Thus apparently the earliest extant dated edition is from 1825, although the preface suggests an edition was printed in 1798. See Han Cao, "*Shi Gong an* de kanxing niandai," *Gudian wenxue zhishi* 1 (1993): 98–99. Liu Yinbo, *Zhongguo wuxia xiaoshuo shi*, 221; cf. the entry for *Shi an qi wen* in Ōtsuka Hidetaka, *Chûgoku tsûzoku shôsetsu shomoku*, 169–71. Wang Hailin lists a number of novels, including *Shi Gong an* and *Green Peony*, as belonging to the genre of martial arts, but does not date them or discuss them in any detail. Wang Hailin, *Zhongguo wuxia xiaoshuo shilüe*, 99, 106.

24. Even the more recent studies by Liu Yinbo and Wang Hailin both spend a considerable amount of space debating the morality of various works. One example is Wang Hailin's response to the standard criticism of Qing martial arts novels as "counterrevolutionary." See his *Zhongguo wuxia xiaoshuo shilüe*, 99, 108–9. Another example is Liu Yinbo's discussion of the "positive and negative influence" of *Shi Gong an*, especially the discussion of Huang Tianba. See his *Zhongguo wuxia xiaoshuo shi*, 221–24. A brief article on *Green Peony* defends it against the generalization that martial arts novels are "the dregs of feudal society" by pointing out "progressive" elements of its ideology. See Zhu Hongbo, "Shilun *Lü mudan* de sixiang yiyun," *Ming Qing xiaoshuo yanjiu* no. 4 (1988): 163–73.

25. For dating and editions, see Ōtsuka Hidetaka, *Chûgoku tsûzoku shôsetsu shomoku*, 166–68; cf. Sun Kaidi, *Zhongguo tongsu xiaoshuo shumu*, 274. *Lü mudan*, rpt., Gu ben xiaoshuo jicheng, 5th ser., vol. 43 (Shanghai: Shanghai guji chubanshe, 1990). Unless otherwise specified, page references to *Green Peony* are to this reprint. The novel *Green Peony* was reprinted under several titles: *Si Wang Ting quan zhuan*, *Longtan Bao Luo qi shu*, *Xu fan Tang zhuan*, *Fan Tang hou zhuan*, and *Hong Bi yuan*.

26. E.g., Liu Yinbo, *Zhongguo wuxia xiaoshuo shi*, 219–21.

27. Wang lists *Ernü yingxiong zhuan*, *Green Peony*, and *Zheng Chun Yuan* among his examples of exceptions to the "court-case adventure," and says even *Xiao wuyi* (The little five brothers), a sequel to *San xia wu yi*, escapes the "cangue" of heroes grouped around a judge. See Wang Hailin, *Zhongguo wuxia xiaoshuo shilüe*, 107–8. Chen Pingyuan suggests that the premise of two separate streams combining is flawed, since court-case fiction and martial arts fiction were never completely independent before the nineteenth century. Chen Pingyuan, *Qiangu wenren xiake meng*, 44–46.

28. Patrick Hanan, "*Judge Bao's Hundred Cases* Reconstructed," 301.

29. Y. W. Ma, "*Kung-an* Fiction: A Historical and Critical Introduction," 214–21. For information on *Longtu's Court Cases* as an adaptation of an earlier collection of court-case tales, see Hanan, "*Judge Bao's Hundred Cases* Reconstructed," 323; and Y.W. Ma, "The Textual Tradition of Ming *Kung-an* Fiction: A Study of the *Lung-t'u kung-an*," 207–8. These tales were written in a vernacular that approaches classical language.

The court-case theme also developed independently in the form of vernacular short stories published in the early seventeenth century.

At around the same time, collections that purported to be actual cases were also published. See Ann Waltner, "From Casebook to Fiction: *Kung-an* in Late Imperial China," 281–89. The relationship between law and literature is explored in Robert E. Hegel and Katherine Carlitz, eds., *Writing and Law in Late Imperial China: Crime, Conflict, and Judgment*. Historical studies of actual court cases are a growing field; see, for example, Thomas Buoye, *Manslaughter, Markets, and Moral Economy*; Melissa Macauley, *Social Power and Legal Culture: Litigation Masters in Late Imperial China*; Matthew Sommer, *Sex, Law and Society in Late Imperial China*; and Janet M. Theiss, *Disgraceful Matters: The Politics of Chastity in Eighteenth-century China.*

30. Y. W. Ma traces the history of court-case fiction across a number of genres, including short, semi-classical tales and full-length novels. See his "*Kung-an* Fiction: A Historical and Critical Introduction," 200–59.

31. Liu Yinbo considers *Cases of Judge Shi* the earliest court-case adventure novel. Liu Yinbo, *Zhongguo wuxia xiaoshuo shi*, 221, 224. The preface to *Cases of Judge Shi* is dated 1798, but the earliest extant edition is from 1825.

32. Pu Tiandiao is a villain in *Shi Gong an* but a hero in *Green Peony*, which speaks to the differences between the two works. The fact that he appears in both is noted in Wen Qiji, introduction to *Lü mudan* (reprint, Shanghai: Shanghai guji, 1993), 2. The sharing of characters between novels is common in the court-case adventure novel in the Qing; *Shi Gong an* shares episodes and characters with *Peng Gong an* (Cases of Judge Peng) and *Yu Gong an* (Cases of Judge Yu), and *Yongqing shengping* (Forever celebrating peace) shares characters with *Peng Gong an*. See Liu Yinbo, *Zhongguo wuxia xiaoshuo shi*, 229, 232.

33. The language and sequence is often very similar to the scenes in which a judge holds court in other novels, including *Cases of Judge Shi.*

34. The interpolation of the judge strikes Wen Qiji as a superficial combination of elements. He says *Sanxia wuyi* was the first novel to shift the focus from court-case fiction to martial arts, but *Green Peony* can be considered a step in this direction. See his introduction to *Lü mudan* (Shanghai: Shanghai guji, 1993), 2–3.

35. Chen Pingyuan, *Xiaoshuo shi,* 211. See also Lu Xun, *Zhongguo xiaoshuo shilüe,* 120.

36. Mikhail Mikhailovich Bakhtin, *The Dialogic Imagination*, 288–92.

37. John Christopher Hamm notes the distinction between episodic court-case novels and novels with more closed plots in his entry on "Wu-hsia hsiao-shuo" in *The Indiana Companion to Traditional Chinese Literature*, 2:189.

38. For instance, in *Green Peony* the villain takes his friend's beautiful wife as his own mistress, a motif central to stories 2, 65, and 66 in *Longtu gongan. Longtu gongan*, 1.4a-7a; 4.15b-19a; 4.19a-21b. In another instance, the hero in *Green Peony* comes into conflict with local bullies over a woman, a motif found in story number 98 in *Longtu gongan*, 5.41b-44a. Another motif the martial romance shares with *Longtu gongan* is the abuse of power by blue bloods. See stories 22, 61, and 62 in ibid., 2.19a-21a, 4.3b-7b, 4.7b-11a. Cf. Y. W. Ma, "Themes and Characterization in the *Lung-t'u kung-an*," 179–202.

The relationship between *Cases of Judge Shi* and *Longtu's Court Cases* is even closer. For example, *Cases of Judge Shi* tells how the judge rights injustice for a man who is dumb, as does story number 48 in *Longtu gongan*, 3.21b-22b. See *Shi an qi wen*, Guben xiaoshuo jicheng (Shanghai: Shanghai guji chubanshe, [1990]), 89–92, 110–15, 118–20. The preface to *Cases of Judge Shi* also borrows heavily from the preface to *Longtu's Court Cases*, often using the exact words but substituting Judge Shi's name for Judge Bao's. This suggests once again how strong a model the collection *Longtu's Court Cases* was for later works in the court-case genre. See Ding Xigen, *Zhongguo lidai xiaoshuo xu ba ji*, 3:1602, 1610–11.

39. Chen Pingyuan, *Qiangu wenren xiake meng*, 46–47.

40. For *chantefables* on *Green Peony*, see appendix. A drum ballad on *Shi Gong an* is listed in Academica Sinica, "Zhongyang Yanjiu Yuan lishi yuyan yanjiu suo suo cang suqu zongmu mulu" (Harvard-Yenching Library, photocopy), 21.

41. A *zidishu* by Yi Geng includes a line in which someone orders copies of *Green Peony* and *Cases of Judge Shi* from Baiben Zhang, so as to surpass the famous storyteller Shi Yukun. Quoted in Guan Dedong, "Shiyin *Qing Menggu Chewangfu cang quben* xu," in Liu Liemao, ed. *Chewangfu quben yanjiu*, 483.

42. In addition, one of the most famous court-case adventure novels, *The Three Heroes and Five Sworn Brothers*, traces back indirectly to oral storytelling. It is closely based on an account recorded from listening to storytelling and published as *Aural Record of Longtu* (*Longtu Erlu*). See Susan Blader, "Introduction" in *Tales of Magistrate Bao and His Valiant Lieutenants*, xiv, xvii-xxiii. A manuscript *chantefable* text entitled *Longtu Gong an* approximates the form of storytelling more closely. See Susan Blader, "A Critical Study of San-hsia Wu-yi and Relationship to the Lung-t'u Kung-an Song-book" (unpublished doctoral thesis, University of Pennsylvania, 1977).

43. They both misread the topic "Rhyme-prose on the peony," and one of the villains does not realize it when a poem ghost-written for him mocks him. Wu Bing, *Lü mudan*, edited by Luo Sining (Shanghai: Shanghai guji chubanshe, 1985), 6, 92, 99, 120.

44. The man traveling to marry his fiancée is one of the plots that structures *Qun Ying Jie* and also appears briefly in *Green Peony*. In nearly every novel in the group the woman narrowly escapes abduction or marriage to another man: An imposter tries to marry the fiancée in *Qun Ying Jie*, *Zheng Chun Yuan*, and *Da Han san he mingzhu bao jian quan zhuan*; the villain tries to force another's fiancée to marry him in *Yun Zhong Yan san nao Tai Ping Zhuang*, and *Da Han san he mingzhu baojian quan zhuan*; and in *Shan e tu* and *Li he jian lianzi ping*, the fiancée's family refuses to recognize her fiancé when he has come down in the world, and betrothe her to another. In almost every case the girl flees (often disguised as a man).

45. I am grateful to Chen Jianhua for this way of formulating it. Lin Chen suggests something similar; cf. Lin Chen, *Mingmo Qingchu xiaoshuo shulu* (Shenyang: Chunfang wenyi, 1988), 83.

46. Ibid., 74–79.

47. Cao Xueqin, *Honglou meng*, 1:5. For an English translation see Cao Xueqin, *The Story of the Stone*, trans. David Hawkes, 1:50.

48. *Green Peony*, 201. The title for many adaptations of *Green Peony* to the drama, *Hong Bi yuan* (The marriage destiny of [Luo] Hong[xun] and [Hua] Bi[lian]), suggests its success as a romance. This title was also used for at least one edition of the novel in the Republican era, *Xiaqing xiaoshuo Hong Bi yuan* (n.p., n.d.).

49. *Zhong yi Shuihu zhuan* (Suzhou: Yuan Wuya, 1611?) in the Harvard-Yenching Library. In the tales of the Yang Family Generals, the woman warrior Mu Guiying starts a battlefield romance. See *Nan Bei Song zhizhuan*, reprinted in Guben xiaoshuo jicheng (Shanghai: Shanghai guji, [1990]), 796–97; and *Yang Jia Fu yanyi* (Suzhou, 1606), reprinted in Guben xiaoshuo jicheng (Shanghai: Shanghai guji, [1990]), 392–95.

50. C. T. Hsia, "The Military Romance," 373.

51. Ailian jushi preface, in Ding Xigen, ed., *Zhongguo lidai xiaoshuo xu ba ji*, 3:1539.

52. Wen Qiji makes this observation in his introduction to a reprint edition of *Lü mudan*, 1. For the novels on the Tang, see Yuanhu yusou, *Shuo Tang yanyi quan zhuan*, Guben xiaoshuo jicheng, 4th ser., vol. 126–27 (Shanghai: Shanghai guji, [1990]). *Shuo Tang yanyi* has a preface dated 1736. See Sun Kaidi, *Zhongguo tongsu xiaoshuo shumu*, 48; and Ōtsuka Hidetaka, *Chûgoku tsûzoku shôsetsu shomoku*, 207–9. *Yishuo Fan Tang quan zhuan* was published in 1753. See Ōtsuka Hidetaka, *Chûgoku tsûzoku shôsetsu shomoku*, 214–16. *Yishuo Fan Tang quan zhuan*, Guben xiaoshuo jicheng (rpt. Shanghai: Shanghai guji, [1990]).

53. Y. W. Ma, "The Chinese Historical Novel," 281.

54. C. T. Hsia, "The Military Romance," 339. Ji Dejun suggests there are other formal models for historical novels based on alternate forms of history, such as biography. See Ji Dejun, *Ming Qing lishi yanyi xiaoshuo yishu lun*, 9, 14–17.

55. Y. W. Ma, "The Chinese Historical Novel," 278.

56. Ibid., 287.

57. Ji Dejun, *Ming Qing lishi yanyi xiaoshuo yishu lun*, 15.

58. For these reasons Hanan excludes those narratives from consideration as novels. See his "Early Chinese Short Story," 182–83.

59. C. T. Hsia, "Military Romance," 339.

60. C. T. Hsia sees *Shuo Tang* as burlesque, and Robert Hegel has shown it to be parody, replacing the literati values of its forbear *Romance of the Sui and Tang* with crude caricatures. See C. T. Hsia, "The Military Romance," 379; and Robert Hegel, "Rewriting the Tang: Humor, Heroics and Imaginative Reading," in *Snakes' Legs*, edited by Martin W. Huang, 159–89.

61. The hero is usually idealized as "braver and more virtuous than his historic counterpart." C. T. Hsia, "The Military Romance," 344.

62. C. T. Hsia, "The Military Romance," 358, 371–78. One of the few women warriors to appear in the historical record is Yang Miaozhen, but although aspects of her story resemble the fictions of the women warriors, her legend was hardly developed in fiction or drama. See Pei-Yi Wu, "Yang Miaozhen: A Woman Warrior in Thirteenth-century China," *Nan nü* vol. 4 no. 2, 2002: 137–169.

63. *The Tale of the Tang* generated a sequel, *Shuo Tang hou zhuan* (Later tale of the Tang); a third novel, *Yishuo Hou Tang zhuan sanji* (Another tale of the later Tang, third collection) picks up where *Later Tale of the Tang* left off; and *Yishuo Fan Tang quan zhuan* (Another tale of rebellion against the Tang, 1753 preface) continues *Later Tang Third Collection* in turn. All four are tied to one man, Rulian jushi, who edited *Shuo Tang hou Zhuan* and signed prefaces to the other three novels. For information on editions, see Ōtsuka Hidetaka, *Chûgoku tsûzoku shôsetsu shomoku*, 207–16.

64. *Green Peony* was published under the title *Fan Tang quan zhuan xiuxiang Lü mudan quan zhuan* (The complete tale of rebellion against the Tang: Green peony) as early as 1831, thus recognizing its ties to the novel *Yishuo Fan Tang quan zhuan* (Another tale of rebellion against the Tang).

65. The term "paraleptic continuation" is from Gérard Genette, *Palimpsests: Literature in the Second Degree*, 177.

66. James J. Y. Liu, *The Chinese Knight-errant*, 81–82.

67. Chen Pingyuan, *Qiangu wenren xiake meng*, 47, 49–50. Interestingly, James J. Y. Liu includes *Shuihu zhuan* in the category of martial arts (he calls it a "chivalric romance"). He does not seem to apply his own criteria to this case. James J. Y. Liu, *The Chinese Knight-errant*, 108–16. Liu Yinbo includes it as well in his *Zhongguo wuxia xiaoshuo shi*, 162–77.

68. *Green Peony*, 582–83.

69. For example, the *nanyin* from Fujian on *Green Peony* center around three scenes: the woman warrior's exhibition of her martial skills at Peach Blossom Knoll, her attempts to catch a monkey on a rooftop at Four Gazes Pavilion, and the martial arts tournament. See Wang Fansen et al., eds., *Su wenxue congkan*, 368: 333–406. Those scenes were also widespread in drama; see Ji Lu, ed., *Si Wang Ting quan zhuan*, Chuantong xiqu quyi yanjiu cankao ziliao congshu, 375–79.

70. Sun Kaidi, *Zhongguo tongsu xiaoshuo shumu*, 5–6, 11–13. Sun uses the term *jiangshi*, which usually refers to storytelling on historical subjects, to refer to the historical novel.

71. Ferdinand Brunetière, *L'évolution des genres dans l'histoir de la littérature*, quoted in Heather Dubrow, *Genre*, 79.

72. Dubrow, *Genre*, 116.

Chapter 2. Formation of a Formula

1. Since I am suggesting a roughly chronological progression, a word about dating is in order. While it is always possible that earlier editions of these novels will be found, I am encouraged by the fact that the dating in general is corroborated by internal evidence within the novels. The language, content, and structure seem to be more or less consistent within a particular chronological group.

2. *Zhenben Tianbao tu quan zhuan* (Feichun ge, 1776), Shoudu Tushuguan in Beijing. Hereafter this work will be cited as *Tianbao Lute Ballad*. The title on the first page of each *juan*, *Xin ke zhenben tanci changkou Tianbao tu quan zhuan* (Newly carved

authentic lute ballad for singing the complete story of the picture of Tianbao), explicitly identifies the work as a lute ballad. See appendix for a list of other ballads related to *Tianbao tu*.

3. Li Dou, *Yangzhou huafang lu*, 258.

4. [*Guci*] *chaoben Lü mudan*, (Green peony manuscript [drum ballad], n.d.) survives in the collection of the office responsible for dramatic entertainment for the palace, the Nan Fu or Shengping Shu. When established in the beginning in the Kangxi era it was called the Nan Fu, but after reorganization in 1827 its name changed to Shengping Shu. *Guci chaoben Lü mudan*, reprinted in Gugong zhenben congkan: Qing dai Nan Fu yu Sheng Ping Shu juben yu dangan, vol. 712. References to *Green Peony Drum Ballad* are to this edition.

5. On women's *tanci*, see Hu Siao-chen "Literary *Tanci*"; and Ellen Widmer, *The Beauty and the Book*, 14, 71–101, 285–89.

6. Nancy Hodes, "Strumming and Singing the 'Three Smiles Romance': A Study of the *Tanci* Text," 9.

7. On the lute ballad (*tanci*), see Zheng Zhenduo, *Zhongguo su wenxue shi*, 2:352–81. The lute ballad as a form must have been well established by the late Qianlong period; not only are there a number of printed lute ballad texts from this era, but the first Suzhou lute balladeers' guild was also founded in 1776. See Hodes, "Strumming and Singing the 'Three Smiles Romance,'" 6.

On printed *nanyin* see Tan Zhengbi, *Mu yu ge, Chaozhou ge xu lu*, 5–7, 22–28.

As for the drum ballad (*guci*), the prolific vendor of performance texts, Baiben Zhang, set up shop in Beijing during the Qianlong era, and drum ballads were a significant category of his wares. See Cui Yunhua, *Shuzhai yu shufang zhi jian: Qingdai zidishu yanjiu*, 149–50. Scholars have paid relatively little attention to drum ballad texts. The main discussion of written drum ballads concerns whether the earliest extant drum ballad texts were literati imitations. See Hu Shiying, *Huaben xiaoshuo gailun*, 2:373; Zhao Jingshen, *Guci xuan*, 3; and Ni Zhongzhi, *Zhongguo quyi shi*, 307–12.

8. Zheng Zhenduo, *Zhongguo su wenxue shi*, 2:397.

9. Perhaps a slight change in perspective would help us better understand these performance-related texts. Instead of looking for orality within the text and speculating on the degree to which these texts record an oral tradition, we might regard oral performance as conditioning their reading context. In this view, the particular tradition of oral performance invoked by each of these texts guides the reader to understand the text in light of that performance tradition, with which he or she was already familiar. Thus the characteristic use in *chantefable* texts of prose and verse, as well as themes and formulae reminiscent of oral performance, establishes a horizon of expectations that cues the reader in to how to read and interpret the text. See Anne E. McLaren, *Chinese Popular Culture and Ming Chantefables*, 38; and Franz Bäuml, "Medieval Texts and the Two Theories of Oral-Formulaic Composition: A Proposal for a Third Theory," 41–43.

10. *Tianbao tu* (Xiamen: Xiamen Fengsheng shufang, 1814). See also *Tianbao tu* (reprint, Shanghai: Shanghai guji chubanshe, 1995). All page references are to this reprint. For information on editions, see Ōtsuka Hidetaka, *Chûgoku tsûzoku shôsetsu*

shomoku, 105. Its similarity to a later lute ballad is noted in Jiangsu Sheng Shehui Kexue Yuan Ming Qing xiaoshuo yanjiu zhongxin wenxue yanjiusuo, ed., *Zhongguo tongsu xiaoshuo zongmu tiyao*, 620.

11. *Tianbao tu*, 123; cf. *Tianbao Lute Ballad* 6.9b.

12. *Tianbao tu*, 12; cf. *Tianbao Lute Ballad*, 1.7b.

13. *Tianbao Lute Ballad*, 2.7ab.

14. *Tianbao tu*, 28–30. For other similar figures of speech preserved in the novel, see *Tianbao Lute Ballad*, 3.11a, 4.4b, 6.4a; cf. *Tianbao tu*, 65, 71, 112.

15. Zhang Jun, *Qingdai xiaoshuo shi*, 324.

16. Inconsistencies in the text due to omissions also indicate that the lute ballad was the prior text. There are no glaring inconsistencies in the novel *Tianbao tu*, but in one case the maid inexplicably knows the hero is hungry. See *Tianbao Lute Ballad*, 6.9a, 6.10a; cf. *Tianbao tu*, 121, 124.

17. For example, two parallel lines of verse in the lute ballad are kept as parallel lines of monologue in the novel: see *Tianbao tu*, 94, and *Tianbao Lute Ballad*, 5.5a.

18. *Tianbao Lute Ballad*, 6.10b.

19. *Tianbao tu*, 124.

20. See Patrick Hanan, "The Early Chinese Short Story: A Critical Theory in Outline," 173–75. On this "simulated context" of storytelling in vernacular fiction, see Hanan, "The Making of *The Pearl-Sewn Shirt* and *The Courtesan's Jewel Box*," 136.

21. Hanan, "The Early Chinese Short Story," 174.

22. For example, *Tianbao Lute Ballad*, 1.2a-3a and *Tianbao tu*, 1–2. In this case the lute ballad allows the character to introduce himself (as he would in drama), while the novel's narrator gives his background in the third person. Nancy Hodes notes the self-introduction of characters in both of the performance-related lute ballad texts she studies. See Hodes, "Strumming and Singing,'" 159–60, 193–200. For more about the differing aesthetics of the *chantefable* and the novel, see Margaret Baptist Wan, "The *Chantefable* and the Novel: The Cases of *Lü mudan* and *Tianbao tu*."

23. Sun Kaidi, *Zhongguo tongsu xiaoshuo shumu*, 274.

24. I suspect that the *Green Peony Drum Ballad* manuscript in the palace collection is a copy of a printed text. At the beginning of each fascicle, the small title just before the text begins reads *Xiuxiang Lü mudan* or *Huitu Lü mudan* (Illustrated Green Peony). Since there are no illustrations, and such a title is unusual for a manuscript but conventional for printed works, it suggests a printed text may have been its source.

25. *Green Peony Drum Ballad*, 174. Cf. *Green Peony*, 3.

26. *Green Peony*, 434–35.

27. *Green Peony Drum Ballad*, 294.

28. *Green Peony Drum Ballad*, 176 and 179, respectively. *Ba* must be followed by some kind of verb complement to be grammatical. See Liu Yuehua et al., *Shiyong xiandai Hanyu yufa*, 469–71.

29. *Green Peony Drum Ballad*, 278; *Green Peony*, 357.

30. *Green Peony Drum Ballad*, 325. Cf. *Green Peony*, 500–501.

31. The use of verse to depict emotion is not unheard of in vernacular fiction. However, in the most famous example, *Jin Ping Mei*, songs rather than poems serve this purpose. See Patrick Hanan, "Sources of the *Chin P'ing Mei*," 60–62.

32. Liu Yinbo, *Zhongguo wuxia xiaoshuo shi*, 244.

33. For example, *Xiyou ji*, 3:908.

34. *Green Peony Drum Ballad*, 205.

35. *Green Peony*, 91–93.

36. *Green Peony*, 228.

37. This is not necessarily the case with all martial arts novels. One of the most famous examples, *The Three Heroes and Five Sworn Brothers*, traces back indirectly to oral storytelling. It is closely based on an account recorded from listening to storytelling and published as *Aural Record of Longtu* (*Longtu Erlu*). See Susan Blader, "Introduction" in *Tales of Magistrate Bao and His Valiant Lieutenants*, xiv, xvii-xxiii; and idem., "A Critical Study of San-hsia Wu-yi and Relationship to the Lung-t'u Kung-an Songbook." The preface to *Yongqing shengping* (Forever celebrating peace, 1892) states that it is recorded from memories of storytelling. See Ding Xigen, *Zhongguo lidai xiaoshuo xu ba ji*, 3:1559.

38. Including lute ballads (*tanci*), Yangzhou storytelling (*Yangzhou pinghua*), and drum ballads (*guci*).

39. *Shan e tu*, Gu ben xiaoshuo jicheng, vol. 181 (reprint, Shanghai: Shanghai guji, [1990]). *Shan e tu* is not dated. See Sun Kaidi, *Zhongguo tongsu xiaoshuo shumu*, 273.

40. *Tianbao tu*, 9–10.

41. *Shan e tu*, 117–18.

42. *Shan e tu*, 35; cf. *Green Peony*, 1.

43. *Shan e tu*, 59–60. The absence of dialogue markers is translated here as indirect speech, but is actually closer to dialogue in drama.

44. *Green Peony*, 15–16.

45. Ibid., 18–19. Cf. *Shan e tu*, 63–64.

46. *Green Peony*, 22–23.

47. *Shan e tu*, 65–66.

48. Ibid., 66–69, 76–90. The whole trial scene is an inversion of justice, but it also introduces a major martial character. The villain is the reverse image of the judge; he is given the power to report traitors but uses it to his own ends. The first time the villain Li Lei abuses his power and rapes two women, he is taken to court. He not only convinces his superior that he is innocent but uses his position to arrange for a bandit to be freed. Just like the judge in *Longtu gongan*, the villain is impressed with the defendant's looks, so he finds a way to help him. *Shan e tu*, 83–85. Li Lei is told that the bandit, nicknamed Robber King Chong, gave himself up. Li Lei meets with him and tells him he can arrange for him to be freed. Chong then lies to the judge that he was framed and is released. *Shan e tu*, 90. Deceit rather than truth comes out in the court.

49. *Shan e tu*, 653–70.

50. *Tianbao tu*, 28–36.

51. *Green Peony*, 53–54.

52. *Tianbao tu*, 38, 45, 47; *Green Peony*, 59, 63, 66–67.

53. *Tianbao tu*, 52.

54. Ibid., 56–57.

55. Liangyan Ge considers a similar phenomenon typical of the oral provenance of *The Water Margin*. Liangyan Ge, *Out of the Margins: The Rise of Chinese Vernacular Fiction*, 64–100.

56. Patrick Hanan, "*Judge Bao's Hundred Cases* Reconstructed," 317. Although there are certain similarities between Western detective fiction and Chinese court-case fiction, it is important to be aware of their differences. As Y. W. Ma notes, "Didactic teachings, interventions of the supernatural, and solutions reached by coincidence, three of the most forbidden taboos in Western detective literature, for example, are not just omnipresent but, more often than not, are of paramount importance in *kung-an* stories, while at the same time crimes (murders in particular), criminals, and logical detection of crimes, which are indispensible components of Western detective literature, are not absolutely essential in this Chinese genre." Y. W. Ma, "Themes and Characterization in the *Lung-t'u kung-an*," 179.

The single largest group of criminals is composed of the privileged sons of high officials, the officials themselves, and the wealthy in general. Eunuchs also appear as criminals, but they are a relatively small group in the *Longtu gongan*. Y. W. Ma, "Themes and Characterization in the *Lung-t'u kung-an*," 195–97. Most of the villains in the martial romance are either spoiled sons of high officials or eunuchs.

57. For example, in story number 2 a woman and her husband are being held captive in a monastery (the monks have trapped the husband under a bell). When Judge Bao arrives in the area, he dreams of Guanyin leading him to a bell. He finds the man and wife and rescues them. Even in this case, two crimes (kidnapping and rape) have already been committed before another crime (murder) is prevented. See *Longtu gongan*, 1.4a-7a.

58. Examples include stories 2, 3, 4, 7, 11, 24, and 40 in *Longtu gongan*, 1.4a-7a, 1.7a-11a, 1.11a-17a, 1.28a-32a, 1.39a-42b, 2.23a-24b, 3.7a-8b. Hanan notes, "[I]njustices announce themselves through dreams, by whirlwinds, [and] by the behavior of animals and birds." See Hanan, "*Judge Bao's Hundred Cases* Reconstructed," 315.

59. Y. W. Ma, "Themes and Characterization," 201.

60. Idem, "*Kung-an* Fiction: A Historical and Critical Introduction," 207.

61. Much martial material is inserted into *Shan e tu*, but it almost never comes to a conclusion on its own. The first hero to confront the villain Li Lei dies; the second battle also has casualties; and afterward the martial heroes are dependent on immortals to save them. In chapter 25 the villain's retainer and a martial hero match skills; the retainer recognizes the hero as his sworn brother and martial "classmate" (*shi xiong*) but refuses to help the hero because he must be loyal to Li Lei for recognizing his worth. *Shan e tu*, 509–10.

62. Martial adventures can also be sandwiched within a chain of crime, mistrial, and justice.

63. Even a court-case novel such as *Shi Gong an* follows the general structure of court-case tales in that the crime is usually a fait accompli before the judge or any of his entourage is called in.

64. There are a few examples of this narrative method in the early stories in *Longtu gongan*; however, even in the Chinese court-case tradition this narrative method is very unusual. Stories number 24, 48, and 73 are examples of this style of narration in *Longtu gongan*. See *Longtu gongan*, 2.23a-24b, 3.21b-22b, 4.32a-33b. Y. W. Ma attributes this narrative style to Pu Songling, much later. Y. W. Ma, "Kung-an Fiction," 233–35.

65. *Tianbao tu*, 405. Besides the judge, several other major characters are not introduced until the second half of the book, including the title character. Moreover, three characters who have been central to the action of the first half of the book die late in the first half (chapter 18) or early in the second half (chapter 23). This discontinuity in characters significantly weakens the structure of the novel. Any unity of structure *Tianbao tu* has is a result of a feud that strings together nested grievances and revenge. After the initial disaster with the woman warrior Shi Bixia described above, the villain Hua Zineng's interest turns to revenge rather than abducting women.

66. For example, the emperor gives Judge Tian a precious sword and the right to pass judgment, including executions (*xian kan hou zou*). *Tianbao tu*, 405. This motif circulated in fiction in the fifteenth century; see Anne McLaren, *Chinese Popular Culture and Ming Chantefables*, 180.

67. This fluidity of role is played upon in *Green Peony*; see chapter 4.

68. *Shan e tu*, 93–94; *Tianbao tu*, 281–86. Despite the heavy use of the supernatural as a linking device in *The Chart of Good and Evil*, a wonderful scene in chapter 35 negates its importance. Judge Tang prays at Guandi Temple and asks why villains like Li Lei are allowed to persist. The statue moves "as if to say" it has jurisdiction only over the netherworld; what happens on earth is the officials' affair. *Shan e tu*, 725.

69. Chen Pingyuan, *Qiangu wenren xiake meng*, 44, 114.

70. For the dating of *Qun Ying Jie*, see Ōtsuka Hidetaka, *Chûgoku tsûzoku shôsetsu shomoku*, 96–97. References below will be to *Qun Ying Jie*, Guben xiaoshuo jicheng (reprint, Shanghai: Shanghai guji, [1990]).

The first edition of *Wanhua Lou* was published in Guangzhou by Changqing Tang in 1808. See C. T. Hsia's discussion on dating this novel in "The Military Romance," 384–85. Cf. Ōtsuka Hidetaka, *Chûgoku tsûzoku shôsetsu shomoku*, 234–35. References below will be to Li Yutang, *Wanhua Lou*, Guben xiaoshuo jicheng (reprint, Shanghai: Shanghai guji, [1990]).

For information on dating and editions of *Zheng Chun Yuan* see Sun Kaidi, *Zhongguo tongsu xiaoshuo shumu*, 212; and Ōtsuka Hidetaka, *Chûgoku tsûzoku shôsetsu shomoku*, 102–4. References below will be to *Zheng Chun Yuan*, Guben xiaoshuo jicheng (reprint, Shanghai: Shanghai guji, [1990]).

71. Any classification is somewhat arbitrary, and there will always be works that do not fit neatly into the categories established. *Qun Ying Jie* lies somewhere between

the first and second group of martial romances. Its use of the supernatural echoes the first group of martial romance novels, as does the tendency toward additive repetition in its structure. However, in other respects it fits squarely with the second group of martial romances.

72. Similar objections on the servant's part occur in *Sanxia wuyi* and oral performances of that cycle. See Susan Blader, "'Yan Chasan Thrice Tested': Printed Novel to Oral Tale," *CHINOPERL Papers* 12 (1983): 95–97.

73. *Qun Ying Jie*, 19–20. The servant who plots against his master on a trip also figures in *Tianbao tu*, 486–89. Cf. story number 42 in *Longtu gongan*, 3.10b-13a.

74. *Qun Ying Jie*, 41–45.

75. Hybridization is also apparent here. Even though their actions resemble those in court-case fiction, the parties are motivated by concern for their family reputation, a matter especially of concern in the scholar-beauty romance.

76. This would strike a note of realism in its day. As Melissa Macauley demonstrates, dead bodies were often used to accuse an enemy of murder. See her *Social Power and Legal Culture*, 4, 152, 195–214 passim, 258–59.

77. *Qun Ying Jie*, 159–67.

78. Ibid., 77–88. Cf. lists of villain's misdeeds in *Shan e tu*, 19–20; and *Tianbao tu*, 9–11.

79. Di Qing was mentioned as a subject for storytellers in *Zuiweng tanlu* by Luo Ye, and figured in early drama. See C. T. Hsia, "The Military Romance," 342.

80. This is similar to the standard background of a hero C. T. Hsia delineates for the military romance: "We are usually told of their astral origin, the unusual circumstances attending their birth and infancy, their tutelage under a human or celestial master, their acquisition of a steed and weapons which will stand them in good stead in their years of military glory, their sworn brotherhood with several lifelong friends and their persecution by villains enjoying powerful positions at court, and their initial participation in a public contest which attracts more than transient attention." Ibid., 359–60.

81. Some of Di Qing's misadventures resemble the youthful adventures of Qin Shubao in *Forgotten Tales of the Sui* (*Sui shi yiwen*), which was later incorporated into *Romance of the Sui and Tang*. See Robert E. Hegel, *The Novel in Seventeenth-century China*, 124–28.

82. C. T. Hsia also notes the importance of court-case fiction to this novel. See "The Military Romance," 389. While the effectiveness of suspense in this novel has been praised, actually it is very similar to court-case fiction in that the reader always knows ahead of time what will happen (even if the characters do not) but not exactly how it will happen.

83. Li Yutang, *Wanhua Lou*, 84.

84. Ibid., 89–90.

85. In the early martial romance novel *Green Peony*, the ceremony already acknowledges its source in *Three Kingdoms*, but there it is part of another motif: The

villain swears brotherhood to gain access to someone else's wife (see chapter 3, below). The other early martial romance novels presume sworn brotherhood but do not portray the ceremony.

86. The brotherhood is even given supernatural justification. In the opening chapter of *Zheng Chun Yuan*, a Daoist gives the martial hero Hao Luan three precious swords and sends him on a quest to find two other heroes on whom to confer the swords. While looking for heroes worthy of them, Hao Luan forms the brotherhood of nine.

87. *Zheng Chun Yuan*, 62 ("*Qingyuan yitong sheng si*"), and 181–82 ("*yuan tong sheng si*"). The third time the vows are not explicitly given. See ibid., 270–72. For the vow in *Three Kingdoms*, see Chen Xizhong, Song Xiangrui, and Lu Yuchuan, eds., *Sanguo yanyi huiping ben*, 6.

88. *Zheng Chun Yuan*, 310–48. He presents himself at court and willingly goes to jail to protect the innocent but also intentionally frames a doctor by planting a severed head in his house in order to secure medical care for his sworn brother who is ailing in jail. Later he clears the doctor.

89. Ibid., 863–64.

90. Ibid., 917–21.

91. Chen Pingyuan, *Xiaoshuo shi*, 217.

92. In both *Zheng Chun Yuan* and *Wanhua Lou*, enmity with a powerful official's son stems from a conflict in a pleasure pavilion. Each novel takes its name from this pleasure pavilion or the garden in which it stands, suggesting the importance of this episode to the overall structure of each novel. *Zheng Chun Yuan*, 16–45; *Wanhua Lou*, 91–101.

93. Y. W. Ma, "The Chinese Historical Novel," 284.

94. Ibid., 285.

95. *Zhongguo tongsu xiaoshuo zongmu* notes that *Qun Ying Jie* is similar to the content of a *nanyin* edited by Shaoyan Banxing Jushi, published by Foshan Wen Guang Lou. See Jiangsu Sheng Shehui Kexue Yuan Ming Qing xiaoshuo yanjiu zhongxin wenxue yanjiu suo, *Zhongguo tongsu xiaoshuo zongmu tiyao*, 708. For versions of *Qun Ying Jie* in the *nanyin* tradition, see appendix below. All of the *nanyin* versions listed are different editions (or volumes) of the same text. None of them are clearly dated, though the Art Deco cover art on the Fudan University edition (published by Wu Gui Tang) suggests a Republican date.

96. Tan Zhengbi, *Muyu ge, Chaozhou ge xulu*, 18, 69–70. The earliest surviving printed texts in this tradition are from late in the Kangxi reign period. Ibid., 5.

97. See *Xin ke Wanhua Lou Di Qing chushen quan ben*, Wu Gui Tang edition, vol. 1, 1.2a.

A different version, in the Fudan University Library and the Shanghai Municipal Library, bears no clear textual relationship to the novel: *Guben Wanhua Lou quan ge* (The ancient edition complete ballad of the Pavilion of Myriad Flowers), (Chaozhou: Li Wanli edition). For a list of songbook editions known to me, see appendix.

98. C. T. Hsia, "The Military Romance," 343.

99. For an overview of the scholarship, see Moss Roberts, "Afterword: About *Three Kingdoms*," in *Three Kingdoms: A Historical Novel*, 946–65. Cf. Boris Riftin, *Sanguo yanyi yu minjian wenxue*.

100. *Qun Ying Jie*, 261–82. Mu Guiying was the most popular figure to emerge from the Yang Family Generals saga; see C. T. Hsia, "The Military Romance," 375. There is a long tradition of magic warfare in the historical novel, at least as early as *Three Kingdoms*.

101. The title "Showing his evil the third time Monk Hua calls up demons; Once again commanded General Mu Guiying defeats the battle formation" precedes the central title of the ballad text *Si xu Qun Ying Jie* (Fourth sequel to the gathering of heroes). See appendix. The novel *Wanhua Lou* also circulated under titles that highlighted its legendary characters, such as *Wanhua Lou Yang Bao Di yanyi* (The Pavilion of Myriad Flowers: The tale of Yang, Bao, and Di), and *Hou xu Da Song Yangjiang wenwu quxing Bao Gong Di Qing chu zhuan* (Later sequel on the Great Song Dynasty: The beginning story of Yang Generals, civil and martial stars Judge Bao and Di Qing).

102. This case was circulating in the oral tradition as early as the fifteenth century. It survives in the Judge Bao *chantefables*, and is reprinted in *Bao gongan cihua bazhong*, Guben xiaoshuo congkan 22:4 (reprint, Beijing: Zhonghua, 1992), 1474–1510. Cf. Anne McLaren, *Chinese Popular Culture and Ming Chantefables*, 174–75. It also figures in the later martial arts novel *Sanxia wuyi*, which was derived indirectly from oral storytelling. C. T. Hsia sees the coincidence of this legend's appearance in both *Wanhua Lou* and *Sanxia wuyi* as "symbolic of the transition from one popular genre of fiction to another." See C. T. Hsia, "The Military Romance," 384.

103. C. T. Hsia, "The Military Romance," 384–85.

104. The commentary to *Wanhua Lou* points out its technique in terms similar to those used by the seminal fiction critic Jin Shengtan, such as "creating a thread for the later text" (*wei xiawen zuo zhenxian*), "leading in" (*yin*), and "reflecting" (*ying*). See *Wanhua Lou*, 18, 153, 180, 193, 220, and 880.

105. C. T. Hsia, "The Military Romance," 384, 390.

106. Ibid., 373, 378.

107. For information on editions, see Sun Kaidi, *Zhongguo tongsu xiaoshuo shumu*, 273–74; and Ōtsuka, *Chûgoku tsûzoku shôsetsu shomoku*, 171–72. Alternate titles for *San he jian* include: (*Xiuxiang*) *San he jian* (*quan zhuan*), *Xin ke San he mingzhu baojian quan zhuan*, and *Di shi caizi shu*. Calling a work a "book of genius" (*caizi shu*) was a tactic used by booksellers to elevate their wares by associating them with Jin Shengtan; but there was no fixed list, so other novels also called themselves *Di shi caizi shu*. See Li Mengsheng's preface to the Shanghai guji reprint of *Da Han san he mingzhu baojian quan zhuan*, Guben xiaoshuo jicheng (rpt. Shanghai: Shanghai guji chubanshe, [1990]), 1. Li Mengsheng also suggests *San he jian* was written by a hack writer and discusses the tendency from the mid-Qing on to "militarize" the scholar-beauty romance and insert immortals. See ibid. A performance genre text with a very similar title, *San he mingzhu fang lun*, bears no relation to the novel.

108. Examples of motifs that disappear in this third group include: the Daoist giving the hero a sword; the husband who is jailed so the villain can get his wife; the hero who is broken out of jail; and the list of the villain's evil deeds.

109. Whereas this group of novels is increasingly self-conscious about the material it draws from other works, understanding is no longer truly dependent on knowledge of other specific stories. In other words, the reader no longer needs knowledge of certain sagas (as opposed to generic conventions).

110. The flood motif also appears in the military romance on Yue Fei. See C. T. Hsia, "The Military Romance," 360.

111. *Yun Zhong Yan san nao Taiping Zhuang quan zhuan*, 113–16; *San he jian*, 25–26; *Da Ming quan zhuan Xiu qiu yuan*, 76.

112. The trend I have traced toward an ever more perfect happy ending may lend some credence to the modern critique of martial arts fiction as fairy tales for adults. I would suggest that despite the term's original derogatory intent, where it means little more than "escapist" literature, it can be a useful way of looking at the genre. John G. Cawelti suggests popular fiction deals with contemporary issues while allowing a space for wish fulfillment. See John G. Cawelti, "The Concept of Formula in the Study of Popular Literature," 87–92; and Cawelti, *The Six-Gun Mystique*. In this light I see the development from tragic elements to a happy ending as a significant move in the development of this popular genre.

113. It is not unheard of for a man to dress as a woman to get close to a woman he is interested in. It occurs in story number 28 of *Longtu gongan*, 2.29a-31a. It also occurs in several scholar-beauty romances. The difference here is that the hero is forced into it, and meeting the girl is a surprise.

114. The preface by Zhuhu Yuyin in the Daoguang 29 (1849) edition printed by Lang Huan shuwu claims to be printing an older manuscript. Cao Guangfu, the editor of the Shanghai guji modern reprint, credits Zhuhu Yuyin with reworking the novel, based on the statement in the preface that he read over and fixed (*yueding*) the text. See the preface by Cao Guangfu to *Yun Zhong Yan san nao Taiping Zhuang quan zhuan*, Guben xiaoshuo jicheng (rpt. Shanghai: Shanghai guji, 1990), 1. For information on editions see Sun Kaidi, *Zhongguo tongsu xiaoshuo shumu*, 212–13; and Ōtsuka Hidetaka, *Chûgoku tsûzoku shôsetsu shomoku*, 108.

115. *Yun Zhong Yan*, 259–65.

116. Heather Dubrow, *Genre*, 37.

117. *Shan e tu*, 20–23.

118. Ibid., 31–53. There is a venerable tradition of wise mothers in historical fiction who protest their sons' bad choices. One example is the episode in *Three Kingdoms* in which Cao Cao takes Xu Shu's mother hostage to win his allegiance. It works, but the mother lectures her son on his poor judgment in serving an unworthy lord just to save her life, and commits suicide to reprimand him. Chen Xizhong, ed., *Sanguo yanyi huiping ben*, 452–61.

119. *Shan e tu*, 494–96.

120. Robert Hegel notes the type of the bumbling *haohan* in *Sui shi yiwen* (Forgotten Tales of the Sui). See Hegel, *Novel in Seventeenth-century China*, 130, 132–37.

121. David Rolston makes a similar observation about this period in general. "The gradual disappearance of the near-mythic figures in early novels might be connected to a decline in the influence of oral culture." David Rolston, *Traditional Chinese Fiction and Fiction Commentary: Reading and Writing between the Lines*, 209 n1.

122. The text reads *haoyou*, but the context and parallelism suggests this is a misprint for *haodai*. *Qun Ying Jie*, 13. A parallel situation occurs in modern storytellers' versions of *Sanxia wuyi*. There the servant is not evil, he just cannot understand his master's noble gestures and finds himself in a practical predicament since funds are running out. See Blader, "'Yan Chasan Thrice Tested,'" 95–97.

123. *Tianbao tu*, 316.

124. Ibid., 628–30, 646.

125. Ibid., 697–98.

126. *Zheng Chun Yuan*, 259.

127. Ibid., 268, 270–71.

128. Ibid., 506. What follows is clearly reminiscent of the episode in *The Water Margin* when Shi Xiu jumps down from a tavern to save Lu Junyi. He is unsuccessful, though, and both are jailed. Chen Xizhong, Hou Zhongyi, and Lu Yuchuan, eds., *Shuihu zhuan hui ping ben*, 1143.

129. Zhang Jun, *Qingdai xiaoshuo shi*, 418–19. For edition information on *Da Ming quan zhuan Xiu qiu yuan*, see Sun Kaidi, *Zhongguo tongsu xiaoshuo shumu*, 213; and Ōtsuka Hidetaka, *Chûgoku tsûzoku shôsetsu shomoku*, 108.

130. *Sword and Vase* was published in 1842, but after the table of contents it gives the date Qianlong 51 (1786), so Sun Kaidi believes it to be a Qianlong work. See Sun Kaidi, *Zhongguo tongsu xiaoshuo shumu*, 200; cf. Ōtsuka Hidetaka, *Chûgoku tsûzoku shôsetsu shomoku*, 93. In the preface to the Shanghai guji reprint of *Li he jian lianzi ping*, Liu Yucai concurs; cf. *Li he jian lianzi ping*, Guben xiaoshuo jicheng (Shanghai: Shanghai guji chubanshe, 1990), 1.

Sword and Vase shares some characteristics with the first group of martial romances, including use of Yangzhou dialect and particular motifs and verses, while its tighter structure and play on the reader's expectations correspond with later stages. Court-case fiction provides its framework and motifs, but it uses this material in a more self-conscious manner than *The Chart of Good and Evil* or *The Picture of Tianbao*. A single prophecy sets the entire novel in motion, shaping a series of expectations that seem to be fulfilled but then are disproved. The misunderstandings unify much of the novel, in the process highlighting the conventions and roles borrowed from court-case tales. For example, several tales in *Longtu's Court Cases* tell of an unsuspecting woman who remarries, only to find out years later that the man she married has killed her first husband. She then takes him to court to seek retribution. (Cf. story number 36 in *Longtu gongan*, 3.1a-4a.) In *Sword and Vase*, not only does the wife know beforehand, she takes justice into her own hands. Instead of bringing the villain to court, she kills him herself. See *Li he jian lianzi ping*, 119–37.

131. In this motif he is more gallant than the heroes in *Zheng Chun Yuan* or *Wanhua Lou*, where pride or friendship seems to be the motivating factor. *San he jian*, 9–12. This situation seems in some ways closer to *Shan e tu* than to either of the other two novels under discussion.

132. *Shuihu quan zhuan*, 85–88.

133. *San he jian*, 162–166. Another episode evoking and rejecting *The Water Margin* occurs in *Yun Zhong Yan*. A loyal official rescues a man's daughter from a group of bandits. He makes the bandits surrender to him and swear brotherhood. *Yun Zhong Yan*, 715–17.

134. Sun Kaidi, *Zhongguo tongsu xiaoshuo shumu*, 13.

Chapter 3. Parody and Roles in *Green Peony*

1. *Green Peony*, 327.

2. Cf. ibid., 301.

3. The narrator comments, "Later, this case would only be understood when they met with a talented, broadly learned scholar conversant with ancient and modern times." Ibid., 333. This serves as prolepsis, referring to Luo Binwang's explanation to Judge Di in chapter 45. Ibid., 440.

4. See Margaret Rose, *Parody: Ancient, Modern, and Post-modern*, 33–34, 51, 117, 135; and idem, *Parody//Metafiction*, 33–34. Cf. Mikhail Mikhailovich Bakhtin, *The Dialogic Imagination*, 364.

5. Bakhtin, *The Dialogic Imagination*, 55. Cf. Margaret Rose, *Parody: Ancient, Modern, and Post-modern*, 146.

6. Bakhtin, *The Dialogic Imagination*, 398.

7. Cf. Ibid., 413.

8. Ibid., 407–8.

9. Cao Xueqin, *Honglou meng*, 1:4–5. The translation is from Cao Xueqin, *The Story of the Stone*, trans. David Hawkes, 1:49–50.

10. Ding Xigen ed., *Zhongguo lidai xiaoshuo xu ba ji*, 2:887. Cf. translation and discussion in Anne Elizabeth McLaren, "Constructing New Reading Publics in Late Ming China," 154.

11. Translation from McLaren, "Constructing New Reading Publics in Late Ming China," 157–58. Cf. Ding Xigen, ed., *Zhongguo lidai xiaoshuo xu ba ji*, 2:887.

12. Translation modified from McLaren, "Constructing New Reading Publics in Late Ming China," 158. Cf. Ding Xigen, ed., *Zhongguo lidai xiaoshuo xu ba ji*, 2:887.

13. McLaren, "Constructing New Reading Publics in Late Ming China," 157–58; Cf. Rolston, *Traditional Chinese Fiction and Fiction Commentary*, 108–9, 131–65.

14. Preface by Rulian jushi from the 1801 edition, in Ding Xigen, *Zhongguo lidai xiaoshuo xu ba ji*, 2:963.

15. See translation and discussion of the "Great Preface" in Stephen Owen, *An Anthology of Chinese Literature: Beginnings to 1911*, 64–67; and of "Fishhawk" in ibid., 30–31. "The poems of the *Book of Songs* were meant to give paradigmatic expression to human feeling, and those who learned and recited the *Songs* would naturally internalize correct values." Stephen Owen, *Readings in Chinese Literary Thought*, 39. From its use in "Fishhawk," *haoqiu* literally means a "fit mate," but I follow the title of the early "translation" of the novel into English.

16. Ding Xigen, *Zhongguo lidai xiaoshuo xu ba ji*, 3:1331–33.

17. Preface from 1776 edition, in Ding Xigen, *Zhongguo lidai xiaoshuo xu ba ji*, 3:1601–2.

18. Ann Waltner, "From Casebook to Fiction: *Kung-an* in Late Imperial China," 283.

19. Preface from 1839 edition, in Ding Xigen, *Zhongguo lidai xiaoshuo xu ba ji*, 3:1610–11.

20. "In the most famous works like *Haoqiu zhuan* or *Yu Jiao Li*, there is no question of the lovers touching before marriage, or even thinking of touching." In other scholar-beauty romances, the beauty rebuffs the scholar's advances. Keith McMahon, *Misers, Shrews, and Polygamists* (Durham: Duke University Press, 1995), 127.

21. *Haoqiu zhuan*, Guben xiaoshuo jicheng (Shanghai: Shanghai guji, [1990]), 120–29.

22. In this regard *Haoqiu zhuan* anticipates the development of the genre. With the incorporation of martial elements from the historical novel, the standard protagonist of the scholar-beauty romance evolves into a hero skilled in both literary and martial endeavors. Lin Chen, *Mingmo Qingchu xiaoshuo shulu*, 83.

23. Chen Pingyuan, personal communication, April 11, 1997.

24. On the historical novel as popularized or fictionalized historiography, see Martin Weizong Huang, "Dehistoricization and Intertextualization: The Anxiety of Precedents in the Evolution of the Traditional Chinese Novel," 54–55. Regarding fiction as moral exemplar, Wilt Idema suggests the early military romance had a similar purpose and audience as *shanshu* (morality books). Idema, *Chinese Vernacular Fiction: The Formative Period*, xxx.

25. See Lin Chen's discussion of the evolution of the scholar-beauty romance novel (*caizi jiaren*), in his *Mingmo Qingchu xiaoshuo shulu*, 83. The classic scholar-beauty romance up to the Kangxi period was only concerned with appropriate marriages, but from about 1671 on, the scholar-beauty romance began to deemphasize exams and allow the brilliant scholar to gain position by fighting pirates or convincing bandits to serve in the government.

The love stories incorporated into the *Romance of the Sui and Tang* were mostly the author Chu Renhuo's original contribution, in contrast to the materials he compiled from other sources. See Robert E. Hegel, "*Sui Tang Yen-I*: The Sources and Narrative Techniques of a Traditional Chinese Novel," 122, 220.

26. C. T. Hsia, "The Military Romance," 371–78. C. T. Hsia argues that as the military romance evolved further and further from textbook history, the element of romance became de rigueur. Ibid., 373.

27. Mu Guiying appears in two related narratives published by the Wanli era of the Ming dynasty, *Nan Bei Song zhizhuan* and *Yang Jia Fu yanyi.* For information on editions see Ōtsuka Hidetaka, *Chûgoku tsûzoku shôsetsu shomoku*, 219–25.

28. *Yang Jia Fu yanyi*, Guben xiaoshuo jicheng (Shanghai: Shanghai guji, [1990]), 392.

29. *Yang Jia Fu yanyi*, 395.

30. The problematic relationship between *qing* and *yu* animates much Chinese fiction. See Martin Huang, *Desire and Fictional Narrative in Late Imperial China.*

31. *Yishuo Hou Tang zhuan sanji: Xue Dingshan zheng Xi Fan Lihua quan zhuan*, Guben xiaoshuo jicheng (Shanghai: Shanghai guji, [1990]), 127–34. References hereafter will read *Hou Tang san ji.* Sun Kaidi lists a 1768 edition. See Sun Kaidi, *Zhongguo tongsu xiaoshuo shumu*, 48–49; Ōtsuka Hidetaka, *Chûgoku tsûzoku shôsetsu shomoku*, 213–14. Alternate titles include *Shuo Tang sanzhuan.*

32. *Hou Tang san ji*, 158–62.

33. *Hou Tang san ji*, 205–71.

34. C. T. Hsia, "The Military Romance," 377–78.

35. *Hou Tang san ji*, 219–20.

36. Ibid., 243. Her father died fighting her over her decision to marry Xue Dingshan, and she then killed her brothers. C. T. Hsia suggests that "Ting-shan rejects her not because of her disloyal and unfilial behavior but because she is his superior as a warrior and he finds it difficult to adjust his sense of male superiority to this reality." See "The Military Romance," 377.

37. *Hou Tang san ji*, 244. His mother criticizes him as "lacking sentiment and righteousness" (*wu qing wu yi*), implicitly reversing the traditional father's views by accepting sentiment (*qing*) as a virtue.

38. *Hou Tang san ji*, 319–31.

39. *Hou Tang san ji*, 211.

40. C. T. Hsia, "The Military Romance," 373.

41. *Green Peony*, 3–4.

42. Keith McMahon notes that in the paradigmatic scholar-beauty romance *Yu Jiao Li* the scholar is an only child with only one living parent; so is the beauty. See his *Misers, Shrews, and Polygamists: Sexuality and Male-Female Relations in Eighteenth-century Chinese Fiction*, 115.

43. Most of the time when Luo is called *yingxiong* (hero) it is directly related to the romance plot. Hua Bilian looks over to Luo and Ren when they cheer her tightrope routine and sees these *yingxiong*; *Green Peony*, 19–20. Hua Bilian tells her mother she saw this hero (*yingxiong*), and her mother knows she is in love; ibid., 27. The crowd praises Luo as a hero (*yingxiong*) for catching Hua Bilian; ibid., 199. Bao Jinhua knows of him as a hero (*yingxiong*) before she goes to his room; ibid., 250.

44. *Green Peony*, 279. Luo's inexperience is also taken into consideration in the assignment of tasks in the restoration; he is told, "You've actually never experienced a really formidable foe," and is sent to keep the city gates open for the gang's escape. Ibid., 567. A similar phrase (*wei jingguo da di*) refers to useless green soldiers in *Yishuo Fan Tang quan zhuan*, 266.

45. A conventional trope for a beauty, originating in the *Han History* biography of Lady Li, "One look could topple a city of men, another look could topple a country of men."

46. Another conventional figure for a beauty, originating in *Zhuangzi*, Qi Wu Lun.

47. Literally, green butterfly powder. "Butterfly powder" was a kind of makeup for palace ladies in the Tang.

48. The three birds are explained in a commentary to the "Nine Laments" (Jiu tan) of the *Chuci* (Songs of Chu) as the messengers who accompanied the Queen Mother of the West when she appeared to Emperor Wu, suggesting a romantic tryst. They acted as messengers thereafter. Another account specifies the three birds as the oriole, the crane, and the swallow. For the very erudite poem that is the source of this allusion see David Hawkes, trans., *Ch'u Tz'u: The Songs of the South* (London: Oxford University Press, 1959), 162.

49. To dip to one side of the horse. *Hanyu da cidian*, 11:1398.

50. The story of Taigong being recruited by the emperor while catching fish is found in *Han Feizi*, Yulao. Cf. *Zhuangzi*, Shanmu.

51. *Green Peony*, 18–20.

52. The nickname "tigress" (*mu dachong*) is also used of Mistress Gu the Tigress (Gu Dasao) in *Shuihu quan zhuan*, 810.

53. *Green Peony*, 29.

54. As I discussed above in chapter 1, Lin Chen schematizes the possibilities for how the couple meets in a scholar-beauty romance novel. See his *Mingmo Qingchu xiaoshuo shulu*, 75–76.

55. In "classic" scholar-beauty romances the heroines can take considerable initiative, but by the time *Green Peony* appeared they took more passive roles. See, for example, Keith McMahon's remarks on *Zhuchun yuan xiaoshi*, in *Misers, Shrews, and Polygamists*, 119.

56. *Green Peony*, 192–93.

57. In contrast, the women warrior Fan Lihua argues with her father when he opposes her chosen match and accidentally kills him. Cf. *Hou Tang san ji*, 222.

58. She is not entirely forthcoming even with her mother, and continues to pretend to be unconscious in hopes of hiding her improper action. *Green Peony*, 209–10.

59. The idiom "monkey of the heart and horse of the will" (*xinyuan yima*) for runaway desires supports this reading.

60. *Green Peony*, 278. In contrast to this statement, marrying a hero is Hua Bilian's ambition; cf. ibid., 29.

61. Ibid., 121. This Confucian ideal forms a clear contrast to the heroic ethic, which Chen Pingyuan summarizes as "punish evil and encourage good." See his *Qiangu wenren xiake meng*, 149.

62. *Green Peony*, 186–87. The reprint reads *zheng* for *zhen*. Chen Pingyuan suggests *haohan* ties of friendship should be as strong as kinship. See his *Qiangu wenren xiake meng*, 150.

63. *Green Peony*, 199. Luo's immediate reaction is to save her. The narrator's explanation echoes *Mencius* 4A:17 (using one's hand to save your drowning sister-in-law); "as soon as he saw Hua Bilian falling from the roof, he had to save her quickly; how could he still consider the separation of male and female?" *Green Peony*, 201. *Green Peony* uses this reference to *Mencius* playfully, in contrast to scholar-beauty romances like *Haoqiu zhuan* that invoke this concept in all seriousness to excuse bending the rules. See also *Mencius* 2A:6, on people's immediate reactions to a child falling in the well.

64. *Green Peony*, 308.

65. Ibid., 439.

66. Ibid., 249–58.

67. As mentioned above, the trope of fighting and then marrying is referred to earlier in the novel when the narrator gives the Hua family's background: Hua Bilian's parents met on the road, fought, fell in love, and married. Ibid., 28.

68. Chapter titles for chapters 23 and 24, in ibid., 229 and 240, respectively.

69. Throughout most of the novel, poetry is limited to end-of-chapter couplets.

70. Ibid., 252–53. In some later editions, the verb in the second line is changed from "fight" to "meet." This makes the whole line consistent with the expectations of a scholar-beauty romance, but loses the juxtaposition of genres that is both present in the scene and encapsulated in the original clash between nouns and verb.

71. Ibid., 253. This suggests a link to chapter 9—the chapter title uses the same term (*xi*) about Madam He's flirtation with Luo. Ibid., 87.

72. Ibid., 253–54. Her reaction, "This fellow doesn't know when he's being promoted!" is the same as Hua Zhenfang's reaction when Luo refuses his proposal the third time. Ibid., 279.

73. Margaret Rose, *Parody: Ancient, Modern, and Post-modern*, 171.

74. *Green Peony*, 16–20.

75. Ibid., 32–35.

76. Ibid., 64.

77. Ibid., 188.

78. Ibid., 192–97.

79. Ibid., 519.

80. In contrast to later novels like *Moral Heroes and Heroines*, once Hua Bilian is married, she can switch between the roles of proper beauty and woman warrior as the situation demands.

81. Ibid., 563. The place the exams are held is labeled "military examination hall" in big letters, but in the center there is a "pavilion for military performance" *yan wu ting*.

82. Ibid., 52. This element of the scene appears in both the novel and drum ballad. *Green Peony Drum Ballad,* 190.

83. *Green Peony*, 52–53. This passage is added by the novel; it does not appear in the drum ballad.

84. *Shuihu quan zhuan*, 797–98. Cf. Chen Xizhong, et al., eds., *Shuihu zhuan huiping ben*, 892. In the added chapters of *Shuihu zhuan,* a similar scene is played out in which the woman warrior Qiongying dazzles her (male) opponents. See chapter 98 of *Shuihu quan zhuan*, 1542–43.

85. *Green Peony*, 42.

86. Ibid., 119.

87. Ibid., 121. Hua quotes the crucial phrase "hiding the bad and disclosing the good" from section 6 of the *Doctrine of the Mean*, and paraphrases Zhu Xi's commentary on chapter 1, verse 7 of the *Analects*. His lecture is even in semiclassical parallel style, using classical grammar particles!

88. Ibid., 124–26. The ailing Hua Bilian recovers when told of the plan, since Ren and Luo are "fast friends" and Ren would be "eternally grateful" to her dad for saving him.

89. Liu Yinbo notes that Hua and Bao do not live up to one's expectations for a martial hero (*xia*) because they are avaricious and destructive. See his *Zhongguo wuxia xiaoshuo shi*, 244.

90. Interestingly, when Hua first awakens Ren, Ren cries "thief!" and Hua has to protest his innocence. *Green Peony*, 132.

91. Ibid., 138.

92. Ibid., 159.

93. Ibid., 161.

94. In *The Water Margin* a single-handed jailbreak is always dismissed as too risky. When Mistress Gu suggests she and her husband attempt to break her cousins out of jail, he insists they get military support and a good plan. *Shuihu quan zhuan,* 812.

95. *Green Peony*, 163.

96. Ibid., 137.

97. Ibid., 152.

98. Bakhtin, *The Dialogic Imagination*, 55.

99. C. T. Hsia, "The Military Romance," 381.

100. *Green Peony*, 170.

101. Ibid., 212.

102. Ibid., 190–94.

103. Ibid., 225.

104. *Sheng hua meng*, 32–36. Ōtsuka lists a 1673 edition. Ōtsuka Hidetaka, *Chûgoku tsûzoku shôsetsu shomoku*, 94. See also Lin Chen, *Mingmo Qingchu xiaoshuo shulu*, 360–62. The trope of an assassin pardoned also appears in *Shi Gong an*; a failed assassination attempt leads to Huang Tianba's adoption by Judge Shi. See *Shi Gong an*, 137–40, 153–55.

105. *Green Peony*, 218.

106. Ibid., 378–79. For other examples of Bao Zi'an's greed, see the discussion of the fake wedding below.

107. Ibid., 131–32, 162, and 311. The thief's kit or outfit is described in "Song Si Gong da nao 'Jinhun' Zhang," story number 36 in Feng Menglong, ed., *Gu jin xiaoshuo*, 1394; and "Nao Fanlou duoqing Zhou Shengxian," story number 14 in Feng Menglong, ed., *Xingshi hengyan*, 787.

108. *Shuihu quan zhuan*, 86.

109. Another criterion is the hero's ability to eat strong meat such as beef. *Green Peony* outdoes *Shuihu zhuan* on that count, serving tiger meat to distinguish the "superheroes" from the merely skilled. *Green Peony*, 277.

110. *Shuihu quan zhuan*, 744–45.

111. Ibid., 702.

112. Ibid., 619.

113. *Sanguo yanyi huiping ben*, 308. This is a test of Guan Yu's virtue. He surrendered on three conditions embodying the proper relations between lord and minister, man and woman, and sworn brothers. Through this situation, Cao Cao is testing both the relation of lord and minister and that of man and woman. In *Green Peony*, Yu Qian fails on two of the three counts: he becomes preoccupied with the distinction between man and woman and thus does not fulfill his obligations to his master, which soon leads to problems between the sworn brothers Ren and Luo.

114. *Green Peony*, 85–92.

115. Ibid., 182.

116. Ibid.

117. Ibid., 101–5.

118. Ibid., 132.

119. Ibid., 148–51. The plot to get a hero drunk before capturing him echoes the incident in *The Water Margin* with Li Kui described above. *Shuihu quan zhuan*, 702.

120. There are many attempts to rework *Shuihu zhuan*. The most famous is Jin Shengtan's own seventy-chapter revision of *Shuihu zhuan* itself. Later authors challenged *Shuihu zhuan*'s values by writing sequels or rewriting it under new titles. One such attempt is *Dangkou zhi*.

121. Wang explicitly refers to the oath in *Three Kingdoms* in suggesting that they swear brotherhood. *Green Peony*, 66–67. Cf. Chen Xizhong et al., eds., *Sanguo yanyi huiping ben*, 6.

122. In discussing the ideological contradictions within *Green Peony*, Zhu Hongbo also notes the parody of *Three Kingdoms* to be found in Wang Lun's interactions. See Zhu Hongbo, "Shilun *Lü mudan* de sixiang yiyun," 165.

This parody of the ceremony and bond of brotherhood in *Green Peony* may have been influenced by a similar parody of brotherhood in *Jin Ping Mei*. For the implications, see below. Cf. stories 2, 65, and 66 in *Longtu gongan*, in which a man sees his friend's wife and plots to commit adultery and do away with his friend. *Longtu gongan*, 1.4a-7a; 4.15b-19a; 4.19a-21b.

123. *Green Peony*, 66.

124. Ibid., 69.

125. Ibid., 70.

126. See Martin Huang, "Dehistoricization and Intertextualization," 65–66.

127. *Jin Ping Mei cihua*, 100, 129–35.

128. *Green Peony*, 80.

129. Cf. Shi Xiu's story in *Shuihu quan zhuan*, 722–64.

130. *Green Peony*, 278–79.

131. *Yu Jiao Li*, Guben xiaoshuo jicheng (reprint, Shanghai: Shanghai guji, [1990]), 603–7. Lin Chen believes *Yu Jiao Li* is the first scholar-beauty novel, written by Tianhua Zang Zhuren in the late Ming. No Ming editions survive. See Lin Chen, *Mingmo Qingchu xiaoshuo shulu*, 91, 142, 242–44. Cf. Sun Kaidi, *Zhongguo tongsu xiaoshuo shumu*, 182; Ōtsuka Hidetaka, *Chûgoku tsûzoku shôsetsu shomoku*, 64–67. The title is composed by taking a word from each of three characters' names.

132. *Shuihu quan zhuan*, 551–53, 556–57.

133. *Green Peony*, 340–41.

134. Ibid., 351–52.

135. *Sanguo yanyi huiping ben*, 452–61.

136. *Yishuo Fan Tang quan zhuan*, Guben xiaoshuo jicheng 4th ser., vol. 129–31 (Shanghai: Shanghai guji, [1990]). Ōtsuka Hidetaka notes a 1753 edition. See his *Chûgoku tsûzoku shôsetsu shomoku*, 214–16. C. T. Hsia notes this novel is the "direct sequel" of *Yishuo Hou Tang zhuan sanji: Xue Dingshan zheng Xi Fan Lihua quan zhuan*. See his "Military Romance," 340 n1. Xue Gang's three trips to pay respects at his parents' grave are almost a dare to the officials to catch him. The novel goes by many titles including *Fan Tang quan zhuan*, indicating that this is the novel to which some editions of *Green Peony* claim to be a sequel under the alternate title *Fan Tang hou zhuan*.

137. In contrast, *Green Peony Drum Ballad* casts Luo unambiguously as a filial son. In the drum ballad, the letter tells Luo his mother disappeared after the house burned down and no one was certain whether she was dead or alive. Luo faints away at the news, and when he is revived he leaves for home immediately. Once he arrives in his hometown he cannot eat or sleep until he learns his mother was "rescued" by the bandit gang. See *Green Peony Drum Ballad*, 273–74.

138. *Green Peony*, 350.

139. *Green Peony*, 347.

140. Critiques by other characters explicitly point to Hua as the root of Luo's troubles on more than one occasion. Yu Qian says as much to Hua when they meet at the inn, while Bao Zi'an traces Luo's clash with the Ba brothers to Hua's scheming. *Green Peony*, 118, 515–16.

141. Heather Dubrow, *Genre*, 32.

142. *Hou Tang san ji*, 319–25.

143. *Green Peony*, 541–44.

144. *Shuihu quan zhuan*, 82–87.

145. Chen Xizhong et al., eds., *Sanguo yanyi huiping ben*, 675. It originally was supposed to be a trap, but "the false came true" and they married.

146. *Shuihu quan zhuan*, 1248–49.

147. Ibid., 1249.

148. *Green Peony*, 326. The Chinese phrase is different in *Green Peony* (*wanwan*) than in *The Water Margin* (*xianshua*).

149. Ibid. 327; cf. the officials' trial in ibid., 301.

150. The use of torture is prominent in court-case tales; here it is made ridiculous (though it is still effective).

151. Ibid., 329; cf. narrator explanation in ibid., 296. The idea of having Bao overhear the conversation may have been inspired by the trope of the judge going undercover in the court-case collections.

152. *Shuihu quan zhuan*, 546.

153. The closest analogue is in *Yishuo Hou Tang zhuan san ji: Xue Dingshan zheng Xi Fan Lihua quan zhuan*, where Judge Di convinces Xue Gang to help restore Luling Wang. See *Hou Tang san ji*, 639–40. Cf. *Fan Tang*, in which Judge Di gives instructions for the restoration of the Tang in brocade bags before he dies. *Fan Tang*, 410–11.

154. *Green Peony*, 440, 556. Even Judge Di does not insist on the letter of the law but is more interested in the outlaws' power.

155. Ibid., 444–53.

156. *Green Peony*, 521–25. In *Rebellion against the Tang*, revenge is still swift and gruesome. *Fan Tang*, 294–96.

157. *Green Peony*, 549–58.

158. Ibid., 237–43.

159. *Shuihu quan zhuan*, 597–98.

160. Chen Pingyuan, *Qiangu wenren xiake meng*, 44.

161. *Green Peony*, 560–62.

162. See Y. W. Ma, "The Chinese Historical Novel," 281, in which Empress Wu's reign is discussed as "an infringement of the divine order and a political sin of the highest magnitude, with devastating chaos as the inevitable result." C. T. Hsia also mentions Empress Wu as clearly evil in "The Military Romance," 363.

163. See *Green Peony*, 175–78, 527–28, and 598–605, respectively.

164. Some parallel could be drawn to Don Quixote in the second part of that novel. I pursue this parallel in chapter 5.

165. Martin Huang, "Dehistoricization and Intertextualization," 45–68.

166. Katherine Carlitz, *The Rhetoric of Chin P'ing Mei*.

167. While Plaks argues in *The Four Masterworks of the Ming Novel* that these novels all have a neo-Confucian worldview, other scholars argue that *Journey to the West* is Daoist, or that *Jin Ping Mei* projects the conservative Confucian philosophy of Xunzi. On *Journey to the West* see Shao Ping, "Monkey and Chinese Scriptural Tradition: A Rereading of the Novel 'Xiyou ji'." On *Jin Ping Mei* see David Tod Roy, "Introduction," in *The Plum in the Golden Vase*, 1:xviii-xix, xxiii-xlii.

Katherine Carlitz demonstrates that the appropriation of previous literary discourse in *Jin Ping Mei* is often used to raise moral issues, although there is some slippage between their meaning in previous contexts and in *Jin Ping Mei*. See *The Rhetoric of Chin P'ing Mei*, 77 and passim.

168. Jin Shengtan has "a conviction that the books' major statement is about morality, although the moral should not be stated too obviously." Widmer, *Margins of Utopia*, 103.

169. "[U]nder the assumption of one correct reading, there is nothing more to the text than the kinds of things one can know about it after reading it carefully several times, for it is simply a puzzle to be unravelled, like a detective story." Ibid., 99–100.

170. Plaks mentions that irony turns on itself to foster indeterminacy in "Full-length *Hsiao-shuo* and the Western Novel: A Generic Reappraisal," 174.

171. Jonathan Culler, *Structuralist Poetics: Structuralism, Linguistics, and the Study of Literature*, 157.

Chapter 4. Metafiction in *Green Peony*

1. Bakhtin, *The Dialogic Imagination*, 413.

2. Ibid., 289.

3. Ibid., 382, 385.

4. Ibid., 314. The emphasis on values is corroborated in another passage, cf. ibid., 416.

5. Ibid., 412.

6. Margaret Rose discusses Bakhtin's ideas of parody, the Second Line novel, and their relationship to metafiction in *Parody: Ancient, Modern, and Post-modern*, 125–70, especially 138–40.

7. The term "metafiction" was apparently invented by William Gass in 1970. The first major critical use of the term was by Robert Scholes in a 1970 article arguing that contemporary novels incorporate criticism. See Robert Scholes, "Metafiction," in Currie, *Metafiction*, 29. On metafiction and realism, see ibid., and Robert Alter, *Partial Magic: The Novel as a Self-conscious Genre*. For an overview of the term and its usage

see Patricia Waugh, *Metafiction: The Theory and Practice of Self-conscious Fiction*. See also Mark Currie, *Metafiction*; Linda Hutcheon, *Narcissistic Narrative: The Metafictional Paradox*; and Margaret Rose, *Parody//Metafiction*.

8. Patricia Waugh, *Metafiction*, 2.

9. Hutcheon, *Narcissistic Narrative: The Metafictional Paradox*, 71, 73–74.

10. Y. W. Ma, "The Chinese Historical Novel," 290 n34, paraphrasing John J. Richetti, *Popular Fiction before Richardson: Narrative Patterns, 1700–1739* (Oxford, 1969).

11. Both the drum ballad and the novel begin like a historical novel, but whereas the drum ballad uses adequate transitions to keep the historical framework going and link subsequent material into it, the novel omits such transitions, resulting in three beginnings.

12. *Green Peony* largely preserves the historical poem in the *Green Peony Drum Ballad*.

13. The preface to the 1522 edition of *Three Kingdoms* (*Sanguo tongsu zhi yanyi*) follows suit. See Rolston, *Traditional Fiction and Fiction Commentary*, 244. Cf. Ding Xigen, ed., *Zhongguo lidai xiaoshuo xu ba ji*, 2:889.

14. *Green Peony*, 3.

15. After being referred to in the introduction and suppressed, the Xue Family Generals material reappears at the end of the novel. In some sense it serves as a familiar frame to the novel, a common technique. The relationship between *The Water Margin* and *Jin Ping Mei* is an obvious example, but many of the eighteenth-century military romances also grew by means of sequels or "prequels." A similar technique is also used in the prologues to *The Story of the Stone* and *Jinghua yuan* (Flowers in the mirror); by figuring the writing of the whole novel into the prologue, the reader is given hints of the ending before the plot proper begins.

16. *Green Peony*, 3–4.

17. Lord Yuchi was a founding general of the Tang.

18. *Green Peony*, 5.

19. The first line appears in two court-case tales of crime and punishment: "The Insoluble Murder," #21 in Ling Mengchu, *Erke pai'an jingqi*, 1032; and "Cheng Chaofeng meets a headless woman once, Wang Tongpan twice solves a mystery" #28 in ibid., 1339.

20. *Qing Feng Zha* is based on *Jingshi tongyan* #13. Cf. Y. W. Ma, "*Kung-an* Fiction," 252.

21. *Qing Feng Zha*, 10.

22. Indeed, the attention to structure and multiple beginnings in *Green Peony* call to mind similar techniques in the great works of Chinese fiction. Most of the masterworks play multiple prologues off one another to create a nuanced perspective on the subject. The prime example is *The Story of the Stone*, which devotes the first thirteen chapters or so to introduction. Cf. David Rolston, *Traditional Fiction and Fiction Commentary*, 335. *Green Peony* is hardly on the same level of complexity, but by juxtaposing

these three beginnings and endings it does go beyond the conventions of the previous genres it drew on.

23. See Heather Dubrow, *Genre*, 31.

24. Wen Kang, *Ernü yingxiong zhuan*, Guben xiaoshuo jicheng (Shanghai: Shanghai guji, [1990]), 4:1981.

25. This reference appears in the Guangxu 14 Hongbao zhai lithographic edition of *Rulin waishi*, in Li Hanqiu, ed., *Rulin waishi huijiao huiping ben* (Shanghai: Shanghai guji, 1987), 816.

26. *Hong Bi yuan* (Xin wenhua shushe, 1935), 1a. The preface is dated 1917.

27. For Jin Shengtan and Zhang Zhupo, "the first chapter is a minature model of all basic principles and relations further elaborated in the novelistic text and a nucleus of all further relations in the novelistic structure." Milena Dolezelova-Velingerova, "Seventeenth-century Chinese Theory of Narrative: A Reconstruction of Its System and Concepts," 146.

28. See Plaks, "Terminology and Central Concepts," in Rolston, ed., *How to Read the Chinese Novel*, 112. Verisimilitude was an important concept for the novel since *Shuihu zhuan*; see Martin Huang, "Dehistoricization and Intertextualization," 55 n41.

In the traditional Chinese novel, the simulated context of the oral storyteller dramatically influences the way a tale is told. As Linda Hutcheon suggests, "The presence of an 'authorial' narrating figure as mediator between reader and novel world demands recognition of a subsequent narrative distance. This results in an added emphasis on diegesis, on the act of storytelling." See her *Narcisstic Narrative*, 51. C. T. Hsia's *The Classic Chinese Novel* holds each of the masterworks up to the standard of Western realism in turn, and finds most wanting. Hsia says that in the absence of a tradition of literary realism, *The Water Margin* fails from historical undernourishment, and the heteroglossia in *Plum in a Golden Vase* strikes him as tampering with realism. C. T. Hsia, *The Classic Chinese Novel: A Critical Introduction*, 75–76, 82–85, 166, 170. Ironically, Hsia finds *The Story of the Stone* (*Honglou meng*) to be the "supreme work of psychological realism" in China. It may be, but it is also relentlessly metafictional.

Despite these differences, the question of the relationship between fiction and reality does seem to be relevant in the Chinese tradition. The earliest novels in China all have some relation to history, and much has been made of the question of how factual they are. From an early critic of *The Three Kingdoms* who criticized it as "seven parts fact and three parts fiction" to C. T. Hsia, the "reality" behind the novel has been an issue. This issue received sophisticated treatment in *The Story of the Stone*. Since the original commentary to the novel also insists on its basis in actual events, an extraordinary amount of scholarship has been concerned with issues external to the novel, which attempt to map the incidents in the novel onto the life of its author Cao Xueqin.

29. Some scholars deny Jin Shengtan's commentary the status of theory, calling it practical criticism or faulting it for not meeting modern standards of literary criticism. John C. Y. Wang considers Jin Shengtan's commentary practical criticism rather than theory. John Ching-yu Wang, *Chin Sheng-t'an*, 39. Chen Xiang attacks Jin Shengtan for failing to measure up to modern standards of literary criticism. Cited in Rolston, *Traditional Chinese Fiction and Fiction Commentary*, 6 n9, and 50 n68.

30. Plaks, "Terminology," in *How to Read the Chinese Novel*, 75.

31. Cf. Rolston, *Traditional Chinese Fiction and Fiction Commentary*, 25–102.

32. Dolezelova-Velingerova, "Seventeenth-century Chinese Theory of Narrative," 137–38.

33. For a discussion of repetition in the Chinese literary tradition, see Yenna Wu, "Repetition in *Xingshi yinyuan zhuan*," 55–87. The article effectively demonstrates the intentional use of repetition in the Chinese novel "to structure the story, achieve coherence in the narrative, enrich the meaning of the text, reinforce the author's moral message, and augment the reader's pleasure." Ibid., 57.

34. Jin Shengtan calls this technique "snake in the grass or discontinuous chalk line" (*cao she hui xian fa*). See Chen Xizhong et al., eds., *Shuihu zhuan huiping ben*, 20, 417–25, and 433–49. Cf. David Rolston, ed., *How to Read the Chinese Novel*, 140–41.

35. Jin Shengtan calls this technique "The otter's tail" (*tawei fa*). See Chen Xizhong et al., eds., *Shuihu zhuan huiping ben*, 21; Cf. David Rolston, ed., *How to Read the Chinese Novel*, 142–43. For an example, see Chen Xizhong et al., eds., *Shuihu zhuan huiping ben*, 426–27.

36. Jin Shengtan calls this technique "clouds cutting the mountains in half" (*hengyun duan shan fa*). See Chen Xizhong et al., eds., *Shuihu zhuan hui ping ben*, 22; Cf. David Rolston, ed., *How to Read the Chinese Novel*, 144–45. For an example, see Chen Xizhong et al., eds., *Shuihu zhuan hui ping ben*, 898–914.

37. Patrick Hanan, "The Composition of the *P'ing yao chuan*," 215.

38. Ibid., 216. See also the analysis of repeated motifs in *The Water Margin* and their relationship to the oral tradition in Liangyan Ge, *Out of the Margins*, 64–100.

39. Rolston, *Traditional Chinese Fiction and Fiction Commentary*, 211.

40. Chen Xizhong et al., eds., *Shuihu zhuan huiping ben*, 232. Jin Shengtan goes on to give a detailed analysis of this example of "partial repetition" (*lüe fan*), referring to Lin Chong buying a sword in chapter 6 and Yang Zhi selling a sword in chapter 11.

41. Rolston, *Traditional Chinese Fiction and Fiction Commentary*, 47. It is hard to underestimate the importance of criticism to the aesthetic of *The Water Margin*; "the critics . . . do sometimes point out subtlety and significance in patterns of repetition that might also be taken as uninspired at first glance." Rolston, ed., *How to Read the Chinese Novel*, 100.

42. Chen Xizhong et al., eds., *Shuihu zhuan huiping ben*, 468.

43. Ibid., 21; Cf. David Rolston, ed., *How to Read the Chinese Novel*, 143.

44. Chen Xizhong et al., eds., *Shuihu zhuan huiping ben*, 853–55. Differences in motivation apparently do not extend to the adulteresses. Jin Shengtan states that the reason Pan Qiaoyun slanders Shi Xiu is precisely the same reason Jinlian had previously slandered Wu Song. Jin Shengtan does note that there is no proof that Pan Qiaoyun would ever go so far as to kill her husband, even though Shi Xiu accuses her of it.

Besides differences in characterization and motivation, Jin Shengtan also calls attention to differences in narrative technique between repetitions. The interlinear commentary points out how the Pan Qiaoyun episode avoids repeating the Pan Jinlian episode by effectively using summary rather than scene. Thus Shi Xiu thinks to himself that Pan Qiaoyun has flirted with him in the past; this summary takes the place of the famous scene in the Pan Jinlian story in which she flirts with Wu Song. The interlinear commentary also notes a shift in the point of view between the two episodes. Pan Jinlian's story is told largely from the point of view of the go-between, Mrs. Wang, so the emphasis is on the seduction, while Pan Qiaoyun's story is told largely from Shi Xiu's point of view, so the emphasis is on the discovery of the affair. Ibid., 833. The two examples show almost no verbal correspondence.

45. E. M. Forster, *Aspects of the Novel*, 130, paraphrased in Brian Attebery, *Strategies of Fantasy*, 52.

46. For a discussion of the Western ontology of repetition as imitation or difference, see J. Hillis Miller, *Fiction and Repetition: Seven English Novels*, 1–21.

47. Rolston, ed., *How to Read the Chinese Novel*, 119.

48. Chen Xizhong et al., eds., *Shuihu zhuan huiping ben,* 20; the translation is from Rolston, ed., *How to Read the Chinese Novel*, 141.

49. Chen Xizhong et al., eds., *Shuihu zhuan huiping ben,* 16; the translation is from Rolston, ed., *How to Read the Chinese Novel*, 133.

50. Cf. Dolezelova-Velingerova, "Seventeenth-century Chinese Theory of Narrative: A Reconstruction of Its System and Concepts," 147.

51. Mao Zonggang concurs about the importance of patterning even though he has a different take on the issue of fictionality versus fact in narrative.

52. Hua Laura Wu, "The Concept of Parallelism: Jin Shengtan's Critical Discourse on the Water Margin," in *Poetics East and West*, edited by Milena Dolezelova-Velingerova (Toronto: Toronto Semiotic Circle, Victoria College in the University of Toronto, 1989), 177–78. On the function and significance of repetition to Jin Shengtan, see also Widmer, *The Margins of Utopia*, 92–96; and Plaks, "Terminology," in *How to Read*, 88, 90, 95–96, 99–100.

53. The incorporation of criticism includes narrators who talk like commentators, and commentary by the authors. Rolston, *Traditional Chinese Fiction and Fiction Commentary*, 9–10.

54. *Green Peony*, 54. There is another reference to the book as a book in ibid., 217. The term *zhaoying* appears in traditional literary criticism; for an example see Mao Zonggang's "Du *Sanguo zhi* fa," in Chen Xizhong et al., eds., *Sanguo yanyi huiping ben*, 17.

55. Charles Hucker, *A Dictionary of Official Titles in Imperial China*, 529.

56. *Green Peony*, 489–90. The reprinted text is corrupt; it reads *mian* 面 for *hui* 回. For the correct text, see the first edition of *Lü mudan quan zhuan* (San huai tang, 1800), 51.1a.

57. *Green Peony*, 2.

58. Ibid., 201.

59. The original phrasing is "*qiangu hanwen.*" Ibid., 197.

60. Ibid., 222–23. Significantly, Yu Qian initially dismisses the challenge as conventional: "Yu Qian said, 'Men of the rivers and lakes (*jianghu*) who make a living playing with fists and clubs all talk this way, so don't blame him. Let him go.'"

61. Ibid., 224.

62. Ibid., 226.

63. Ibid., 344–96.

64. Ibid., 344–45.

65. Ibid., 353.

66. Ibid., 354.

67. Ibid., 355–56.

68. Ibid., 356.

69. Ibid., 358.

70. Ibid., 381.

71. Ibid., 383–84. This ability to recognize the formula one is in and play it to one's own advantage occurs occasionally in *The Water Margin.* See, for example, *Shuihu quan zhuan*, chapter 27, 427–29. Wu Song knows the wine is drugged, pretends to succumb, and pins Sun The Witch to the ground. In other examples of the same formula the victims talk about drugged wine, but they take no precautions. Jin Shengtan has no specific comments on the technique. Cf. Chen Xizhong et al., eds., *Shuihu zhuan huiping ben*, 515–18.

72. In some cases this full-blown recounting is added by the novel; the drum ballad simply states the character "told them what had happened." In chapter 28 and chapter 31 the novel fleshes a very brief statement out into a full-blown recounting. The notable exception is Luo's recounting to Hua of Wang's adultery in chapter 12 of the novel; there the drum ballad includes a long passage of retelling (449 characters long) which the novel trims down to 130 characters. The function of the brief analepses in the drum ballad is simply to prompt the listener to action.

73. This resembles a phenomenon Vladimir Propp notes in the folktale: The characters must all know what happened before the action may proceed. Thus the hero tells his plight and gains a helper. See Propp, *Morphology of the Folktale*, 73.

74. *Green Peony,* 122–75.

75. Gérard Genette, *Narrative Discourse: An Essay in Method*, 56.

76. *Green Peony,* 212. In contrast, in chapter 12 of the drum ballad Hua retells the whole incident. *Green Peony Drum Ballad*, 238.

77. *Green Peony*, 280–81.

78. In referring to the two halves of the tale here, Bao uses the terms *qian ban jie* and *hou ban jie*, which were also used by fiction critics to discuss the structure of a text. Plaks notes that in fiction criticism the synonymous terms *shang ban jie, xia ban jie* refer to halves of the text. In Rolston, ed., *How to Read the Chinese Novel*, 89. In another instance, Bao Zi'an labels his comments about causality as "criticism" (*ping*) and launches into primarily classical diction. *Green Peony,* 515–16.

79. This is reminiscent of the Zhiyan zhai commentary to *The Story of the Stone*, which actually changed the way the novel was written. Of course similar tendencies were inherent in commentary; Jin Shengtan had no compunction about changing anything he disliked, and praising the results.

80. *Green Peony*, 158–60 and 313–14, respectively.

81. Ibid., 318.

82. Ibid., 486.

83. Ibid., 308–9.

84. Umberto Eco, "The Narrative Structure in Fleming," 57.

85. Hanan, "The Composition of the *P'ing yao chuan*," 215–16; C. T. Hsia, "The Military Romance," 345, 352, 378.

86. Hegel, "*Sui T'ang Yen-I*: The Sources and Narrative Techniques of a Traditional Chinese Novel," 253.

87. Margaret Rose, *Parody//Metafiction*, 96.

88. Ibid., 83.

89. One of the difficulties with sequels is "escaping" the original. Thus Shuhui Yang argues that *Quell the Bandits* (*Dangkou zhi)*, a sequel written specifically to correct the morality of *The Water Margin*, ends up falling into the same pattern. See his essay "Growing from the Waist" in Martin Huang, ed., *Snakes' Legs*, 143–58.

90. The use of settings is meticulously related to the pattern of the plot. *Green Peony* incorporates six major settings: the capital, Dingxing County (in Hebei), Shandong, Yangzhou, Zhenjiang (in Jiangsu), and Jiaxing (in Zhejiang). The progression of the action is from north to south for the first half of the novel, whereupon it reverses and proceeds steadily from south to north for the second half. Each new setting (except Yangzhou) alternates with a known setting. Moreover, for the bulk of the novel (chapters 11–56), each plot sequence switches back and forth between an outlaw's lair and a nearby city.

91. Linda Hutcheon, *Narcissistic Narrative*, 71.

92. Rudiger Imhof, *Contemporary Metafiction: A Poetological Study of Metafiction in English since 1939*, 113.

93. Bao Jinhua is also labeled a "beauty" (*jiaren*) in the drum ballad, but the novel adds the conversation "If you weren't married" to frame their meeting in terms of the romance, and it also adds the chapter titles that mismatch subjects and verbs from two different genres. Finally, she is not portrayed as a shrew in the drum ballad, so the label "beauty" is not so obviously wrong.

94. *Green Peony Drum Ballad*, 195.

95. Roger Chartier, *The Cultural Uses of Print in Early Modern France*, 287, 335–36.

96. See Margaret Baptist Wan, "The *Chantefable* and the Novel: The Cases of *Lü mudan* and *Tianbao tu*," 367–97.

97. The nineteenth century appears to be an important moment in the conception of the novel, or at least in its reception. While metafictional novels like *The Story of the*

Stone were written earlier in the eighteenth century, if one looks at publication dates, it is not until 1791 that *The Story of the Stone* was finally printed. The next thirty years saw the publication of quite a number of metafictional works, including *Green Peony* and *Flowers in the Mirror*. Once published, they quickly gained a national audience and were frequently reprinted throughout the rest of the Qing dynasty. This suggests that a market for metafiction developed by the early nineteenth century, one that extended to popular fiction.

98. For an exception, see Ellen Widmer's discussion of how reading is figured within the sequels to *Story of the Stone* in her "*Honglou meng* Sequels and their Female Readers in Nineteenth-century China," in Huang, ed., *Snakes' Legs*, 116–42, especially 128 and 131.

99. Robert E. Hegel, *Reading Illustrated Fiction*, 328.

100. Cao Xueqin, *Honglou meng*, 445–46; Cf. *Story of the Stone*, 2:131–32. *Moral Heroes and Heroines* critiques "living according to literature" in *Story of the Stone* by praising He Yufeng's refusal to think in terms of the conventions of the scholar-beauty romance for her own life (on the occasion of the exchange of inkstone and bow). The digression is begun by an interruption of the narrator by the "audience," who has already made the association of the objects with the conventions of love tokens and is incredulous that He Yufeng had not. Furthermore, this critique is interpolated into the discourse in which Zhang Jinfeng uses precisely the exchanged objects to convince He Yufeng that she is fated to fulfill her "Heavenly" destiny as beauty (*jiaren*) and marry An Ji. Wen Kang, *Ernü yingxiong zhuan*, Guben xiaoshuo jicheng (Shanghai: Shanghai guji, [1990]), 1134–37.

101. Robert E. Hegel, *Reading Illustrated Fiction*, 328. For discussions of the self-conscious and metafictional nature of *Story of the Stone*, see also Wai-yee Li, *Enchantment and Disenchantment*; Anthony Yu, *Rereading the Stone*; Qiancheng Li, *Fictions of Enlightenment*, 134–64, 167; and Ming Dong Gu, *Chinese Theories of Fiction*, 153–80.

102. *Green Peony* is credited with incorporating "romance" into the martial arts novel, which laid the ground for *Moral Heroes and Heroines*. See Wen Qiji, introduction to *Lü mudan*, 3. Chen Pingyuan argues that structurally, *Green Peony* is more typical than *Moral Heroes and Heroines* for the incorporation of the romance plot into martial arts fiction, a combination that later produced "countless" works. Chen Pingyuan, *Qiangu wenren xiake meng*, 59.

103. Stephen Roddy, *Literati Identity and Its Fictional Representations in Late Imperial China*, 282 n6.

104. See *Green Peony*, 3; and Li Ruzhen, *Jinghua yuan*, Guben xiaoshuo jicheng (Shanghai: Shanghai guji, 1990), 146.

105. *Green Peony* reads "*raoluan da Tang gangji*," 2; Cf. "*raoluan Tang shi*" in Li Ruzhen, *Jinghua yuan*, 32.

106. *Green Peony*, 529–30.

107. Li Ruzhen, *Jinghua yuan*, 62.

108. Ibid., 63–64.

109. Ibid., 99–100.

110. *Sui Tang yanyi*, Guben xiaoshuo jicheng, 1903–4. As Ying Wang notes, such ambiguity is allowed in historical accounts, such as Sima Qian's account of Empress Lu in *Shi ji*, as part of their truth claim. See Ying Wang, "The Voices of the Re-readers: Interpretations of Three Late-Qing Rewrites of *Jinghua yuan*," in Huang, ed., *Snakes' Legs*, 224.

111. See Y. W. Ma, "The Chinese Historical Novel," 281.

112. *Green Peony*, 553–54.

113. Ibid., 451.

114. Maram Epstein, *Competing Discourses*, 266–67, 270; Stephen Roddy, *Literati Identity*, 173, 175, 180. See also Ellen Widmer's discussion of the "unstable ironies" regarding Empress Wu and the issue of loyalty in *Jinghua yuan*. Ellen Widmer, *Beauty and the Book*, 40–41.

115. He Yufeng belongs to a different tradition of martial heroines than Hua Bilian. While Hua Bilian is a female general (*nüjiang*) with ties to the heroines of the military romances, He Yufeng is more closely associated with female knight-errants (*nüxia*) going back to classical tales from the Tang dynasty. On the distinction, see Roland Altenburger, "The Sword or the Needle: The Female Knight-errant (*Xia*) in Traditional Chinese Fiction," 17–25. The "substitution" in *Moral Heroes and Heroines* is necessitated by the gender inversion in the second iteration of the romance trope. Because in this instance it is the woman, not the man, who is reluctant to marry and devoted to duty and the sword, the associations of the female knight errant fit the needs of the plot better than the forward female general.

116. Cf. Patrick Hanan, "The Narrator's Voice before the 'Fiction Revolution,'" in *Chinese Fiction of the Nineteenth and Early Twentieth Century*, 31 n5.

117. Wen Kang, *Ernü yingxiong zhuan*, 1105–66.

118. David Wang, *Fin-de-siècle Splendor: Repressed Modernities of Late Qing Fiction, 1849–1911*, 160–61.

119. Wen Kang, *Ernü yingxiong zhuan*, 1981.

Chapter 5. Placing the "Popular" Novel in the Qing

1. Roger Chartier, *Forms and Meanings*, 88–89.

2. Ibid., 92.

3. Anne E. McLaren, "Ming Audiences and Vernacular Hermeneutics," 51–80.

4. See Wei Shang, *"Rulin Waishi" and Cultural Transformation in Late Imperial China*; and Stephen Roddy, *Literati Identity and Its Fictional Representations in Late Imperial China*.

5. See, for example, Wilt Idema, *Chinese Vernacular Fiction: The Formative Period*, x-xii. Idema does make an exception for *The Water Margin* and *Three Kingdoms*, which he says are of "universal appeal." Idema refuses to use the term popular fiction to describe China's traditional vernacular fiction, since "if one wants to call specific kind of *texts* popular, one first has to know how large the reading public might have been in

premodern China." He believes the literacy rates could not have been high enough to justify the use of the term "popular fiction," and that much fiction was also prohibitively expensive. Ibid., xlvii-lxiv.

6. Cynthia Brokaw, *Commerce in Culture*, 553; Cf. idem, "Woodblock Printing and the Diffusion of Print in Qing China," 17.

7. Based on surviving evidence, the military romance was far and away the most popular genre of fiction in Sibao. One surviving account book shows orders totaling 114 copies for six military romance titles. This compares favorably with the orders for 105 copies of the basic educational text *San zi jing* (Three character classic). Next would come the Four Masterworks, if one includes the combined edition of *The Water Margin* and *Three Kingdoms* titled *Yingxiong pu* (A register of heroes). *Three Kingdoms* appears to have been by far the most popular of the four; then *The Water Margin*, *Journey to the West*, and *Jin Ping Mei* (only one edition recorded). After the masterworks, the next most popular group is historical fiction, followed by scholar-beauty romances. Court-case fiction, martial romances, and Pu Songling's *Liaozhai zhiyi* also sold well. Surprisingly, *Story of the Stone* only appears once in the extant Sibao publishing records, although Sibao's productions include four sequels or prequels to *Story of the Stone*.

Besides *Green Peony*, other martial romances—*Zheng Chun Yuan*, *San he jian*, and *Wanhua Lou*—were also among Sibao productions. Indeed, most of the titles and genres of the novel that the martial romance drew on were also produced in Sibao; they were genuinely popular texts with a wide audience. See Brokaw, *Commerce in Culture*, 476–98 and Appendix G.

8. Cynthia Brokaw notes that the Sibao imprint of *Sanguo yanyi*, titled *Di yi caizi shu*, includes commentary spuriously attributed to Jin Shengtan. Brokaw, *Commerce in Culture*, 478–81.

9. For the situation in the Ming, see Anne E. McLaren, "Ming Audiences and Vernacular Hermeneutics," 51–80. It is useful to distinguish between classifying a work by its author and intended audience and classifying it based on the actual audience for a work, as David Johnson suggests. David Johnson, "Communication, Class and Consciousness," 41.

10. Shang Wei, *"Rulin waishi" and Cultural Transformation in Late Imperial China*, 314.

11. Kang Baocheng, "Zidishu zuozhe 'He Lü Shi' shengping, jiashi kaolüe," 128–44.

12. Later in one of his *zidishu*, Yi Geng mentions ordering copies of *Green Peony* and *Cases of Judge Shi* from Baiben Zhang, so as to surpass the storyteller Shi Yukun. Quoted in Guan Dedong, "Shiyin *Qing Menggu Chewangfu cang quben* xu," in Liu Liemao, ed. *Chewangfu quben yanjiu*, 483. Since Baiben Zhang was primarily a purveyor of drama and *chantefable* manuscripts, this probably refers to the drum ballad version of *Green Peony*.

13. According to Cynthia Brokaw, Sibao publishers sold *Green Peony*, although no editions survive. Personal communication, May 18, 2003. See also Brokaw, *Commerce in Culture*, 494 and Appendix G, page 20.

14. I borrow the term "reading public" from Anne E. McLaren, "Constructing New Reading Publics in Late Ming China," 153.

15. Preface from Songde Xuan edition of *Shan e tu*, in Ding Xigen, ed., *Zhongguo lidai xiaoshuo xu ba ji*, 3:1537.

16. Preface from 1849 edition of *Yun Zhong Yan san nao Taiping Zhuang*, in Ding Xigen, ed., *Zhongguo lidai xiaoshuo xu ba ji*, 3:1597

17. *Tianbao tu*, 6. The adaptation of this novel from a lute ballad suggests a possible reason why the preface might be signed by a woman. For more on women audiences in this period, see Ellen Widmer, *The Beauty and the Book: Women and Fiction in Nineteenth-century China*.

18. Preface from the 1819 edition of *Qing Feng Zha*, in Ding Xigen, ed., *Zhongguo lidai xiaoshuo xu ba ji*, 3:1624–65.

19. The publisher's aspirations came true only in part. Although *Qing Feng Zha* was "passed down" and reprinted, it never seems to have "gone far" and was reprinted only in Yangzhou during the Qing dynasty. On the storyteller Pu Lin, see Li Dou, *Yangzhou huafang lu,* 258. For more on this novel and its audience, see Margaret B. Wan, "Local fiction of the Yangzhou region: *Qingfengzha*," in Lucie Olivová and Vibeke Børdahl, eds., *Lifestyle and Entertainment in Yangzhou* (Copenhagen: Nordic Institute of Asian Studies Press, 2008).

20. Preface by Rulian jushi from the 1801 edition of *Shuo Tang quanzhuan*, in Ding Xigen, *Zhongguo lidai xiaoshuo xu ba ji*, 2:963.

21. Brokaw, *Commerce in Culture*, 556–59. On the different ways the "same" texts might be read, see idem, "Reading the Best-Sellers of the Nineteenth Century."

22. The *Green Peony Drum Ballad* (*Guci chaoben Lü mudan*, n.d.) seems to be a copy of an earlier printed work; the title at the beginning of each fascicle (*Xiuxiang Lü mudan* or *Huitu Lü mudan*) indicates an illustrated work even though there are no illustrations in the manuscript.

23. The surviving volume (*juan* 51) entitled *Lü mudan* in the rare book room of the Beijing Normal University Library is an example of late Qing drum ballad treatments of this story. Stamps on the cover identify it as having been rented by Xing Long Zhai; writing in a different hand dates it to the Guangxu reign period (1875–1908). This is quite plausible; Fu Xihua dates the activities of the Xing Long Zhai rental shop to the Tongzhi-Guangxu reign periods (1862–1908). See Fu Xihua, "Bai Ben Zhang xiqu shuji kaolüe," 317–31. In addition, three different stamps on the cover of the Xing Long Zhai manuscript explicitly warn both men and women not to damage, lose, or rent out the book to others. This suggests that its audience included women. An example of one of the stamps appears in the above article by Fu Xihua.

24. Brokaw notes the military romance "constituted by far the most popular of the fiction genres that Sibao published, with at least twenty titles in the Cuiyun tang inventory. Military romances were also, along with primers, the Four Books, and the Five Classics, the works most commonly mentioned by informants as part of Sibao's regular stock." Brokaw, *Commerce in Culture*, 485.

25. Just because a work claims membership in a performance genre does not mean it has any relationship to performance. There are whole genres of imitations, such as "literary lute ballads," which were written and copied primarily as reading materials rather than for performance. Nancy Hodes is careful to note that even "performance-related" lute ballad texts are "fakes," written to be read, and cannot be proven to be either scripts or transcriptions of performance; nonetheless, they bear a closer relationship to performance than the "literary" lute ballads. Nancy Hodes, "Strumming and Singing the 'Three Smiles Romance': A Study of the *Tanci* Text," 9. Be that as it may, these texts provide valuable information on the reading habits of local audiences. Similarly, the Cantonese ballad form called *muyu shu* (or *nanyin*) included very different forms, some written for reading and considered proper reading material for women, others intended for performance in brothels. See Sai-shing Yung, "Mu-Yu Shu and the Cantonese Popular Singing Arts," *The Gest Library Journal* 2, no. 1 (1987): 19; and Bell Yung, "Popular Narrative in the Pleasure Houses of the South," *CHINOPERL Papers* 11 (1982): 126–49.

26. Academica Sinica, *Zhongyang Yanjiu Yuan lishi yuyan yanjiu suo suo cang suqu zongmu mulu.*

27. One historian suggests "the most effective agency of popular education in Qing China . . . was the rural theatrical troupes." Alexander Woodside, "Some Mid-Qing Theorists of Popular Schools: Their Innovations, Inhibitions, and Attitudes toward the Poor," 33.

28. This would change; when *chantefables* were printed in lithographic editions in late Qing Shanghai, illustrations became the norm.

29. Anne E. McLaren, *Chinese Popular Culture and Ming Chantefables,* 112–13.

30. Brokaw, *Commerce in Culture*, 504.

31. McLaren, *Chinese Popular Culture and Ming Chantefables*, 52.

32. Ibid.

33. Ibid., 42.

34. *Zhenben tianbao tu quan zhuan*, 1.5a. Cf. *Tianbao tu*, 3.

35. A notable exception are "literary lute ballads" (*wenci* or *nü tanci*), which tend to be extremely long and often circulated privately in manuscript.

36. Similar stamps on the fronts of these manuscripts from various rental shops tell us about how they were generally rented. The patron would make a large deposit up front, and was supposed to return a volume every day to get the next installment. Patrons who failed to return it within half a month would lose their deposit, and those who failed to return it for over a month would pay a fine. According to a note on the book *Tian ci fu* rented by San Mei Zhai, each rental cost nine cash (*wen*) in the Guangxu era. A note on *Sanguo zhi guci* from Jiwen Zhai says a lost volume would cost one string of cash (*diao*) [100 cash (*wen*)]. See Li Jiarui, "Qingdai Beijing mantou pu zulin changben de gaikuang," 135.

37. See appendix for information on editions. One of these *chantefables* includes "Acapella" (*qing chang*) in the title, suggesting it was published to aid amateur performance.

38. Research has shown that *zidishu* and one type of lute ballad (known as "literary" *tanci*) appeal to an elite, well-educated audience. The lute ballad *Zaisheng yuan* was read by the *guixiu* author's mother, friends, and relatives; she wrote in it, "I don't want to publish my manuscripts for ordinary people to read. They are meant for well-educated and extraordinary women." See Marina H. Sung, "T'an-Tz'u and T'an-Tz'u Narratives," 18. The female author of the lute ballad *Zaizaotian* was an impoverished member of the social elite who imagined an audience of *guixiu* readers, and the lute ballads she edited carried endorsements by elite women. Ellen Widmer, *The Beauty and the Book*, 75–86. See also Mark Bender, "Tan-ci, Wen-ci, Chang-ci," 121–24. For the audience and aesthetic of *zidishu*, see Andrea S. Goldman, "The Nun Who Wouldn't Be: Representations of Female Desire in Two Performance Genres of 'Si Fan'," 71–138.

39. The analogy of dialogue markers to punctuation I make here is inspired by a study of the reading contexts of Old English verse. "In a study of the ways in which Old English poetry is accommodated by and assimilated within the literate frameworks of the transmission of information, the presence and distribution of points [punctuation] directly measures a need for increased visual information in the reading of verse." Early practice did not need punctuation because of its close relationship to performance–"the early paucity of pointing speaks to a tacit understanding that a reader of verse brought the necessary interpretive information to the text, aided by memory and by a deep familiarity with the formulaic conventions of Old English verse. Increasingly consistent pointing in the manuscripts of Old English verse indexes the growing textuality of the verse and the distance of the reader from vital oral tradition." Katherine O'Brien O'Keefe, *Visible Song*, 153–54.

40. Vibeke Børdahl's work on actual storyteller's scripts of Yangzhou storytelling supports this point of view; dialogue markers are completely absent in these true aides-memoire. Vibeke Børdahl, "Storytellers' Scripts in the *Yangzhou Pinghua* Tradition," 255, 269. The use of such dialogue markers may be genre-specific. See Børdahl's discussion of the use of dialogue markers in a drum tale (*dagu*) text in idem, "A Drum Tale on 'Wu Song Fights the Tiger'", 80–82.

41. Cf. Patrick Hanan, "The *Yün-men Chuan*: from *Chantefable* to Short Story," 302.

42. *Green Peony Drum Ballad*, 179 and 180, respectively. The latter allusion refers to Lady Li of the Han dynasty.

43. While *Green Peony* does not explicitly refer to *Story of the Stone*, links to both in *Moral Heroes and Heroines* suggest a common audience. *Moral Heroes and Heroines* openly reacts to *Story of the Stone*, and it mentions *Green Peony* in chapter 39. See Wen Kang, *Ernü yingxiong zhuan*, 4:1981.

44. *Shuihu quan zhuan*, 735; *Jin Ping Mei cihua*, 82–83; cf. David Tod Roy, trans., *The Plum in the Golden Vase*, 1:167, 501 n43.

45. Gérard Genette, *Palimpsests*, 16–17.

46. *Jin Ping Mei cihua*, 82; cf. Roy, *The Plum in the Golden Vase*, 1: 167, 500 n42.

47. *Yishuo Hou Tang zhuan san ji Xue Dingshan zheng Xi Fan Lihua quan zhuan*, 633; *Yishuo Fan Tang quan zhuan*, 867.

48. Mikhail Mikhailovich Bakhtin, *The Dialogic Imagination*, 41–83.

49. See *Green Peony Drum Ballad*, 273–74.

50. Gérard Genette, *Palimpsests*, 152.

51. Genette notes that contamination (double or multiple imitation) is a technique of transformation that can create a new genre. *Palimpsests*, 210.

52. Since each genre "speaks for itself," it still can be seen as somewhat admirable.

53. Plaks, "Full-Length Hsiao-Shuo," 172.

54. A familiar example is Ang Lee's film *Crouching Tiger, Hidden Dragon* (2000). Like *Green Peony, Crouching Tiger, Hidden Dragon* uses the conventions of another genre—the romance—to critique what Ang Lee felt was missing or "repressed" in the martial arts films and novels he grew up on. The characters are aware of the roles they play, but often are ambivalent toward them. The film invokes and displays the genre conventions through the characters' understanding of them: Yu Jiaolong (Jen) initially aspires to be like the heroes in the martial books she reads, while Li Mubai and Yu Xiulian (Yu Shu Lien) are trying to escape such expectations. Still, Li Mubai and Yu Xiulian are portrayed as admirable for adhering to the martial code despite their disillusionment. This is not to say that the film sides with a particular character, genre, or value system. The ambiguity created by the juxtaposition of genres is never resolved, thanks to the enigmatic ending, leaving the interpretation of the film up to the viewer.

55. Indeed, the beginnings of genre hybridization can be seen even in the scholar-beauty romance and the historical novel. The increasing consciousness of the genres played upon in the martial romance suggests a distancing from the values embodied in them. Cf. McKeon, "The very capacity of seventeenth-century [English] narrative to model itself so self-consciously on established categories bespeaks a detachment sufficient to imagine them *as* categories, to parody and thence to supercede them." McKeon, *The Origins of the English Novel*, 268.

56. Bakhtin, *Dialogic Imagination*, 388.

57. The other martial romance novels that still feature the civil service examination, like *San he jian*, *Yun Zhong Yan*, and *Xiu qiu yuan*, are precisely those novels that have most clearly undermined the values of the scholar.

58. Martin Huang notes that "suicide . . . was ultimately a feminine act of helplessness and despair, reflecting a man's incompetence. Though viewed by many as an act of heroism, suicide . . . paradoxically often reflected the absence of the spirit of *yingxiong* and the painful reality of men being feminized." Huang, *Negotiating Masculinities in Late Imperial China*, 92.

59. In *Flowers in the Mirror*, "men who leave the Confucian fold entirely are able to foster their talents primarily because they escape the deleterious influence of literati institutions." The young men abandon civil for military arts. Stephen Roddy, *Literati Identity and Its Fictional Representations in Late Imperial China*, 185. Similar ideas appear in the eighteenth-century novel *Yesou puyan* (The Humble words of a rustic), although it posits not an abandonment but a fusion of the two ideals in its "painstaking attempts to construct a Confucian superhero and . . . its re-envisioned masculinity

based on the perfect union between *ernü* and *yingxiong*." Martin Huang, *Negotiating Masculinities*, 158.

In the eighteenth century, the scholar-beauty romances also evolved to deemphasize the civil service examinations and put the scholar on the battlefield; Martin Huang notes this often makes the scholars seem "somewhat pathetic as military heroes." Ibid., 156.

60. By way of illustrating this point, my research finds that only two of the novels on Robert Hegel's table of "Frequently Printed Novels of the Ming and Qing" (*Reading Illustrated Fiction*, 65, Table 2.4) do not show clear influence of Jin Shengtan or *pingdian* commentary: *Shuo Tang houzhuan* and *Zui Puti*. While *Shuo Tang houzhuan* is a military romance and *Zui Puti* concerns the supernatural, the absence of obvious influence is not determined by thematic genre. The supernatural novel *Fengshen yanyi* carries commentary, and the military romance *Nan Bei Song zhizhuan* claims commentary in the title of many editions. Cf. Han Xiduo, *Xiaoshuo shufang lu*, 10, 15, 17, 26, 219; and Rolston, "List of Commentary Editions of Traditional Chinese Fiction Other than the Six Novels," in *How to Read the Chinese Novel*, 485–87.

Rolston notes deliberate obfuscation to suggest that Jin Shengtan wrote the commentary on *Sanguo*, *Xiyou ji* and *Jin Ping Mei*. See his *Traditional Chinese Fiction and Fiction Commentary*, 48–49. This suggests the commercialization of Jin Shengtan's name.

61. The court-case story collections may be an exception, since Rolston suggests any commentary found in them is closer to that in handbooks of historical cases than to Jin Shengtan-style commentary. Rolston, *Traditional Chinese Fiction and Fiction Commentary*, 285. However, at least one edition of *Longtu gongan* claims a "Li Zhi" commentary. Rolston, *How to Read*, 486.

While commentary on military romances seems to be fairly rare, many editions of the popular military romance *Nan Bei Song zhizhuan* claim to carry fiction commentary. Han Xiduo, *Xiaoshuo shufang lu*, 10, 15, 17, 26.

62. *Di ba caizi shu Hua jian ji* (The eighth work of genius: The elegant letter, 1714) has a Jin Shengtan-style commentary by Zhong Daicang, noted by Tan Zhengbi in his *Muyu ge, Chaozhou ge xulu*, 5. Plaks notes the existence of eleven *muyu shu* with *caizi shu* titles; see Plaks, "Terminology and Central Concepts," in Rolston, ed., *How to Read the Chinese Novel*, 84–85 n14.

For a discussion of the generic significance of the designation *caizi shu*, see Patricia Sieber, "The Chinese Fictional Canon Reconsidered: The View from European Book Acquisitions, 1720–1860" (unpublished mss).

63. *San he jian*, 1; *Huitu Qun Ying Jie hou Song qi shu* (Shanghai shuju, 1894, in Fudan University Library); *Longtan Bao Luo qi shu* (1892, Shanghai shuju lithographic edition, in Beijing University Library).

64. Preface from 1819 edition of *Zheng Chun Yuan*, in Ding Xigen, *Zhongguo lidai xiaoshuo xu ba ji*, 3:1595–96.

65. The numbers of editions are based primarily on Ōtsuka, supplemented with other editions I have found in libraries or listed in Han Xiduo, *Xiaoshuo shufang lu*.

Although it is always possible that more editions of these novels may be found, I expect the general pattern would hold.

66. With *Qun Ying Jie* it is interesting to note how early the title includes *qi shu*—even in the first edition, which Sun Kaidi thinks is from the Qianlong-Jiaqing period. Its link with local Cantonese literature is intriguing, since a significant number of those songbooks adopted Jin Shengtan's rhetoric early on. *Qun Ying Jie* was also printed as a *nanyin* in Foshan and Guangzhou; see appendix.

67. For these terms, see, for example, "creating a thread for the later text" (*wei xiawen zuo zhenxian*) in *Wanhua lou*, 18; "preparing" (*zuo yi dibu*; ibid., 153); "reflection" (*ying*[1] or *ying*[2]; ibid., 193, 880); and "leading in" (*yin*; ibid., 180, 220). For an example of the use of individual words as foreshadowing, see ibid., 629.

68. For analysis of the repetition of similar plot elements, see the note to chapter 44, in ibid., 603.

69. See *Wanhua lou*, 18 and 153, respectively. Contrast in characterization is also the subject of notes to chapters 29 and 38, on pages 405 and 522.

70. One note says, "Zhang and Li are both called heroes, but if you look at their private discourse, although it is not comparable to the deportment of the evil, Li Yi does lust after glory. Glory and profit put people in a bind." It goes on to contrast behavior of gentleman and petty man; one sees the gentleman hold back his anger toward petty men, but never sees a petty man let a gentleman go. Ibid., 523.

71. "Extraordinary!" appears in ibid., 339. Another comment explains why he did not edit out a weak point by claiming to be copying an "ancient edition." Ibid., 509–10.

The "ancient edition" defense also appears within the novel itself at the end of the last chapter. *Wanhua Lou* is a prequel to two other novels on Di Qing, as C. T. Hsia suggests. In chapter 68, it explicitly justifies the repetition of incidents found in its popular forbear, *Wu Hu ping Xi*: "This explains that this book and *Wu Hu ping Xi* chapter 120 have a lot in common (*lüe duo guanzhao zhi bi*), only Miss Fan finding a husband and getting married is different. But the original ancient edition also wrote this, so I went by the original edition and did not make changes." Ibid., 921. Like certain places in *Green Peony*, this acknowledges the text as a text, but *Wanhua Lou* goes further to explicitly discuss its relationship with another novel. Perhaps its status as a prequel partly explains this. More elaborate discussions of the relationship between particular novels appear in the sequels to *Honglou meng*. See Ellen Widmer, "*Honglou meng* Sequels and Their Female Readers in Nineteenth-century China," 128, 131.

72. *Wanhua Lou*, 207.

73. See Rolston, *Traditional Chinese Fiction and Fiction Commentary*, 186–87.

74. The 1679 edition has a preface signed by Li Yu which may be authentic. "Later editions contain a reworked version of the 1679 preface and it is in this fashion that the 'Chin Sheng-t'an' preface to the popular editions of the novel with commentary ascribed to Mao Tsung-kang came into existence." David Roy, "Introduction: Mao Tsung-kang and His 'Tu *San-kuo chih* fa,'" in Rolston, ed., *How to Read the Chinese Novel*, 149. Both versions of the preface are reprinted in Ding Xigen, *Zhongguo lidai xu ba ji*, 2:897–901.

75. See Ding Xigen, *Zhongguo lidai xu ba ji*, 2:898 and 900.

76. Incidentally, both impulses appear in the title of a later novel *Zheng Chun Yuan* influenced, *San he jian: Xiuxiang di shi caizi shu* (Three united swords: The illustrated Tenth Book of Genius). The "sword" in the title marks it clearly as a martial arts novel, while the "Tenth Book of Genius" uses Jin Shengtan's rhetoric to claim its place as art.

77. This is figured nicely in the "erudite" novel *Flowers in the Mirror*: crucial information is given to the characters on a stone tablet in an archaic script that only one person can read, and she can make it out only because she is a reincarnated immortal.

78. Patricia Ebrey, *Confucianism and Family Ritual in Imperial China*, 143–44, 188–89.

79. Ibid, 188.

80. See, for example, Jin Shengtan's "Third Preface" in Chen Xizhong, Hou Zhongyi, and Lu Yuchuan, eds., *Shuihu zhuan huiping ben*, 8–11.

81. The text also was not sacrosanct—Jin Shengtan felt free to change anything he disagreed with.

82. Jin Shengtan also has "a conviction that the books' major statement is about morality, although the moral should not be stated too obviously." Ellen Widmer, *Margins of Utopia*, 103.

83. Patricia Ebrey would argue that ritual itself was similar across classes in the Qing. See Ebrey, *Confucianism and Family Ritual in Imperial China*, 229. There is also evidence of middlebrow authors concerning themselves with ritual issues, for example Hsiung Ping-chen's study, "Treading the Weedy Path: T'ang Cheng (1630–1704) and the World of the Confucian Middlebrow," 195–211. Some of these "middlebrow" ideas gained currency in the nineteenth century. Still, it would seem the core debates of ritualism on the relationship between ritual texts and practice would most concern the educated elite.

84. Margaret Rose, *Parody//Metafiction*, 92–93.

85. Preface to *Lü mudan quan zhuan* (San huai tang, 1800), 1.1b-2a; cf. Ding Xigen, *Zhongguo lidai xiaoshuo xu ba ji*, 3:1538.

86. Cao Xueqin, *Honglou meng*, 5.

87. John Christopher Hamm, *Paper Swordsmen*, 75.

88. John Christopher Hamm, *Paper Swordsmen*, 75. For the comedies of displacement, see ibid., 67–75.

89. Pieter C. A. Keulemans, "Sounds of the Novel: Storytelling, Print-culture, and Martial-arts Fiction in Nineteenth-century Beijing," (unpublished doctoral thesis, University of Chicago, 2004) 52–54, 60–62. On the place of the martial arts novel in late Qing print culture, see also Paize Keulemans, "Listening to the Printed Martial Arts Scene: Onomatopoeia and the Qing Dynasty Storyteller's Voice," *Harvard Journal of Asiatic Studies* (2007): 51–87.

90. Chen Pingyuan notes that one can see in the merging of heroism and romance in *Green Peony* the beginnings of such organizing principles of later martial arts novels;

in this he considers the structure of *Green Peony* much more typical than that of *Ernü yingxiong zhuan*. Chen Pingyuan, *Qiangu wenren xiake meng*, 59.

91. Wilt Idema, *Chinese Vernacular Fiction: The Formative Period*, xliii.

92. Robert Hegel notes that, due to the increasing complexity of Qing works of fiction, scholars tend to turn from genre categorization to themes or intellectual concerns. Hegel, *Reading Illustrated Fiction*, 57.

93. "If we do not recognize the existence of this second context of somebody else's speech and begin to perceive stylization or parody in the same way ordinary speech is perceived, that is, as speech directed only at its referential object, then we will not grasp the phenomena in their essence: stylization will be taken for style, parody simply for a poor work of art." Bakhtin, *Problems of Dostoevsky's Poetics*, 185.

94. Michael McKeon, *The Origins of the English Novel 1600–1740*, 13.

Glossary

Ailian jushi	愛蓮居士
An Ji	安驥
an nu	暗怒
ba	把
Ba Bao	巴豹
Ba Biao	巴彪
Ba Hu	巴虎
ba jia huan	把家還
Ba Long	巴龍
ba Lu Jia guai	把蘆家怪
ba luo da	把鑼打
Baiben Zhang	百本張
Ban Gu	班固
Bao Gang	包剛
Bao Gang	鮑剛
Bao Gong	包公
Bao Jinhua	鮑金花
Bao Zi'an	鮑自安
bian	編
bin	賓
bu tong hu zhongren	不通乎眾人
bu yi le hu	不亦樂乎
bu yi xing hu	不亦幸乎
cailang	才郎
caizi	才子
caizi jiaren	才子佳人

caizi shu	才子書
Cao Cao	曹操
Cao Tianheng	曹天衡
changben	唱本
chen	襯
Chuci	楚辞
dagu	大鼓
da nu	大怒
Dang kou zhi	蕩寇志
Daoguang	道光
daole yipen reshui/ qule yitiao shoujin	倒了一盆热水,取了一条手巾
de	德
Di Qing	狄青
Di Renjie	狄仁傑
Di ba caizi shu Hua jian ji	第八才子書花箋記
Di shi caizi shu	第十才子書
diao	吊
Dingxing	定興
Dong Chao	董超
Dongfang Shuo	東方朔
du	讀
dushu	讀書
Du Xiantong	杜仙童
ernü	兒女
Ernü yingxiong zhuan	兒女英雄傳
Fan Lihua	樊梨花
Fan Tang hou zhuan	反唐後傳
Fan Tang quan zhuan	反唐全傳
Fan Zhongyan	范仲淹
Feng shen yanyi	封神演義
gongan	公案
gongan xiayi	公案俠義
gongzi	公子
Gu Dasao	顧大嫂
guci	鼓詞
guye	姑爺
guan	觀

Guanyin 觀音
Guangxu 光緒
Gui lian meng 歸蓮夢
guixiu 閨秀
Han Wudi 漢武帝
Hao Luan 郝鸞
haodai 好歹
haohan 好漢
haoqiu 好逑
haoyou 好友
He Lü 鶴侶
He Shilai 賀世賴
He Yufeng 何玉鳳
Hong Bi yuan 宏碧緣
Hong Hua 紅花
Hong Niang 紅娘
hou ban jie 後半截
Hou xu Da Song Yangjiang wenwu quxing Bao Gong Di Qing chu zhuan 後續大宋楊將文武曲星包公狄青初傳
Hu Li 胡理
Hu Lian 胡璉
Hu Saihua 胡賽花
Hu Sanniang 扈三娘
Hua Bilian 花碧蓮
Hua Jinzhang 花錦章
Hua Rong 花榮
Hua Saijin 花賽金
Hua Sanqian 華三千
Hua Zhenfang 花振芳
Hua Zineng 花子能
Hua Zining 花子寧
Huang Tianba 黃天霸
Huitu Lü mudan 繪圖綠牡丹
ji 集
jia gongzi 佳公子
Jiaqing 嘉慶
jiaren 佳人

jiaren caizi	佳人才子
Jiaxing	嘉興
jiang	將
jianghu	江湖
jianghu dao ke	江湖刀客
jiang Lu Jia guai le	將盧家怪了
Jiangnan	江南
jiang shen mai	將身賣
jiangshi	講史
jiang tai shang	將台上
jie gong bao si	借公報私
jienü	傑女
Jin Ping Mei	金瓶梅
Jin Shengtan	金聖嘆
Jin tai quan zhuan	金台全傳
Jinghua yuan	鏡花緣
juan	卷
junzi	君子
Kangxi	康熙
kaozheng	考證
kuai	快
lan	覽
Lang Huan shuwu	瑯環書屋
Lao Mei	老梅
laoye	老爺
li	禮
Li Kui	李逵
Li Lei	李雷
Li Mubai	李慕白
Li Rongchun	李榮春
Li Yi	李義
Li Yu	李漁
li zhi	立志
Liaozhai zhiyi	聊齋誌異
Liu Bei	劉備
Longtan Bao Luo qi shu	龍潭鮑駱奇書
Longtu erlu	龍圖耳錄

Longtu gongan	龍圖公案
Lu Junyi	盧俊義
Lu Zhishen	魯智深
Luling Wang	廬陵王
Luan Yiwan	欒鎰萬
lüe duo guanzhao zhi bi	略多關照之筆
lüe fan	略犯
Luo Binwang	駱賓王
Luo Hongqu	駱紅蕖
Luo Hongxun	駱宏勛
Luo Long	駱龍
Luo Ye	羅燁
Ma Jun	馬俊
mai shen	賣身
Mao Zonggang	毛宗崗
Mei Tao	梅滔
mie lun	滅倫
Mu Guiying	穆桂英, 木桂英
mu dachong	母大虫
muyu shu	木魚書
Nan Bei Song zhizhuan	南北宋志傳
Nan Fu	南府
nanyin	南音
nüjiang	女將
nüxia	女俠
nüzi wu cai bian shi de	女子無才便是德
Peng gongan	彭公案
ping	評
pingdian	評點
pinghua	平話
Ping yao zhuan	平妖傳
Pu Tiandiao	濮天雕
Pu Tianpeng	濮天鵬
qi	奇
Qi caizi shu	七才子書
qi shu	奇書
qi zai	奇哉

qian ban jie	前半截
qiangu hanwen	千古罕聞
qian hou bu zhaoying	前後不照應
Qianlong	乾隆
qin	親
qing	情
qing chang	清唱
qingyuan yitong sheng si	情願一同生死
Qiongying	瓊英
raoluan da Tang gangji	擾亂大唐綱紀
raoluan Tang shi	擾亂唐室
reshui dengshi bei yihu/ shoujin yikuai tiao huabu	热水登时备一壶, 手巾一块挑花布
Ren Zhengqian	任正千
Renzong	仁宗
ruci ruci	如此如此
Rulian jushi	如蓮居士
San caizi shu Yu Jiao Li	三才子書玉嬌梨
Sanguo yanyi	三國演義
Sanguo zhi yanyi	三國志演義
Sanhe mingzhu fang lun quanben	三合明珠方倫全本
Sanxia wuyi	三俠五義
San yan	三言
San zi jing	三字經
se	色
shanshu	善書
shang tai	上台
Shao Qing	邵青
Shaoyan Banxing Jushi	少岩半醒居士
Shengping Shu	昇平署
Shi Bixia	施碧霞
Shi Bixian	施必顯
Shi ji	史記
Shi jing	詩經
Shi pai shu	石派書
shi xiong	師兄
Shi Xiu	石秀

Shi Yukun	石玉昆
Shi Zhong	施忠
shou	手
shou	首
si	私
Sibao	四堡
Si caizi shu Ping Shan Leng Yan	四才子書平山冷燕
Si Jie Cun	四傑村
Si Wang Ting	四望亭
Si Wang Ting quan zhuan	四望亭全傳
Sima Xiangru	司馬相如
Sui shi yiwen	隋史遺文
Sui Tang yanyi	隋唐演義
tanci	彈詞
Tang	唐
Tang Ao	唐敖
Tang Guichen	唐閨臣
Tao Tianbao	陶天豹
Tianbao tu	天豹圖
Tian Daxiu	田大修
Tianhua Zang Zhuren	天花藏主人
Tongzhi	同治
Wanhua Lou Yang Bao Di yanyi	萬花樓楊包狄演義
wanwan	玩玩
wang en	忘恩
Wang Aihu	王矮虎
Wang Lun	王倫
Wanli	萬曆
wei jingguo da di	未經過大敵
wei xiawen zuo zhenxian	為下文作針線
wen	文
wen fa	文法
wenyan	文言
wen yi zai dao	文以載道
wu	武
Wu Bing	吳炳
Wu hang ye ke	吳航野客

Wu Hu ping Nan	五虎平南
Wu Hu ping Xi	五虎平西
wuli	無禮
wuqing wuyi	無情無義
Wu Sansi	武三思
Wu Song	武松
wuwei	無味
wuxia	武俠
Wuxia congtan	武俠叢談
wuyong	武勇
Wu Zetian	武則天
Wu Zetian gai Tang yanyi	武則天改唐演義
xi	戲
xijiang yue	西江月
Xixiang ji	西廂記
xia	俠
xiaqing xiaoshuo	俠情小說
xiayi	俠義
Xianfeng	咸豐
xian gu ji er hou you ren	先顧己而後有人
xian kan hou zou	先砍後奏
xianshua	閑耍
xiao	孝
Xiao An	消安
Xiao Ji	消計
xiaosheng	小生
xiaoshuo	小說
Xiao wuyi	小五義
xiao xiaqi	消俠氣
Xiao Yue	消月
Xin ke zhenben tanci changkou Tianbao tu quan zhuan	新刻真本彈詞唱口天豹圖全傳
xinyuan yima	心猿意馬
Xing Long Zhai	興隆齋
Xiuxiang Lü mudan	綉像綠牡丹
Xu fan Tang zhuan	續反唐傳
Xu Shu	徐庶

Xu Songpeng	徐松朋
Xue Dingshan	薛丁山
Xue Gang	薛剛
Xue Kui	薛葵
Xue Rengui	薛仁貴
yanyi	演義
Yang Jia Fu yanyi	楊家府演義
Yang Shen	楊慎
Yang Xiong	楊雄
Yangzhou	揚州
Yangzhou pinghua	揚州評話
Yang Zongbao	楊宗保
yeshi	野史
Yesou puyan	野叟曝言
yi	義
Yi Geng	奕賡
yi guan shi wei ming	以官事為名
yiqi	義氣
yishi	義士
yin	引
ying[1]	應
ying[2]	映
yingxiong	英雄
yingxiong chuanqi	英雄傳奇
yingxiong haojie	英雄豪杰
Yingxiong pu	英雄譜
Yong qing sheng ping	永慶升平
Yong qing sheng ping qian zhuan	永慶升平前傳
yu	欲
Yu gongan	于公案
Yu Jiao Li	玉嬌梨
Yu Jiaolong	玉蛟龍
Yu Qian	余謙
Yu Xiulian	俞秀蓮
yuan tong sheng si	願同生死
Yuan Wuya	袁無涯
yueding	閱定

Yue Fei	岳飛
Yunmen zhuan	雲門傳
Yun Wen	雲文
zan	贊
zei	賊
zeizi	賊子
Zhang Hai	張海
Zhang Jinfeng	張金鳳
Zhang Tianzuo	張天左
Zhang Zhong	張忠
Zhang Zhupo	張竹坡
zhaoying	照應
zhe cai suan zuo haohan	這才算做好漢
zheng fan	正犯
zhiji	知己
zhi xin zhi yu	知心之語
zhong	忠
Zhongguo tongsu xiaoshuo shumu	中國通俗小說書目
Zhongguo xiaoshuo shilüe	中國小說史略
Zhongzong	中宗
Zhou Shun	周順
zhu	主
Zhu Biao	朱彪
Zhuchun yuan xiaoshi	駐春園小史
Zhu Hu	朱虎
Zhuhu Yuyin	珠湖漁隱
Zhu Long	朱龍
Zhuolao	拙老
zidishu	子弟書
Zizhi tongjian	資治通鑑
Zuiweng tanlu	醉翁談錄
Zui puti	醉菩提
zuo yi dibu	作一地步

Selected Bibliography

Chinese and Japanese Works

Academica Sinica. *Zhongyang Yanjiu Yuan lishi yuyan yanjiu suo suo cang suqu zongmu mulu* 中央研究院歷史語言研究所所藏俗曲綜目目錄. Harvard-Yenching Library. Photocopy.

Bao gongan cihua bazhong 包公案詞話八種. Guben xiaoshuo congkan, 22:4. Beijing: Zhonghua, 1992.

Cao Xueqin 曹雪芹. *Honglou meng* 紅樓夢. Beijing: Renmin, 1988.

Chen Pingyuan 陳平原. *Qiangu wenren xiake meng* 千古文人俠客夢. Beijing: Renmin wenxue chubanshe, 1992.

———. "Wuxia xiaoshuo yu zhongguo wenhua 武俠小說與中國文化," *Wenshi zhishi* 文史知識, 1990, no. 1:69–75.

———. *Xiaoshuo shi: Lilun yu shijian* 小說史： 理論與實踐. Beijing: Beijing daxue, 1993.

Chen Qinghao 陳慶浩, ed. *Xinbian Honglou meng Zhiyanzhai pingyu ji jiao* 新編紅樓夢脂硯齋評語輯校. Hong Kong: Zhongwen daxue, 1972.

Chen Xizhong 陳曦鐘, Hou Zhongyi 侯忠義, and Lu Yuchuan 魯玉川, eds. *Shuihu zhuan huiping ben* 水滸傳會評本. Beijing: Beijing Daxue, 1987.

Chen Xizhong 陳曦鐘, Song Xiangrui 宋祥瑞, and Lu Yuchuan 魯玉川, eds. *Sanguo yanyi huiping ben* 三國演義會評本. Beijing: Beijing Daxue, 1986.

Chu Renhuo 褚人穫. *Sui Tang yanyi* 隋唐演義. Guben xiaoshuo jicheng. Reprint. Shanghai: Shanghai guji [1990].

Cui Yunhua 崔蘊華. *Shuzhai yu shufang zhi jian: Qingdai zidishu yanjiu* 書齋與書坊之間：清代子弟書研究. Beijing: Beijing Daxue chubanshe, 2005.

Da Han san he mingzhu baojian quan zhuan 大漢三合明珠寶劍全傳. With a preface by Li Mengsheng 李夢生. Reprint. Guben xiaoshuo jicheng, vol. 163. Shanghai: Shanghai guji [1990].

Da Ming qi xia zhuan 大明奇俠傳. 1895.

Da Ming quan zhuan xiu qiu yuan 大明全傳繡球緣. Guben xiaoshuo jicheng, vol. 127. Shanghai: Shanghai guji [1990].

Ding Xigen丁錫根, ed. *Zhongguo lidai xiaoshuo xu ba ji* 中國歷代小說序跋集. Beijing: Renmin, 1996.

Feng Menglong 馮夢龍, ed. *Gu jin xiaoshuo* 古今小說. Shanghai: Shanghai guji, 1987.

———. *Jingshi tongyan* 警世通言. Shanghai: Shanghai guji, 1987.

———. *Xingshi hengyan* 醒世恆言. Guben xiaoshuo congkan. Beijing: Zhonghua [1990].

Fengyue meng 風月夢. Guben xiaoshuo jicheng. Shanghai: Shanghai guji [1990].

Fu Xihua 傅惜華. "Bai Ben Zhang xiqu shuji kaolüe 百本張戲曲書籍考略." In *Zhongguo Jindai chuban shiliao er bian* 中國近代出版史料二編, ed. Zhang Jinglu 張靜廬, 317–31. Shanghai: Qunlian chubanshe, 1954.

Guan Dedong 關德棟. "Shiyin *Qing Menggu Chewangfu cang quben* xu." In Liu Liemao 劉烈茂, ed. *Chewangfu quben yanjiu* 車王府曲本研究, 481–85. Guangzhou: Guangzhou renmin chubanshe, 2000.

Guben Wanhua Lou quan ge 古本萬花樓全歌. Chaozhou: Li Wanli, n.d.

Guci chaoben Lü mudan 鼓詞抄本綠牡丹. Reprint, Gugong zhenben congkan: Qingdai Nan Fu yu Sheng Ping Shu juben yu dangan, vol. 712. Haikou: Hainan Chubanshe, 2001.

Gui lian meng 歸蓮夢. Guben xiaoshuo jicheng. Shanghai: Shanghai guji [1990].

Han Cao 寒操. "*Shi Gong an* de kanxing niandai 《施公案》的刊行年代." *Gudian wenxue zhishi* 1 (1993): 98–99.

Han Xiduo 翰錫鐸 and Wang Qingyuan 王清原, eds. *Xiaoshuo shufang lu* 小說書坊錄. Beijing: Beijing Tushuguan chubanshe, 2002.

Hanyu da cidian 漢語大詞典. Ed. Luo Zhufeng 羅竹風. Shanghai: Hanyu da cidian chubanshe, 1994.

Haoqiu zhuan 好逑傳. Guben xiaoshuo jicheng. Shanghai: Shanghai guji [1990].

Hong Bi yuan 宏碧緣. Xin wenhua shushe, 1935.

Hu Shiying 胡士瑩. *Huaben xiaoshuo gailun* 話本小說概論. Beijing: Zhonghua shuju, 1980.

Huitu Qun Ying Jie hou Song qi shu 繪圖群英傑後宋奇書. Shanghai: Shanghai shuju, 1894.

Ji Dejun 紀德君. *Ming Qing lishi yanyi xiaoshuo yishu lun* 明清歷史演義小說藝術論. Beijing Shifan Daxue Boshi Wenku. Beijing: Beijing shifan daxue chubanshe, 2000.

Ji Lu 季路, ed. *Si Wang Ting quan zhuan* 四望亭全傳. Chuantong xiqu quyi yanjiu cankao ziliao congshu. Beijing: Baowentang shudian, 1986.

Jiangsu Sheng Shehui Kexue Yuan Ming Qing xiaoshuo yanjiu zhongxin wenxue yanjiusuo 江蘇省社會科學元明清研究中心文學研究所. *Zhongguo tongsu xiaoshuo zongmu tiyao* 中國通俗小說總目提要. Beijing: Zhongguo wenlian, 1990.

Jin Ping Mei cihua 金瓶梅詞話. Ed. Mei Jie 梅節. Hong Kong: Xinghai wenhua, 1987.

Jin tai quan zhuan 金台全傳. Guben xiaoshuo jicheng. Shanghai: Shanghai guji [1990].

Kang Baocheng 康保成. "Zidishu zuozhe 'He Lu Shi' shengping, jiashi kaolüe 子弟書作者"鶴侶氏" 生平、家世考略." *Wen Xian*, no. 4 (1999): 128–44.

Li Dou 李斗. *Yangzhou huafang lu* 揚州畫舫錄. Reprint. Taibei: Shijie shuju, 1964.

Li Hanqiu 李漢秋, ed. *Rulin waishi huijiao huiping ben* 儒林外史會校會評本. Shanghai: Shanghai guji, 1987.

Li he jian lianzi ping 離合劍蓮子瓶. With a preface by Liu Yucai 劉玉才. Guben xiaoshuo jicheng, vol. 107. Shanghai: Shanghai guji [1990].

Li Jiarui 李家瑞, "Qingdai Beijing mantou pu zulin changben de gaikuang 清代北京饅頭鋪租賃唱本的概況." *Zhongguo jin xian dai chuban shiliao* 中國近現代出版史料, ed. Zhang Jinglu 張靜廬, 134–38. Reprint. Shanghai: Shanghai shudian chubanshe, 2003.

Li Mengsheng 李夢生. "Preface." In *Da Han san he mingzhu baojian quan zhuan* 大漢三合明珠寶劍全傳. Reprint. Guben xiaoshuo jicheng, vol. 163. Shanghai: Shanghai guji chubanshe [1990].

Li Ruzhen 李汝貞. *Jinghua yuan* 鏡花緣. Guben xiaoshuo jicheng. Shanghai: Shanghai guji, 1990.

Li Yutang. *Wanhua Lou* 萬花樓. Guangzhou: Changqing Tang [1808].

———. *Wanhua Lou* 萬花樓. Guben xiaoshuo jicheng. Shanghai: Shanghai guji [1990].

Lin Chen 林辰. *Mingmo Qingchu xiaoshuo shulu* 明末清初小說述錄. Shenyang: Chunfeng Wenyi, 1988.

Ling Mengchu 凌濛初. *Erke pai'an jingqi* 二刻拍案警奇. Reprint. Shanghai: Shanghai guji, 1988.

Liu Liemao 劉烈茂, ed. *Chewangfu quben yanjiu* 車王府曲本研究. Guangzhou: Guangzhou renmin chubanshe, 2000.

Liu Yinbo 劉蔭柏. *Zhongguo wuxia xiaoshuo shi* 中國武俠小說史. Shijiazhuang: Huashan wenyi chubanshe, 1992.

Liu Yuehua 劉月華 et al., *Shiyong xiandai Hanyu yufa* 實用現代漢語語法. Beijing: Beijing waiyu jiaoxue yu yanjiu chubanshe, 1983.

Longtan Bao Luo qi shu 龍潭鮑駱奇書. Shanghai: Shanghai shuju, 1892.

Longtu gongan 龍圖公案. Reprint. Taibei: Tianyi, 1974.

Lü mudan guci 綠牡丹鼓詞 [*Green Peony Drum Ballad* 51]. Manuscript. 1 fascicle. Beijing: Xinglong Zhai, Guangxu period (1875–1911). In Beijing Normal University Library.

Lü mudan quan ge 綠牡丹全歌. Reprint. Chaozhou: Ruiwen tang, 1956.

Lü mudan quan zhuan 綠牡丹全傳. n.p.: San huai tang, 1800.

Lü mudan quan zhuan 綠牡丹全傳. Reprint. Guben xiaoshuo jicheng, series 5 vol. 43. Shanghai: Shanghai guji [1990].

Lu Xun 魯迅. *Lu Xun quanji* 魯迅全集. Beijing: Renmin wenxue, 1989.

———. *Zhongguo xiaoshuo shilüe* 中國小說史略. Reprint. Jinan: Qi Lu shushe, 1997.

Luo Lichun 羅立群. "Wuxia xiaoshuo yu minzu wenhua 武俠小說與民族文化." *Anhui Shida xuebao* (*Zhexue shehui kexue ban*) 安徽師大學報 (哲學社會科學版) 18 no. 4 (1990): 395–400.

Nan Bei Song zhizhuan 南北宋志傳. Reprint. Guben xiaoshuo jicheng. Shanghai: Shanghai guji [1990].

Ni Zhongzhi 倪鐘之. *Zhongguo quyi shi* 中國曲藝史. Shenyang: Chunfeng wenyi chubanshe, 1991.

Ōtsuka Hidetaka 大塚秀高. *Chûgoku tsûzoku shôsetsu shomoku* 中國通俗小說書目. Tokyo: Kyuko shoin, 1987.

Qing Feng Zha 清風閘. Reprint. Guben xiaoshuo jicheng, ser. 3 vol. 143. Shanghai: Shanghai guji [1990].

Qun Ying Jie 群英傑 [*Xiuxiang Qun Ying Jie quan zhuan: Hou Song qi shu* 綉像群英傑全傳:後宋奇書]. Guben xiaoshuo jicheng. Shanghai: Shanghai guji [1990].

Riftin, B[oris]. 李福清. *Sanguo yanyi yu minjian wenxue chuantong* 三國演義與民間文學傳統. Trans. Yin Xikang 尹錫康 and Tian Dawei 田大畏. Shanghai: Shanghai guji, 1997.

Rulian jushi 如蓮居士. *Yishuo Hou Tang zhuan san ji*: *Xue Dingshan zheng Xi Fan Lihua quanzhuan* 異說後唐傳三集薛丁山征西樊梨花全傳. Guben xiaoshuo jicheng. Reprint. Shanghai: Shanghai guji [1990].

San he jian: Xiuxiang di shi caizi shu 三合劍: 綉像第十才子書. 1848.

Shan e tu 善惡圖. Guben xiaoshuo jicheng. Reprint. Shanghai: Shanghai guji [1990].

Sheng hua meng 生花夢. Guben xiaoshuo jicheng. Reprint. Shanghai: Shanghai guji [1990].

Shi Gong an 施公案 [*Shi an qi wen* 施案奇聞]. Guben xiaoshuo jicheng. Reprint. Shanghai: Shanghai guji chubanshe [1990].

Shuihu quan zhuan 水滸全傳. Beijing: Renmin, 1954.

Sun Kaidi 孫楷弟. *Zhongguo tongsu xiaoshuo shumu* 中國通俗小說書目. Reprint. Beijing: Renmin wenxue, 1982.

Tan Zhengbi 譚正璧. *Muyu ge, Chaozhou ge xulu* 木魚歌, 潮州歌敘錄. Wen shi zhe yanjiu ziliao congshu. Beijing: Beijing Shumu Wenxian chubanshe, 1982.

Tianbao tu 天豹圖. Xiamen: Xiamen Fengsheng shufang, 1814.

Tianbao tu 天豹圖. Guben xiaoshuo jicheng. Reprint. Shanghai: Shanghai guji [1990].

Tong Shuozhi 佟碩之 [Liang Yusheng 梁羽生]. "Jin Yong Liang Yusheng he lun 金庸梁羽生合論." In *Liang Yusheng ji qi wuxia xiaoshuo* 梁羽生及其武俠小說, 74–115. Hong Kong: Weiqing shudian, 1980.

Tuo Bafeng 拓跋逢, "Wuxia xiaoshuo yuanxing liubian de lunli jiyin 武俠小說原型流變的倫理基因," *Wenshi zhishi* 文史知識, 1990, no. 2: 58–64.

Wang Fansen 王汎森 et al., eds. *Su wenxue congkan* 俗文學叢刊. Taibei: Zhongyang yanjiu lishi yuyan yanjiusuo, 2004.

Wang Hailin 王海林. *Zhongguo wuxia xiaoshuo shilüe* 中國武俠小說史略. With an introduction by Xue Baokun 薛寶琨. Taiyuan: Beiyue wenyi chubanshe, 1988.

Wen Kang 文康. *Ernü yingxiong zhuan* 兒女英雄傳. Guben xiaoshuo jicheng. Reprint, Shanghai: Shanghai guji [1990].

Wen Qiji 文豈几. Introduction to *Lü mudan* 綠牡丹. Shi da gudian gongan xiayi xiaoshuo congshu 十大古典公案俠義小說叢書. Reprint, Shanghai: Shanghai guji, 1993.

Wu Bing 吳炳. *Lü mudan* 綠牡丹. Ed. Luo Sining 羅斯寧. Shanghai: Shanghai guji chubanshe, 1985.

Wu Zongxi 吳宗錫, ed. *Pingtan wenhua cidian* 評彈文化詞典. Shanghai: Hanyu da cidian chubanshe, 1996.

Xiyou ji 西遊記. Beijing: Renmin wenxue chubanshe, 1984.

Xiaqing xiaoshuo Hong Bi yuan 俠情小說弘碧緣. N.p., n.d.

Xin ke Lü mudan quanzhuan 新刻綠牡丹全傳 [also titled *Xin ke Lü mudan guci* 新刻綠牡丹鼓詞 and *Xiuxiang Lü mudan quanzhuan* 繡像綠牡丹全傳]. Shanghai: Jinzhang tushuju [1919].

Xin ke Wanhua Lou Di Qing chushen quan ben 新刻萬花樓狄青出身全本. Wu Gui Tang. In the Fudan University Humanities Library.

Yang Jia Fu yanyi 楊家府演義. Guben xiaoshuo jicheng. Shanghai: Shanghai guji [1990].

Yishuo Fan Tang quan zhuan 異說反唐全傳. Guben xiaoshuo jicheng. Reprint. Shanghai: Shanghai guji [1990].

Yishuo Hou Tang zhuan san ji: Xue Dingshan zheng Xi Fan Lihua quan zhuan 異說後唐三集 薛丁山征西樊梨花全传. Guben xiaoshuo jicheng ser. 3, vol. 80. Shanghai: Shanghai guji [1990].

Yu Jiao Li 玉嬌梨. Guben xiaoshuo jicheng. Reprint. Shanghai: Shanghai guji [1990].

Yu Wanchun 俞萬春. *Dang kou zhi* 蕩寇志. Reprint. Guben xiaoshuo jicheng, Shanghai: Shanghai guji [1990].

Yuanhu yusou 鴛湖漁叟 . *Shuo Tang yanyi quan zhuan* 說唐演義全傳. Guben xiaoshuo jicheng. Reprint. Shanghai: Shanghai guji [1990].

Yun Zhong Yan san nao Taiping Zhuang quan zhuan 雲鍾雁三鬧太平莊全傳. With a preface by Cao Guangfu 曹光甫 . Guben xiaoshuo jicheng. Reprint. Shanghai: Shanghai guji, 1990.

Zhang Jun 張俊. *Qingdai xiaoshuo shi* 清代小說史. Zhongguo xiaoshuo shi congshu. Hangzhou: Zhejiang guji chubanshe, 1997.

Zhao Jingshen 趙景深. *Guci xuan* 鼓詞選. Beijing: Zhonghua shuju, 1959.

Zhenben Tianbao tu quan zhuan 真本天豹圖全傳 [also titled *Xin ke zhenben tanci changkou Tianbao tu quan zhuan* 新刻真本彈詞唱口天豹圖全傳]. n.p.: Feichun Ge, 1776.

Zheng Chun Yuan 爭春園. Guben xiaoshuo jicheng. Reprint. Shanghai: Shanghai guji [1990].

Zheng Zhengduo 鄭振鐸. *Zhongguo su wenxue shi* 中國俗文學史. Reprint. Shanghai: Shanghai shudian, 1987.

Zhong yi Shuihu zhuan 忠義水滸傳. Suzhou: Yuan Wuya, ca. 1611.

Zhu Hongbo 竺洪波. "Shilun *Lü mudan* de sixiang yiyun 試論綠牡丹的思想意蘊." *Ming Qing xiaoshuo yanjiu* 明清小說研究, no. 4 (1988): 163–73.

Western Works

Altenburger, Roland. "The Sword or the Needle: The Female Knight-errant (*Xia*) in Traditional Chinese Fiction." Habilitationsschrift Philosophische Fakultät der Universität Zurich, 2000.

Alter, Robert. *Partial Magic: The Novel as a Self-conscious Genre*. Berkeley: University of California Press, 1975.

Ashley, Bob, ed. *The Study of Popular Fiction: A Source Book*. London: Pinter, 1989.

Attebery, Brian. *Strategies of Fantasy*. Bloomington and Indianapolis: Indiana University Press, 1992.

Bakhtin, Mikhail Mikhailovich. *The Dialogic Imagination*, ed. Michael Holquist. Austin: University of Texas Press, 1981.

———. *Problems of Dostoevsky's Poetics*. Trans. Caryl Emerson. Minnesota, 1984.

Bäuml, Franz. "Medieval Texts and the Two Theories of Oral-Formulaic Composition: A Proposal for a Third Theory," *New Literary History* 16, no. 1 (1984): 31–49.

Bender, Mark. "Tan-ci, Wen-ci, Chang-ci." *Chinese Literature: Essays, Articles, Reviews* 6, no. 1–2 (1984): 121–24.

Blader, Susan. "A Critical Study of *San-hsia Wu-yi* and Relationship to the *Lung-t'u Kung-an* Song-book." Unpublished doctoral thesis, University of Pennsylvania, 1977.

———. "Introduction." In Shi Yukun, *Tales of Magistrate Bao and His Valiant Lieutenants: Selections from* Sanxia wuyi, trans. Susan Blader. Hong Kong: Chinese University Press, 1998.

———. "'Yan Chasan Thrice Tested': Printed Novel to Oral Tale," *CHINOPERL Papers* 12 (1983): 84–111.

Børdahl, Vibeke. "A Drum Tale on 'Wu Song Fights the Tiger.'" *CHINOPERL Papers* 27 (2007): 61–106.

———. *The Oral Tradition of Yangzhou Storytelling*. Nordic Institute of Asian Studies Monograph Series, No. 73. Surrey, Great Britain: Curzon Press, 1996.

———. "Storytellers' Scripts in the *Yangzhou Pinghua* Tradition." *Acta Orientalia* 66 (2005): 227–96.

Brokaw, Cynthia. *Commerce in Culture: The Sibao Book Trade in the Qing and Republican Periods.* Cambridge, Mass.: Harvard University Asia Center, 2007.

———. "Reading the Best-Sellers of the Nineteenth Century: Commercial Publishing in Sibao." In Cynthia Brokaw and Kai-wing Chow, eds., *Printing and Book Culture in Late Imperial China*, 184–234. Vol. 28, *Studies on China.* Berkeley: University of California Press, 2005.

———. "Woodblock Printing and the Diffusion of Print in Qing China." Unpublished manuscript.

Buoye, Thomas. *Manslaughter, Markets, and Moral Economy.* Cambridge: Cambridge University Press, 2000.

Cao Xueqin. *The Story of the Stone.* Trans. David Hawkes. New York: Penguin, 1973.

Carlitz, Katherine. *The Rhetoric of Chin P'ing Mei.* Bloomington: Indiana University Press, 1986.

Cawelti, John G. "The Concept of Formula in the Study of Popular Literature." In *The Study of Popular Fiction: A Source Book*, ed. Bob Ashley, 87–92. London: Pinter, 1989.

———. *The Six-Gun Mystique.* Bowling Green, Ohio: Bowling Green University Popular Press, n.d.

Chartier, Roger: *The Cultural Uses of Print in Early Modern France.* Trans. Lydia G. Cochrane. Princeton: Princeton University Press, 1987.

———. *Forms and Meanings: Text, Performance, and Audience from Codex to Computer, New Cultural Studies Series.* Philadelphia: University of Pennsylvania Press, 1995.

Culler, Jonathan. *Structuralist Poetics: Structuralism, Linguistics and the Study of Literature.* Ithaca, N.Y.: Cornell University Press, 1975.

Currie, Mark. *Metafiction.* New York: Longman, 1995.

Dolezelova-Velingerova, Milena. "Seventeenth-century Chinese Theory of Narrative: A Reconstruction of Its System and Concepts." In *Poetics East and West*, ed. Milena Dolezelova-Velingerova, 137–57. Toronto: Toronto Semiotic Circle, Victoria College in the University of Toronto, 1989.

Dubrow, Heather. *Genre.* New York: Methuen, 1982.

Ebrey, Patricia. *Confucianism and Family Ritual in Imperial China.* Princeton: Princeton University Press, 1991.

Eco, Umberto. "The Narrative Structure in Fleming." In Oreste Del Buono and Umberto Eco, eds., *The Bond Affair.* London: MacDonald, 1966.

Epstein, Maram. *Competing Discourses: Orthodoxy, Authenticity, and Engendered Meanings in Late Imperial Chinese Fiction.* Cambridge, Mass. and London: Harvard University Asia Center, 2001.

Forster, E. M. *Aspects of the Novel.* New York: Harcourt, 1927.

Ge, Liangyan. *Out of the Margins: The Rise of Chinese Vernacular Fiction.* Honolulu: University of Hawaii Press, 2001.

Genette, Gérard. *Narrative Discourse: An Essay in Method.* Trans. Jane E. Lewin. Ithaca, N.Y.: Cornell University Press, 1980.

———. *Palimpsests: Literature in the Second Degree.* Trans. Channa Newman and Claude Doubinsky. Lincoln and London: University of Nebraska Press, 1997.

Goldman, Andrea S. "The Nun Who Wouldn't Be: Representations of Female Desire in Two Performance Genres of 'Si Fan.'" *Late Imperial China* 22, no. 1 (2001) 71–138.

Goody, Jack. *The Interface between the Written and the Oral.* Cambridge: Cambridge University Press, 1987.

Gu, Ming Dong. *Chinese Theories of Fiction: A Non-Western Narrative System.* Albany: State University of New York Press, 2006.

Hamm, John Christopher. *Paper Swordsmen: Jin Yong and the Modern Chinese Martial Arts Novel.* Honolulu: University of Hawaii Press, 2005.

———. "Wu-hsia hsiao-shuo." In William H. Nienhauser, ed., *The Indiana Companion to Traditional Chinese Literature.* Bloomington: Indiana University Press, 1998, 2:189.

Hanan, Patrick. "The Composition of the *P'ing yao chuan,*" *Harvard Journal of Asiatic Studies* 31 (1971): 201–19.

———. "The Early Chinese Short Story: A Critical Theory in Outline." *Harvard Journal of Asiatic Studies* 27 (1967): 168–207.

———. "*Judge Bao's Hundred Cases* Reconstructed." *Harvard Journal of Asiatic Studies* 40 (1980): 301–23.

———. "The Making of *The Pearl Sewn Shirt* and *The Courtesan's Jewel Box.*" *Harvard Journal of Asiatic Studies* 33 (1973): 124–53.

———. "The Narrator's Voice before the 'Fiction Revolution.'" In *Chinese Fiction of the Nineteenth and Early Twentieth Century: Essays by Patrick Hanan.* New York: Columbia University Press, 2004.

———. "Sources of the *Chin P'ing Mei.*" *Asia Major* 10 (1963): 23–67.

———. "The *Yün-men chuan*: From *Chantefable* to Short Story." *Bulletin of the School of Oriental and African Studies,* vol. XXXVI part 2 (1973): 299–308.

Hawkes, David, trans. *Ch'u Tz'u: The Songs of the South.* London: Oxford University Press, 1959.

Hegel, Robert E. *The Novel in Seventeenth-century China.* New York: Columbia University Press, 1981.

———. *Reading Illustrated Fiction in Late Imperial China.* Stanford, Calif.: Stanford University Press, 1998.

———. "Rewriting the Tang: Humor, Heroics and Imaginative Reading." In *Snakes' Legs,* ed. Martin W. Huang, 159–89. Honolulu: University of Hawaii Press, 2004.

———. "*Sui T'ang Yen-I*: The Sources and Narrative Techniques of a Traditional Chinese Novel." Doctoral thesis, Columbia University, 1973.

Hegel, Robert E. and Katherine Carlitz, eds. *Writing and Law in Late Imperial China: Crime, Conflict and Judgment.* Seattle: University of Washington Press, 2007.

Hodes, Nancy. "Strumming and Singing the 'Three Smiles Romance': A Study of the *Tanci* Text." Unpublished doctoral thesis, Harvard University, 1990.

Hsia, C. T. *The Classic Chinese Novel: A Critical Introduction*. Reprint. Ithaca, N.Y.: Cornell University Press, 1996.

———. "The Military Romance: A Genre of Chinese Fiction." In *Studies in Chinese Literary Genres*, ed. Cyril Birch, 339–390. Berkeley: University of California, 1974.

Hsiung, Ping-chen. "Treading the Weedy Path: T'ang Cheng (1630–1704) and the World of the Confucian Middlebrow." In *Imagining Boundaries*, ed. Kai-wing Chow, On-cho Ng, and John B. Henderson, 195–211. Albany: State University of New York Press, 1999.

Hu Siao-chen. "Literary *Tanci*." Unpublished doctoral thesis, Harvard University, 1984.

Huang, Martin Weizong. "Dehistoricization and Intertextualization: The Anxiety of Precedents in the Evolution of the Traditional Chinese Novel." *Chinese Literature: Essays, Articles, Reviews* 12 (1990): 45–68.

———. *Desire and Fictional Narrative in Late Imperial China*. Cambridge, Mass.: Harvard University Asia Center, 2001.

———. *Negotitating Masculinities in Late Imperial China*. Honolulu: University of Hawaii Press, 2006.

———, ed. *Snakes' Legs: Sequels, Continuations, Rewritings and Chinese Fiction*. Honolulu: University of Hawaii Press, 2004.

Hucker, Charles. *A Dictionary of Official Titles in Imperial China*. Palo Alto: Stanford University Press, 1988.

Hutcheon, Linda. *Narcissistic Narrative: The Metafictional Paradox*. New York: Routledge, 1980.

———. *A Theory of Parody*. New York: Methuen, 1985.

Idema, Wilt. *Chinese Vernacular Fiction: The Formative Period*. Vol. 13, *Sinica Leidensia*. Leiden: Brill, 1974.

Imhof, Rudiger. *Contemporary Metafiction: A Poetological Study of Metafiction in English since 1939*. Heidelberg: Carl Winter, Universitätsverlag, 1986.

Johnson, David. "Communication, Class and Consciousness in Late Imperial China." In *Popular Culture in Late Imperial China*, ed. David Johnson, Andrew J. Nathan, and Evelyn S. Rawski, 34–74. Berkeley: University of California Press, 1985.

Keulemans, Paize. "Listening to the Printed Martial Arts Scene: Onomatopoeia and the Qing Dynasty Storyteller's Voice." *Harvard Journal of Asiatic Studies* (2007): 51–87.

Keulemans, Pieter C. A. "Sounds of the Novel: Storytelling, Print-culture, and Martial-arts Fiction in Nineteenth-century Beijing." Unpublished doctoral thesis, University of Chicago, 2004.

Li, Qiancheng. *Fictions of Enlightenment: Journey to the West, Tower of Myriad Mirrors, and Dream of the Red Chamber*. Honolulu: University of Hawaii Press, 2004.

Li, Wai-yee. *Enchantment and Disenchantment: Love and Illusion in Chinese Literature*. Princeton: Princeton University Press, 1993.

Liu, James J. Y. *The Chinese Knight-errant.* Chicago: University of Chicago Press; London: Routledge and Kegan Paul, 1967.

Luo Guanzhong. *Three Kingdoms: A Historical Novel.* Trans. Moss Roberts. Berkeley: University of California Press, 1991.

Ma, Y. W. "The Chinese Historical Novel: An Outline of Themes and Contexts," *Journal of Asian Studies* 34, no. 2 (February 1975): 277–93.

———. "*Kung-an* Fiction: A Historical and Critical Introduction." *T'oung Pao* 65 (1979): 201–59.

———. "The Textual Tradition of Ming *Kung-an* Fiction: A Study of the *Lung-t'u kung-an.*" *Harvard Journal of Asiatic Studies* 35 (1975): 190–220.

———. "Themes and Characterization in the *Lung-t'u kung-an,*" *T'oung Pao* 59 (1973): 179–202.

Macauley, Melissa. *Social Power and Legal Culture: Litigation Masters in Late Imperial China.* Stanford: Stanford University Press, 1998.

McKeon, Michael. *The Origins of the English Novel 1600–1740.* Baltimore: Johns Hopkins University Press, 1987.

McLaren, Anne Elizabeth. *Chinese Popular Culture and Ming Chantefables.* Sinica Leidensia, vol. 41. Boston: Brill, 1998.

———. "Constructing New Reading Publics in Late Ming China." In Cynthia Brokaw and Kai-wing Chow, eds., *Printing and Book Culture in Late Imperial China,* 152–183. Berkeley: University of California Press, 2005.

———. "Ming Audiences and Vernacular Hermeneutics: The Uses of the 'Romance of the Three Kingdoms.'" *T'oung Pao* 81, no. 1–3 (1995): 51–80.

McMahon, Keith. *Misers, Shrews, and Polygamists: Sexuality and Male-Female Relations in Eighteenth-century Chinese Fiction.* Durham, N.C.: Duke University Press, 1995.

Miller, J. Hillis. *Fiction and Repetition: Seven English Novels.* Cambridge: Harvard, 1982.

O'Brien O'Keefe, Katherine. *Visible Song: Transitional Literacy in Old English Verse.* Cambridge: Cambridge University Press, 1990.

Ong, Walter. *Orality and Literacy: The Technologizing of the Word.* New York and London: Methuen, 1982.

Owen, Stephen, trans. and ed. *An Anthology of Chinese Literature: Beginnings to 1911.* New York: Norton, 1996.

———. *Readings in Chinese Literary Thought.* Cambridge, Mass.: Harvard University Press, 1992.

Plaks, Andrew. *The Four Masterworks of the Ming Novel.* Princeton: Princeton University Press, 1987.

———. "Full-length *Hsiao-Shuo* and the Western Novel: A Generic Reappraisal." *Xin ya xueshu jikan. New Asia Academic Bulletin* 1 (1978): 163–76.

———. "Terminology and Central Concepts." In *How to Read the Chinese Novel,* ed. David Rolston, 75–123. Princeton: Princeton University Press, 1990.

Propp, Vladimir. *Morphology of the Folktale*. Austin: University of Texas Press, 1968.

Roberts, Moss. "Afterword: About *Three Kingdoms*." In *Three Kingdoms: A Historical Novel*. Trans. idem. Berkeley: University of California, 1991.

Roddy, Stephen. *Literati Identity and Its Fictional Representations in Late Imperial China*. Stanford: Stanford University Press, 1998.

Rolston, David. *How to Read the Chinese Novel*. Princeton: Princeton University Press, 1990.

———. *Traditional Chinese Fiction and Fiction Commentary: Reading and Writing between the Lines*. Stanford: Stanford University Press, 1997.

Rose, Margaret. *Parody: Ancient, Modern and Post-modern*. New York: Cambridge University Press, 1993.

———. *Parody//Metafiction*. London: Croom Helm, 1979.

Roy, David Tod. "Introduction." In David Roy, trans., *The Plum in the Golden Vase, or, Chin P'ing Mei*. Princeton: Princeton University Press, 1993.

———. "Introduction: Mao Tsung-kang and His 'Tu *San-kuo chih* fa.'" In *How to Read the Chinese Novel*, ed. David Rolston, 146–51. Princeton: Princeton University Press, 1990.

Scholes, Robert. *Structuralism in Literature: An Introduction*. New Haven: Yale University Press, 1974.

Shahar, Meir. *Crazy Ji: Chinese Religion and Popular Literature*. Cambridge, Mass.: Harvard University Asia Center, 1998.

Shang Wei. *"Rulin Waishi" and Cultural Transformation in Late Imperial China*. Cambridge, Massachusetts: Harvard University Asia Center, 2003.

Shao Ping. "Monkey and Chinese Scriptural Tradition: A Rereading of the Novel 'Xiyou ji.'" Doctoral dissertation: Washington University, 1997.

Sieber, Patricia. "The Chinese Fictional Canon Reconsidered: The View from European Book Acquisitions, 1720–1860." Unpublished manuscript.

Sommer, Matthew. *Sex, Law and Society in Late Imperial China*. Stanford: Stanford University Press, 2000.

Sung, Marina H. "T'an-Tz'u and T'an-Tz'u Narratives." *T'oung Pao* 79, no. 1–3 (1993): 1–22.

Theiss, Janet M. *Disgraceful Matters: The Politics of Chastity in Eighteenth-century China*. Berkeley: University of California Press, 2005.

Waltner, Ann. "From Casebook to Fiction: *Kung-an* in Late Imperial China." *Journal of the American Oriental Society* 110, no. 2 (1990): 281–89.

Wan, Margaret Baptist. "The *Chantefable* and the Novel: The Cases of *Lü mudan* and *Tianbao tu*," *Harvard Journal of Asiatic Studies* 64, no. 2 (Dec. 2004): 367–97.

———. "Local fiction of the Yangzhou region: *Qingfengzha*." In Lucie Olivová and Vibeke Børdhal, eds., *Lifestyle and Entertainment in Yangzhou*. Copenhagen: Nordic Institute of Asian Studies Press, 2008.

Wang, David. *Fin-de-siècle Splendor: Repressed Modernities of Late Qing Fiction, 1849–1911*. Stanford: Stanford University Press, 1997.

Wang, John Ching-yu. *Chin Sheng-t'an*. New York: Twayne, 1972.

Wang, Ying. "The Voices of the Re-readers: Interpretations of Three Late-Qing Rewrites of *Jinghua yuan*." In *Snakes' Legs*, ed. Martin Huang, 210–36. Honolulu: University of Hawaii Press, 2004.

Waugh, Patricia. *Metafiction: The Theory and Practice of Self-conscious Fiction*. New York and London: Methuen, 1984.

Widmer, Ellen. *The Beauty and the Book: Women and Fiction in Nineteenth-century China*. Cambridge, Mass.: Harvard University Asia Center, 2006.

———. "*Honglou meng* Sequels and Their Female Readers in Nineteenth-century China." In *Snakes' Legs*, ed. Martin Huang, 116–42. Honolulu: University of Hawaii Press, 2004.

———. *The Margins of Utopia:* Shui-hu hou-chuan *and the Literature of Ming Loyalism*. Cambridge, Mass.: Council on East Asian Studies, Harvard University, 1987.

Woodside, Alexander. "Some Mid-Qing Theorists of Popular Schools: Their Innovations, Inhibitions, and Attitudes toward the Poor." *Modern China* 9, no. 1 (1983): 33.

Wu, Laura Hua. "The Concept of Parallelism: Jin Shengtan's Critical Discourse on *The Water Margin*." In *Poetics East and West*, ed. Milena Dolezelova-Velingerova, 169–79. Toronto: Toronto Semiotic Circle, Victoria College in the University of Toronto, 1989.

———. "From *Xiaoshuo* to Fiction: Hu Yinglin's Genre Study of *Xiaoshuo*." *Harvard Journal of Asiatic Studies* 55, no. 2 (1995): 339–71.

Wu, Pei-Yi. "Yang Miaozhen: A Woman Warrior in Thirteenth-century China." *Nan nü* 4, no. 2 (2002): 137–69.

Wu, Yenna. "Repetition in *Xingshi yinyuan zhuan*." *Harvard Journal of Asiatic Studies* 51, no. 1 (June 1991): 55–87.

Yang, Shuhui. "Growing from the Waist: The Problem of Sequeling in Yu Wanchun's *Dangkou zhi*." In *Snakes' Legs*, ed. Martin Huang, 143–58. Honolulu: University of Hawaii Press, 2004.

Yu, Anthony. *Rereading the Stone: Desire and the Making of Fiction in* Dream of the Red Chamber. Princeton: Princeton University Press, 1997.

Yung, Bell. "Popular Narrative in the Pleasure Houses of the South." *Chinoperl Papers* 11 (1982): 126–49.

Yung, Sai-shing. "Mu-Yu Shu and the Cantonese Popular Singing Arts." *The Gest Library Journal* 2, no. 1 (1987): 16–30.

Index